# Footnotes

## THE BAY AREA GUIDE TO DANCE



Beth Witrogen

TWO STEP BOOKS

*Library of Congress Cataloging in Publication Data*

*Witrogen, Beth, 1948-*
*Foot notes.*

*Includes bibliographical references.*
*1. Dancing – California – San Francisco Bay region – Directories. I. Title.*
*GV1587.5.W57 793.3'025'7946 80-5091*
*ISBN 0-931018-04-8*

*Manufactured in the United States of America.*



*Published by,*
***Two Step Books, PO Box 2942, Oakland, California 94618***

*Dedicated to the light above, R.J.M. below.*

*Although the forms of dance change as they evolve, the essence remains: to reach that depth of man called soul, and move it to its brightest expression.*

*I wish to sincerely thank all those who have moved me during the process of researching and writing, in particular:*

*Everyone who responded to my letter of inquiry*

*The San Francisco Bay Area Dance Coalition*

*Examiner photographer, Bob McLeod*

*Marin Scope dance critic Robert Stephens*

*Evelyn Schuert*

*Family and friends.*

*My special thanks to:*

*Myland McRevey, the artistic muse*

*Janet Ruth Gendler, whose flexibility and patience allowed this book to be updated until the final hour and especially*

*my publisher Liza Cohen, whose unwavering enthusiasm and professionalism have been the alpha and omega of my endeavors.*

# Contents

## dance forms

### Ballet

# Contents

# Contents

# Contents

# Contents

# Contents

# Contents

## dance fields

# Contents

# Contents

# Contents

*It wasn't long ago that vendors hawked buckets of fried chicken during intermissions of San Francisco Ballet performances in Concord. While it hasn't exactly become a black tie affair, dance in the San Francisco Bay Area has come of age. No one interested in dance and dance-related arts could fail to notice the boom not only in audience attendance, but especially in the number of students of all ages pouring into dance classes for fun or career training.*

*The growth of dance in the Bay Area mirrors the increased enthusiasm across the nation. Annual attendance at all U.S. dance events now stands near 25 million, a 1500 percent increase in only 10 years. There are about 1,000 dance companies in the U.S., compared with some 450 five years ago. The figures keep rising. In ballet alone, there are now nearly 60 professional companies, versus 35 five years ago. The San Francisco Ballet, formed in 1933, was the first, making the Bay Area an important dance center for more than 40 years.*

*This guide is an attempt, not to be a complete, permanent record, as fluidity is the norm in this art form, but rather to be a resource for dancers and dance lovers throughout the Bay Area. The project was undertaken with the recognition and regret that some data may not have come to our attention. As well, some studios and companies will have folded by publication; others will have been born.*

*The lengthier listings are taken from information returned to me; those that give only the address did not respond by deadline to letters of inquiry. For simplification, studios that offer more than one kind of dance style are listed under ballet, unless information indicated that they specialize in another form. In any case all studios that offer more than one kind of dance are cross-referenced under all forms. Studios with companies are listed first; those without companies follow, even if they offer student performances. In respect for individual needs, interests and tastes, this guide does not make any judgments on quality.*

*Other information related to any one dance form (folk, ballet, etc.) is discussed at the end of the chapter. Geographic categories are Contra Costa County (CCC); East Bay (EB); Marin and Sonoma; Peninsula; San Francisco (SF); San Jose (SJ), Santa Clara, Santa Cruz.*

*The guide also was compiled to share something more lasting with the readers: a discovery of the ingenuity and humanity, the breadth and depth of those who have made dance a medium of exchange from the heart. At a recent ballet performance I overhead an elderly woman remark, "Gee, she's sure graceful for a ballerina." I trust that dance will always be an innocent awakening, and I hope these pages will help broaden the path for those seeking something practical or timeless in this ethereal expression of life.*

# dance forms

Ballet

Ballroom

Belly

Disco

Ethnic/Folk

Jazz

Modern

Tap

Other Dances

# Ballet

*Ballet as a dance/theater form will be 400 years old in 1981. Its roots go back to the 15th century ducal courts of Italy, though more of its present form derives from the court of Louis XIV of France, who established the Royal Academy of Dance in 1661. Ballet remained a European, especially Russian, phenomenon little known to North America until 1910, when the exquisite Anna Pavlova and Diaghilev's Ballet Russe performed in New York.*

*San Francisco Ballet was the first full-fledged professional U.S. company and school, followed by what became the New York City Ballet and American Ballet Theatre. But interest grew faster than professional companies, so a movement unique to the U.S. emerged--the regional (non-professional, civic) ballet company. It began in 1929 with the Atlantic Civic Ballet; by 1971 there were close to 100 such companies plus 200 or more civic or local ballets that were not members of one of the four regional ballet associations. The numbers today reach well into the hundreds.*

*This chapter alphabetically lists studios with ballet companies, then studios which only give classes, within geographical area. A quick reference table of studios emphasizing Cecchetti, Royal Academy or Russian styles follows.*

# Ballet

## *Contra Costa County Companies*

***CONTRA COSTA BALLET CENTER AND Contra Costa Ballet Company, 2040 N. Broadway, Walnut Creek, 94596, 415-935-7984.*** *Donald Eryck, director. Official school of Contra Costa Ballet Company. Faculty: Jocelyn Vollmar (SFB); Suzanne Davis (LRB); Brynar Mehl (Manh School of Dance). Classical ballet at six levels including adagio and three levels of pointe; academic and adult divisions; four levels of jazz for teens and adults, and tap. Special programs for talented students.*

*Company has 18 performances of Nutcracker at Christmas with other seasons. Dancers paid just under union scale. Eight ballets in repertoire with continuous performing lecture/demonstrations in public and private schools, senior citizen and civic groups. Dancers may audition in company class any time; call Eryck in advance. (I'm told you can try two or three times in case you don't do well in the first class.)*

***ORINDA ACADEMY OF BALLET and Orinda Ballet Company, 214 Moraga Way, Orinda 94563, 415-376-6322.*** *Susan Edgren, director and principal teacher; performed with San Francisco Ballet, Oakland Ballet, Oakland Civic Ballet, Richmond Ballet Company. Faculty: Patricia Baldwin, Dita Pepin, Julia Slaight, Judi Stephens. Traditional and contemporary training in ballet; character, pointe, pas de deux, modern and jazz. Curriculum emphasizes suppleness, musicality, discipline, vocabulary and individual attention. Adult beginners taught through St. Mary's College (see EDUCATION). Single classes, privates, class cards.*

*The Orinda Ballet Company is open to dancers by audition for Christmas and spring performances and for the San Francisco Children's Opera. Performance schedule soon will be year round. The Orinda Ballet Guild, Inc. sponsors the company whose purpose is "to add quality professional dance activities to the community." Orinda Ballet Guild, 214 Moraga Way, Orinda 94563.*

***RICHMOND BALLET COMPANY, 322 Harbour Way, Richmond, 415-237-5065.*** *Est. 25 years ago; Harold Garton, director. New location with two large studios.*

# Ballet

## *Contra Costa County Classes*

***THE BALLET SCHOOL, 1295 Boulevard Way, Suite D, Walnut Creek 94595, 415-934-2133.*** *Laureen Fender, director. Specializes in training the young dancer. Adult classes, morning and evening.*

***CERRITO DANCE ARTS CENTER, 1534 Kearney St., El Cerrito, 94530, 415-236-2097.*** *Maryse Gaye Weigand, director. Beg. through adv. ballet; tap, jazz, women's dancersize, character and Hawaiian. Specializes in children and teens; adult classes available. Yearly recital for all students. With Eleanor Edson (see EDSON BALLET STUDIO) choreographs for Contra Costa Civic Theater, for which students are encouraged to audition.*

***CONCORD YOUNG WORLD OF DANCE, 3431 Chestnut Ave., Concord 94519, 415-686-4343.*** *Ballet, tap, jazz.*

***CONTRA COSTA ACADEMY OF DANCING ARTS, 180 Hilltop Crescent, Walnut Creek 94596, 415-934-9201.*** *Megan Baloyra-Samartzis, director. Ballet (Russian, French and Cecchetti, pointe, performances); character (Russian, Spanish, Scottish, Circle); kinder dance (ages 4-5); musical comedy; ballroom; disco; modern jazz; jazz-tap and line work; Spanish and flamenco; yoga. Single classes and cards.*

***DANSE BOUTIQUE, 2846 Fourth St., Livermore 94550, 415-443-4670.*** *Sally Emmert, director. Ballet (beg. through adv. with pointe), modern, creative movement, pre-ballet, dancersize, jazz, music education, gymnastics. Limited class size. Creative movement (3-5 years), modern (6-8), pre-school (3-6), primary (6-8), juniors (8-12), seniors (12-adults). Single classes and monthly cards.*

***EL CERRITO BALLET CENTER, 6712 Portola Drive, El Cerrito 94530, 415-235-1734 or 529-1749.*** *June Boblitt, director. RAD graded classes, pre-school through advanced.*

# Ballet

## *Contra Costa County Classes*

***ELEANORA'S SCHOOL OF DANCE, 1401 Danville Blvd., Alamo and 1948 Oak Park Blvd., Pleasant Hill 94523, 415-938-0192.*** *Ballet and jazz, beg. through prof., pre-school through adult.*

***ENCORE STUDIO OF DANCE AND GYMNASTICS, 4705 Valley View Road, Richmond 94803, 415-223-6450.*** *Established more than 15 years ago; Jeanne Pounds, owner. Ballet, jazz and tap, pre-school through adult. School performance bi-annually.*

*Also at 1104 Seranap Ave., Walnut Creek 94595, 415-932-1033; 8,000 square feet for ballet, tap, jazz, pre-school through adults.*

***HAMILTON STUDIOS OF DANCE AND MUSIC.*** *See TAP, CCC.*

***PEARL KAY STUDIO OF ORINDA, 415-254-3296 or 254-9995.*** *Tap, ballet, jazz and ladies' dancersize, beg. through adv., at Oak Springs Clubhouse, Spring Road, Orinda. Singles and monthly cards.*

***McBRIDE DANCE STUDIO, St. Mary's College, St. Mary's Road, Moraga 94556, 415-820-1475.*** *Mailing address: 297 Oak Road, Danville 94526. Sheri McBride, director and principal instructor; trained locally, soloist with Dancer's Repertory Theatre, Berkeley. RAD syllabus includes musicality, discipline, pointe and vocabulary, basic (all ages) through adv. ballet, with beg. and inter. jazz. Studio features a major production yearly.*

***MISS BARBARA SCHOOL OF DANCE, 1831 Monument Blvd., Concord 94520, 415-687-3024.*** *Ballet, ages 4 through adults.*

***MISS PENNY'S SCHOOL OF DANCE, 7090A Johnson Industrial Drive, Pleasanton 94556, 415-462-5160.*** *Classical ballet.*

# Ballet

## *Contra Costa County Classes*

***NISSEN'S SCHOOL OF DANCE, 3242 Clayton Road, Concord 94519, 415-682-1390.*** *Since 1953. Ballet and tap; member RAD. Ages four through adults; beg. through adv.*

***OAK PARK DANCE ACADEMY, 1948 Oak Park Blvd., Pleasant Hill 94523, 415-933-1174 or 689-2907.*** *Ballet and tap; children and adults.*

***VERNON RUSSEL.*** *See TAP, CCC.*

***SAN RAMON VALLEY DANCE ACADEMY, P.O. Box 141, San Ramon 94683, 415-837-4656.*** *Founded 1969. Faculty: Joan Winton, co-director (classical ballet, body conditioning); Muriel Ruslender, co-director (ballet, pre-school, pre-ballet); Karla Kobelt, co-director (modern jazz, tap); Renee Carey (tap, modern and Afro-jazz, disco); Janne Jackson (classical ballet). Beg. through prof.; master classes. More than 7,000 sq. ft., with 1,900 sq. ft. for expansion. The adjacent Dance Shoppe supplies dancewear.*

# Ballet

## *East Bay Companies*

***ACADEMY OF DANCE and Metropolitan Ballet Company of Oakland, 1512 Webster, Alameda 94501, 415-523-9333.*** *Vern Nerden, director. Classical ballet, pas de deux, advanced pointe, boys' variations; children (beg. 6-9 years old; inter. 9-12) and adults. Company class Saturdays at 12:30 p.m. Working scholarship program; singles, cards and family rates.*

***BALLET ARTS CENTER and Oakland Civic Ballet, 4689 Telegraph Ave., Oakland 94609, 415-658-0684.*** *Raoul Pausé, director; formerly with Pavley-Oukrainsky Ballet, Cincinnati Opera, Chicago and Manh Opera companies. Faculty: Harold Garton, Michele Kaitner, Donald Springer, Linda Kraft, Toni Silver (modern); Connie Collins (jazz). Ballet for adult beg., inter., adv. prof., pre-ballet (4-6), threshold (5-7; rhythmic movement); beg. kids (7-11), junior inter. Combines technique of traditional ballet with freedom of contemporary dance: result is called theater dance. Students are fed into local company performances. Singles, semester rates.*

***VALA BOVIE SCHOOL OF CLASSICAL BALLET, 1805 Grove St., Berkeley 94709, 415-848-2590.*** *Mme. Bovie, founder and director; trained in Russia with Artzebusheva, Karsavina, danced with Paris Opera at age eight, received teaching degree at 15. Performed and choreographed in London, royal courts of Europe and Egypt until age 22. Since then she has taught and choreographed more than 50 ballets.*

*Complete curriculum for students, beg. through prof. Children may begin at age 2½; all under six must audition. Advanced students may begin pointe at 8. School's company, Ballets D'Enfants (1975) performs original classical ballets on a professional level in schools, retirement homes, etc. Admittance by audition only.*

# Ballet

## *East Bay Companies*

*Classes for adults include beg. through adv. ballet, pointe and pas de deux; private classes in ballet theory, partnering, character and expression, for certification through the Conservatory of Paris and/or the British Association of Classical Dance. Adult students may audition for company membership. The school also offers summer master classes and lecture/demonstrations to introduce schoolchildren to ballet and the infinite capacities of the body.*

***THE CLASSICAL BALLET CENTER and Berkeley Ballet Theatre, 2640 College Ave. (Julia Morgan Center for the Arts), Berkeley 94704, 415-531-0323.*** *Janet Carole, director (Pennsylvania Ballet and Les Grands Ballets Canadiens, Montreal). Teaching combines Balanchine and Ballet Russe techniques. Day and evening classes for adults, children and teens in ballet (intro. through adv.), men's and women's technique, pointe and pas de deux, modern (Elin Sowle), and jazz (Julie Lie). New classes, (exercise, dance movement) scheduled, as well as master classes featuring local guest teachers and visiting companies. Studio is 1,500 sq. ft.; sometimes available for rental. Singles and cards.*

*The Berkeley Ballet Theatre debuted summer 1979. Its philosophy is "to develop a unique sense of expression with a solid foundation of classical ballet technique and an intrinsic understanding of modern technique."*

***DANCE REPERTORY THEATRE and Alameda Civic Ballet Company, 1422 Everett St., Alameda 94501, 415-521-3230.*** *Patricia C. Hanna and Jeanne M. Woltering (SFB), directors. Pre-ballet (ages 4-6), beg. to adv. ballet (variations, character, pas de deux); pointe (by invitation); jazz, adult classes and disco. Monthly class cards. Company performances with selected advanced students. Studio also carries apparel, T-shirts, ballet bags, educational materials. Special orders welcome.*

# Ballet

## *East Bay Companies*

***THE DANCE WORKS (formerly JAZ Dance Center), 2212 Parker St., Berkeley 94704, 415-548-5962.*** *Justin Zitler, director. Classes in Ballet I-III, pas de deux. Faculty: Sara Newton, Beth Jahn, Isom, Alexandra Sawicka. See also JAZZ, EB.*

***DANCER'S THEATRE STUDIO, 6034 College Ave., Oakland 94618, 415-658-2035.*** *Jeannde Herst, artistic director. Faculty: Jean Haet (ABT); Susan Watkins (RAD, JB); Michael Davis, Cunningham. Children, adults and professionals, all levels. Studio focuses on ballet; Jeannde Herst Dance Company is modern. The ballet company is called Dancer's Repertory Theatre, and performs at local colleges and universities.*

***EAST BAY BALLET THEATRE, 1800 Dwight Way at Grant, Berkeley 94703, 415-841-8913.*** *Grace Doty, artistic director; former principal with Alan Howard's Pacific Ballet, and with Ballet Spectacular. Faculty includes Howard Sayette, formerly with Ballet Russe and Metropolitan Opera Ballet Co., current ballet master at Oakland Ballet; Deborah Kaufman. Ballet for children, teens, adults, beg. through prof. Morning exercise. Pointe, pas de deux, men's, technique, master classes.*

*Nutcracker, spring seasons. Auditions; requirements include three years of ballet, 11 years old for apprentice company, 14 for company. Classes in ballet technique, summer workshops with area guest teachers. Call 415-841-6500, ext. 481.*

***OAKLAND BALLET ACADEMY and Oakland Ballet Company, 2968 MacArthur Blvd., Oakland 94602, 415-530-7516.*** *Ronn Guidi, founder and artistic director. Classes for boys and men, pointe, variation, pas de deux; pre-ballet for children 4-6; basic, inter., adv., and prof. ballet. Floor exercises supplement all levels to develop turnout, extension and control. Tuition on sliding scale; first class free. Family and professional rates.*

*All children at the academy may belong to the Youth Company, which performs each June. Some children perform with the full company in spring, fall and Nutcracker seasons.*

## *East Bay Companies*

*Company consists of about 50 dancers with a repertoire of 26 pieces by Guidi, Massine, Loring, Pasqualetti, Caravajal, Clifford, Arpino. Applicants may audition any time by taking advanced class with Guidi. Free dance productions and demonstrations available for disadvantaged, senior citizens, handicapped, public schools. For touring information call Robert Friedman Presents, 442 41st Ave., San Francisco 94121, 415-668-4545. For more information call 530-0447 (offices at 2704 MacArthur Blvd., Oakland). Member NEA Dance Touring Program.*

***PIEDMONT BALLET, 4245 Piedmont Ave., Oakland 94611, 415-547-2048.***

# Ballet

## East Bay Classes

***ACT ONE STUDIO, 1708 Lincoln Ave., Alameda 94501, 415-523-0779.*** *Terry Ingram, director. Tap and ballet.*

***ALAMEDA SCHOOL OF DANCE AND GYMNASTICS, 1402 Park St., Alameda 94501, 415-521-2232 or 523-6110.*** *Ballet, tap, pointe, jazz and modern; ages three through adult.*

***ANDRE'S SCHOOL OF DANCE, 1341 Russell Way, Hayward 94541, 415-836-1688 (Dublin).*** *Andre and Beverly Ashour, directors. Classical ballet and pointe, jazz and tap.*

***BALLET ARTS, 4923 Harbord Drive, Oakland 94618, 415-547-9998.*** *Lynette DeFazio, director.*

***THE BALLET SCHOOL, 1402 Park St., Alameda 94501, 415-865-5423 or 522-1888.*** *Joan Vickers Coffey, director; formerly with SFB, ABT; co-established ballet department at University of Utah. Graded classes in ballet for ages four and up. Ballet-oriented exercises for women. Two to three studios; small classes, personal attention.*

***BALLET THEATRE SCHOOL, 377 MacArthur Blvd., San Leandro 94577, 415-635-8077.***

***HELEN CARROLL SCHOOL OF THEATRE DANCE, 13055 Aurora Drive, San Leandro, 415-483-9240; P.O. Box 4274, San Leandro 94579.*** *Ballet, tap, Afro and jazz.*

***CENTRAL OAKLAND DANCE STUDIO.*** *See MODERN, EB.*

***DANCE UNLIMITED, 5640 College Ave., Oakland 94618, 415-654-7009.*** *Ballet (Kirov) for children 7-13 and adults; jazz for adults. Dance conditioning and creative dance for children being added.*

## East Bay Classes

***DANSPACE, A BALLET SCHOOL, 3003 Telegraph Ave., Oakland 94609, 415-834-9219.*** *Beth Jahn, director. Beg., inter., adv., pointe, adults and children.*

***DAVLIN-LOWELL ACADEMY OF DANCE, Davlin Dance and Music School, 2311 Stuart St., Berkeley, 94705, 415-843-9740 or 832-9694.*** *Also known as Center for the Creative Arts. Ann Davlin-Lowell, director, RAD associate. Classical ballet and tap, pre-school to prof.*

***EAST BAY CENTER FOR THE PERFORMING ARTS, 339 11th St., Richmond 94801, 415-234-5624; main office, 1819 Tenth St., Berkeley 94710, 415-841-3100.*** *Community arts school that develops dance programs as well as theater and music classes for adults and children. After-school programs include ballet and creative movement. Call 415-234-5624 between 10 a.m. and 6 p.m. to register. For adults: modern, tap and jazz, technique and choreography (taught by Helen Dannenberg and Betsy Kagan). Monthly newsletter, lecture/demonstrations and performances. Performers auditioned from faculty and classes.*

***EDSON BALLET STUDIO, 825 The Alameda, Berkeley 94707, 415-526-3946.*** *See CERRITO DANCE ARTS CENTER, CCC.*

***EVERYBODY'S DANCE STUDIO.*** *See MODERN, EB.*

***FULL SPECTRUM STUDIO, 6505 Telegraph Place, Oakland 94133, 415-653-7024.*** *Lisa Bullwinkel, manager. Ballet (beg. through adv.), modern, jazz, Afro-jazz, beg. tae-kwan-do, clown theater, salsa, disco, relaxation, dance exercise, clown-mime for children, yoga, and more. Newly remodeled with 25 x 50 hardwood floor, barres, mirrors, stereo and plants. Performing space is 25 x 15. Quarter system, with new teachers accepted any time; contracts for three months. Teachers may take other classes free. Rental $2.50/hr., Sun-Fri., 8 a.m.-4 p.m.; $4.50/hr, Sun.-Fri., 4 p.m. to midnight, and all day Saturday.*

# Ballet

## *East Bay Classes*

***THE GRAND DANCE.*** *See DISCO, EB.*

***LESSER OAKLAND DANCE THEATRE.*** *See OTHER DANCES.*

***LOS AYRES DANCE STUDIOS, 1991 Bancroft Ave., San Leandro 94577, 415-483-2566.*** *Classical ballet.*

***GRACE MANN BALLET CENTER, 452 Santa Clara Ave., Oakland 94610, 415-836-9920 or 652-1728.*** *Grace Mann, director; appeared in "Spectre of the Rose" film on Nijinsky, featured in original Ballet Russe and Colonel de Basil, formed Ballet Valmann. Kirov system emphasized in classes for inter. and adv. students; children's classes three times a week. Mann coaches professionals in classical repertoire, pas de deux. Private classes by appointment. Periodic performances and master classes; studio has hardwood floors.*

***MISS PENNY'S, 21700 Redwood Rd., Castro Valley 94546, 415-581-4460 or 462-5160.*** *Penny Tomasello and Scott Francis, directors. Ballet, jazz, disco, exercise, beg.-adv., adults and children. Most of the 600 enrolled students are between 8-12. Dance Duds (above address and 7090 A Johnson, Industrial Dr., Pleasanton), supply apparel.*

*A new ballet company, Valley Dance Theatre, performs in the East Bay. The 20 dancer troupe is filled by auditions in Sept., Jan. and June.*

# Ballet

## *East Bay Classes*

***ALEXANDRA SAWICKA SCHOOL OF BALLET*, The Redwood Studio, *2212* Parker St., Berkeley *94704, 415-848-8011* or *849-4170* (evenings).** *More than 25 years at this location; day and evening classes taught by Sawicka and Patricia Schoenfield. Sawicka trained with Olga Preobajenska, Anthony Tudor, Margaret Craske and others, performed with Serge Lifar and New York Metropolitan Opera Ballet. Schoenfield trained at Tulsa Ballet Theatre and ABT school. Emphasis is on professional classical training in Cecchetti and Russian styles, with RAD for children. Occasional performances. Standard of training geared to facilitate the joy of dance. Mailing address: 2601 Regent St., Berkeley 94704.*

***SHAWL-ANDERSON MODERN DANCE CENTER, 2704* Alcatraz Ave., Berkeley *94705, 415-654-5921*.** *School founded in 1958; non-profit cultural and educational institution affiliated for credit with the California College of Arts and Crafts (see EDUCATION). Ballet (four levels), modern (three levels), and jazz (three levels); master classes by guest artists from visiting companies in all three styles, with occasional workshops and classes in kinesiology and related topics. Three studios, two 20 x 40, one 38 x 45; hardwood floors.*

*Principal faculty: Frank Shawl, trained with Charles Weidman, Martha Graham, May O'Donnell (with whom he performed for years); Victor Anderson, studied with O'Donnell and others in New York, performed with O'Donnell, Ruth St. Denis, many others; Evelyn Schuert, head of ballet department, studied with Bronislava Nijinska and danced professionally for 12 years, including SFB (classes emphasize Russian technique and building of strength, especially for those who began late); Luisa Pierce, former leading member of Lester Horton Dance Company and formerly with Martha Graham Company. Other teachers: ballet, Larry Grenier, Howard Sayette; jazz, Vicky Buchwald, Mary Kolp, Kathy Sanson, Roberta Williams; modern, Karen Attix, Jan Johnson.*

## *East Bay Classes*

*Full program in modern and ballet for children, with professional teachers. Children placed according to age and interest. Faculty includes Shuert, Jenefer Johnson (also teaches adult ballet), Sheila Kogan and Patricia Lawton. Minimum age for ballet is 8; for modern, 4-5. Enrollment limited, registration advised. Modern dance based on eight week semester; ballet on quarter system. Parents' day performances at end of all sessions.*

*Advanced modern students perform pieces from the Shawl-Anderson Modern Dance Company repertoire.*

***STAMPS SCHOOL OF CLASSICAL BALLET, 1417 Solano Ave., Albany 94706, 415-525-9575.*** *Established more than 20 years ago. Faculty: Jane Stamps, Tina Stamps Zahner, Marianne Woodson. Graded classes plus ballet camp, with ballet, jazz, music, camp activities for those in sixth grade through high school.*

***THE STARR DANCE STUDIO, 1107 MacArthur Blvd., San Leandro 94577, 415-483-6068.*** *Ballet, tap, jazz.*

***WEST COAST DANCE THEATRE.*** *See JAZZ, EB.*

# Ballet

## *Marin / Sonoma Companies*

***BALLET THEATRE WEST Studio and Company, 124 Belvedere St., San Rafael 94901, 415-456-6396 or 457-0996.*** *Barbara Begany, artistic director, formerly with SFB; Ric Mount, tap director; David Jones, jazz director; Ruth Syndon, yoga director; June Richards, drama director. Professional ballet school follows Balanchine pedagogy in which Russian technique is expanded for versatility. Graded courses in ballet, jazz, tap and yoga; threshold classes (ages 4-6); children's (7). Student division with structured syllabus to increase stamina, technique and artistry. Adult division in jazz (beg. through adv. inter.), hatha yoga, tap, professional theater (beg. through adv. acting, improvisation and musical theater). Singles and cards.*

*Three studios, equipped with Marley floors, barres and mirrors. Sizes: 30 x 70, 40 x 40 and 40 x 35. Rental $5 per hour.*

*School shares studios with Ballet Theatre West Company, a showcase for graduates of Ballet Theatre West. Apprenticeship program allows select group to rehearse, with performance possibilities. Limited number of full and partial scholarships available to qualified male students, as determined by director.*

*The company has 10 members; open auditions are held in fall and spring. It has performed 22 original ballets in the past two years, including works by guest choreographers and the company's three resident choreographers. Repertoire includes classical ballets, jazz ballets and modern works.*

***BELROSE STUDIO THEATRE and School of Dance and Performing Arts, 1415 Fifth Ave., San Rafael 94901, 415-454-6422.*** *Established 1955. Home of the Vaudeville Showcase. Ballet, jazz, tap, belly, flamenco, freestyle disco, drama, voice, musical comedy and theater workshop. Faculty: Margie Belrose, Aron Tamaroff, Louise Sims, Lynette Lynch, Rachael Lopez, Rodney Sheriff, Gillian Lovejoy.*

## *Marin/Sonoma Companies*

*Activities include shows and benefits (any student may audition, as well as those outside the studio), theater parties, movies. Each pupil allowed one free lesson a month, and to bring a guest for one free class a month. Length of classes varies according to age. Privates $6.50 per half hour.*

**MARIN CIVIC BALLET SCHOOL and Company, 100 Elm St., San Rafael 94901, 415-435-6705.** *Maria Vegh, school director (former director of Harkness House for Ballet Arts, NYC); Margaret Swarthout, company director (formerly with LRB); Norbert Vesak, company artistic director. More than 100 classes and 14 teachers in ballet, disco, exercise, tap, flamenco, modern, yoga, jazz, pointe, variations, men's ballet classes, pas de deux, dance composition and history. Master classes scheduled throughout the year; teachers have included Leonide Massine and Alexandra Danilova. Academic division classes by registered enrollment; adult classes based on 12 week vouchers. Pre-ballet and beg. ballet also taught under MCB auspices at the San Geronimo Swim and Tennis Club, 1 Garden Way, San Geronimo.*

*Company is an honorary member of the Pacific Regional Ballet Association. Open auditions held twice a year. Dancers must be 13 to be eligible for membership or internship, and must study ballet technique anywhere at least five times a week. All students have a chance to appear at least once a year in a demonstration performance; there are studio workshop performances throughout the year, Nutcracker and other seasons.*

*The school also sponsors summer day camps for boys and girls ages 6-11, in three week sessions that stress the performing arts and culminate in a production.*

*The Marin Civic Ballet Association (415-453-6705) is a non-profit organization offering memberships starting at $10 to sponsor master classes with world renowned teachers and choreographers, summer camp, classes, concerts and scholarships. Since 1972 enrollment has leaped 500% to 700 and more than $53,000 has been given in scholarships. See also DOMINICAN COLLEGE (See EDUCATION) for other MCB-related classes for credit.*

# Ballet

## *Marin/Sonoma Companies*

***PETALUMA SCHOOL OF BALLET, and Petaluma City Ballet, 7 Fourth St., Petaluma 94952, 707-762-3972.*** *Mary Paula, director. Faculty: Harold Christensen, Wendy Holt, Joyce Bierman, Ann Ringstad. Classes at all levels.*

*Petaluma City Ballet is a new group that allows local dancers to perform throughout Sonoma County. Auditions are open to all; performances include Nutcracker, spring and summer seasons.*

***SANTA ROSA BALLET SCHOOL and Company, 645 S. Fourth St., Santa Rosa 95401, 707-545-7167.*** *Susan Borgeson, director, ballet senior division; Margot Torbert, director, junior division, ballet and tap. Pre-dance (4-7); ballet levels I through adv.; adult classes in ballet I & II, jazz I & II, dancersize (includes yoga, ballet and jazz). Annual school recital for junior students. Upper level students perform in workshop productions during the year. Registration by phone or appointment to determine class placement. Singles, privates.*

***TAMALPAIS DANCE CENTER, Tamalpais Dance Theater Company, 10 Olive St., Mill Valley 94941, 415-388-5146.*** *Established 1975. Charles Perrier, director (trained with Leona Norman, Mark Wilde and others, and has choreographed more than 15 works). Faculty: David Jones, Alice Rocky, Patricia Rockwood, Martha Thomson. Professional level dance training for children and adults; ballet at all levels, with emphasis on beginners. Dance For the Very Young is a program for 3½-year-olds (and older) to gain introduction to dance through improvisation, rhythm study and simple dance movements. Studios are 25 x 40 and 20 x 20, and rentable for rehearsals, concerts, etc.*

*The center also offers in-school and community performances for the potential professional. Advanced dancers may join the resident company, which performs seasonally at the center and at some community-sponsored events.*

# Ballet

## *Marin/Sonoma Companies*

*The Tamalpais Dance Guild is a non-profit corporation that solicits funds to support dance events, including the dance history lecture/demonstration that has played to more than 3,000 Marin schoolchildren. The guild sponsors dance films, master classes and scholarships.*

# Ballet

## *Marin/Sonoma Classes*

***AQUARIUS DANCE THEATER.*** *See JAZZ, MARIN.*

***RUBY CHRISTENSEN SCHOOL OF BALLET, Wisteria Bay and Almonte Blvd., Mill Valley 94941, 415-388-9863 or 453-1619.***

***CONSERVATORY OF BALLET AND THEATRE ARTS, 22 Brassie Court, Novato 94947, 415-883-4767 or 883-4306.*** *Jeannie Mullen, director; performed at University of Utah. CCofA certified. Pre-ballet (4-6), academic I (7-9), academic II, inter.-adv., pointe, and teens/adults ballet exercise/jazz. Musical comedy, creative arts, tap, jazz, disco. Guest teachers include Beryl Casazza, David Jones. Singles, class cards.*

***DANCE ACADEMY OF MARIN, 1611 Fourth St., San Rafael 94901, 415-454-4412.*** *Norma Glenn, director. Ballet, jazz, tap for beg. and inter., 4 years old and up.*

***DANCE ARTS OF MARIN, 5603C Paradise Drive, Corte Madera 94925, 415-924-1538.*** *Marilyn Izdebski and Jacklyn Dana, directors. Emphasis on classical ballet; theatrical dance, jazz and tap available. Workshops in musical theater, acting and performance technique. All ages. Ballet emphasis on correct placement, line and musicality. Jazz technique based on Broadway musical styles. Minimum age for tap is 5; theater classes, 10; jazz, 10; ballet, 8.*

***DANCE ARTS STUDIOS, Montecito Shopping Center, 361C Third St., San Rafael 94901, 415-459-1020.*** *Ballet, jazz, disco (NY and LA, beg. through prof.), modern, international style of Latin American and modern ballroom, social dancing, body conditioning. Private lessons by appointment. Faculty: Parrish, Christine Smith, Sandy Meyer, Marin Isabeau, Debbie Obiedo, Luis Arnold and Jerry Youngblood.*

# Ballet

## *Marin/Sonoma Classes*

***LET'S MOVE, INC., 82 Corte Del Coronado, Larkspur 94939, 415-924-6716.***

***MARIN SCHOOL OF DANCE, 419 Via Herbosa, Ignacio 94947, 415-883-6813.***

***MARVELEEN DANCE STUDIO.*** *See TAP, MARIN.*

***REC RUSSEL DANCE STUDIO.*** *See JAZZ, MARIN.*

***SAN GERONIMO SWIM AND TENNIS CLUB.*** *See BALLET, MARIN.*

## *Peninsula Companies*

***PACIFIC DANCE CENTER and Palo Alto Dance Theater, 514 High St., Palo Alto 94301, 415-32D-ANCE (322-2222).*** *Richard L. Gibson, director. Complete ballet training, beg. to adv., six days a week, Sept. through June, with intensive six week summer workshop. Pre-ballet, basic I-III, inter. I-III, adv., pointe, character, adult beg. and basic; modern. Company offers a bridge of commitment between student and professional. School located in a historical landmark, one block from bus and train depots.*

*Gibson was director of Peninsula Ballet Theater, leaving to direct the Royal Conservatory in Holland. Ballet master and choreographer for the Netherlands Dance Theater, Joffrey Ballet company teacher. Currently artistic director of the new Palo Alto Dance Theater and SFB company teacher. Company has several performances a year.*

***PENINSULA BALLET THEATRE SCHOOL and Company, 333 South B, San Mateo 94401, 415-343-8485.*** *Anne Bena, director. Official school of the Peninsula Ballet Theatre Company. Full classical ballet curriculum for beg. through prof. from Sept. through June, with six-week summer session. Three studios.*

*Company repertoire covers classical ballet, modern and jazz. It performs at Spangenberg Theatre, 780 Arastradero Road, Palo Alto, and at the San Mateo Performing Arts Center, 650 N. Delaware, San Mateo. Seasons in fall, Nutcracker, spring and summer (outdoor).*

***THE SAN CARLOS DANCE COLLECTIVE (formerly The Dance Institute), 1144 Holly St., San Carlos 94070, 415-595-5733.*** *Judy Johnson, director. Ballet, tap, jazz, belly, disco. Performing line of dancers, "The Collectibles."*

# Ballet

## *Peninsula Classes*

***ANABEL'S SCHOOL OF BALLET, P.O. Box 392, San Carlos 94070, 415-367-0806.*** *Established in 1945 by Anabel Mueller "to provide the best classical ballet foundation to prepare young people for futures in dance or dance academics." Ronda Tennison Rush, director. Faculty: Karen Rush, Wendy Lufrano. Classical ballet (beg. through adv.) with pointe and pas de deux in Casa de Flores building, 737 Walnut St., San Carlos 94070. Recitals expose students to traditional and new choreography, related theater arts.*

***BALLET ARTS CENTER OF PALO ALTO, 3825 Middlefield Road, Palo Alto 94303, 415-493-2195.*** *Lorna Affleck, director. Faculty: Leilani Krainer-Strelis (Maryland Ballet); Sandra Scheinberg (Miami Ballet). Eleven grades of ballet, jazz (three levels), pointe and pas de deux. Monthly cards, professional and family rates.*

***THE BALLET SCHOOL, 601 Escuela Ave., Mountain View 94040, 415-965-0895.*** *Connie Schwarze, director; training includes Bolshoi and Vaganova schools. Pre-ballet (5-7) for rhythm, coordination; beg. through adv. ballet. Minimum age 8. Syllabus includes terminology, music, character dance, technique and performance ability. Adult ballet and body conditioning classes. Summer workshop at inter. and adv. levels with ballet, pointe, character, jazz and variations. Singles and monthly cards.*

*Classes limited in size. Excursions offered for ballet arts appreciation. One major performance each spring, plus smaller ones at end of workshop. Studio space rentable, rates depending on equipment needs.*

***BEAUDOIN'S SCHOOL OF DANCE, 464 Colorado Ave., Palo Alto 94306, 415-326-2184.*** *Flo and Heston Beaudoin, directors and teachers. Member DMofA and California CCofA. Ballet, jazz, tap, disco and ballroom, children and adults, group and private. Students perform for hospitals and convalescent homes, etc.*

# Ballet

## *Peninsula Classes*

***CALIFORNIA ACADEMY OF BALLET, 961 Laurel St., San Carlos 94070, 415-592-0421.*** *Juliette Fischer, director (National Ballet of Canada). Specializes in ballet, with classes in jazz and folk. Workshops, guest teachers, small performances. Creative dance (age 5), basic I-III, beg. through adv. for adults, privates and teacher training. Two large studios. Parents may watch at start of each month.*

***CONSERVATOIRE DE BALLET, 141 Cambridge Lane, San Bruno 94066, 415-589-4409.*** *Ballet, jazz, summer workshops; beg. through prof., children and adults.*

***DANCE ARTS CENTER AT MARLIN COVE, 1020 Foster City Blvd., Foster City 99404, 415-574-2001.*** *Berle Davis, director, teaching jazz and tap; Jayne Zaban, (soloist, Atlanta Ballet), ballet and children's jazz. Davis also directs and choreographs for The Jazz Set, a professional performing company based at the center; members are auditioned from inter. and adv. classes. Studios are 45 x 33 and 21 x 21. A professional-oriented school with emphasis on musical theater; voice and drama.*

***STEVE AND MICKI GRANGER'S DANCE THEATRE WORKSHOP, 649 San Mateo Ave., San Bruno 94066, 415-583-5980.*** *Classical ballet, modern ballet, stylized tap, ballroom.*

***SONIA IVANOVA ACADEMY OF CLASSICAL BALLET, 651 University Ave., Palo Alto 94301, 415-329-0134.***

***THE ROBERT KIRKPATRICKS' SCHOOL OF DANCE EDUCATION, 24 Second Ave., San Mateo 94401, 415-342-3313 or 341-3535.*** *Pre-school (3-5); ballet with tap (6 and up); Cecchetti style (8 and up); modern jazz. Teens and adults welcome.*

# Ballet

## *Peninsula Classes*

***KIROV-CORDELLE SCHOOL OF CLASSICAL BALLET, 395 First St., Los Altos 94022, 415-948-3603 or 736-2229.*** *Lucilla Cordelle, ballet mistress. Imperial Russian (Bolshoi) tradition of classes; tots, beginners, career-minded, pointe, beg. adults, teens.*

***LEE LANE DANCE STUDIO, 384 Broadway, Millbrae 94030, 415-697-7163.*** *Specialize in children's classes; special adult classes. Ballet, tap, modern jazz, character.*

***MAJOR DANCE STUDIO.*** *See DISCO, Peninsula.*

***MENLO PARK ACADEMY OF DANCE, 1163 El Camino Real, Menlo Park 94025, 415-323-5292; also 1665 Fernside, Redwood City 94061.*** *Established 1947. Rose Ann Sayler, director (RAD, CCofA, DMofA). Classical ballet, stage dancing, tap, jazz. Special boys' classes.*

***NANCY'S DANCE STUDIO.*** *See TAP, Peninsula.*

***SHEILA NELSON SCHOOL OF DANCING, 1144 Holly, San Carlos 94070, 415-593-5275.*** *Member RAD and British Dance Teachers of America. Ballet and jazz, group or private.*

***SAN JUAN SCHOOL OF DANCE, 140 Third St., Los Altos 94022, 415-948-6287.*** *Jean San Juan, director. RAD children's examiner; RAD associate; fellow Imperial Society Teachers of Dancing, London; member DMofA. Daily classical ballet, jazz, tap and folk.*

***SAN MATEO CITY PARKS DEPT.*** *See GROUPS/SPONSORS--CITY.*

***GLEN SHIPLEY SCHOOL OF THE DANCE.*** *See TAP, Peninsula.*

# Ballet

## *Peninsula Classes*

***SUGANO-JONSSON SCHOOL OF BALLET, 131 Mira Way, Menlo Park 94025, 415-854-6169 or 324-4521.*** *Kimiko Sugano-Jonsson; trained with Vera Volkova, Olga Preobrajenska. Classical ballet, beg. through adv. (pointe) based on Cecchetti and Vaganova (Kirov).*

*Classes in Redwood City and Atherton, under aegis of Town Atherton, Redwood City Parks and Recreation Department. Recital in late spring, Canada College auditorium. Talented students are encouraged to take master classes at nearby Stanford, and to audition with the SFB school (all pupils who auditioned summer, 1978, were accepted). Fees adjusted for number of children in family and classes per week. Full and partial scholarships for boys and girls "with motivation and promise."*

***MARLENE THERKELSEN DANCE STUDIO.*** *See MODERN, Peninsula.*

***JUDY TOROK SCHOOL OF BALLET, 890 Laurel, San Carlos 94070, 415-592-9666 or 591-3989.*** *Formerly teacher in Budapest and at Troyanoff Ballet Academy. Pre-ballet through adv. adult.*

***ZOHAR SCHOOL OF DANCE, 655 Arastradero Rd., Palo Alto 94306, 415-858-2161.*** *Faculty includes Uta Enders (SFB), Marilyn Trounson (LRB, Stuttgart Ballet). Two studios with wood floors. Space available for community arts events.*

# Ballet

## *San Francisco Companies*

***ARABESQUE CONCERT DANCE, 2184 Greenwich St., SF 94123, 415-922-2755.*** *Pepper Smith, director and principal choreographer; Tance Johnson, choreographer. Contemporary ballets with jazz influence. Beginning choreographers encouraged. Ballet and modern for adults. Touring, workshops, program for kids. Company performs at 456 Post, SF 94102, 397-3764 (BART-Powell). See also SMITH STUDIOS, below.*

***CHILDREN'S BALLET THEATRE and School, 3569 Sacramento St., SF 94118, 415-921-9777.*** *Productions include Wizard of Oz.*

***JANINA CYWINSKA'S BALLET School and Company, 2900 Judah St., SF 94122, 415-681-3560.*** *Janina Cywinska, director; trained in Leningrad. Classes limited in size and emphasize correct technique, health-giving benefits of a disciplined body, balanced living. Company class, children I-II, adult classes, partnering and variations. Singles, monthly and unlimited cards.*

***PACIFIC BALLET CENTER Studio and Company, 1519 Mission St., SF 94103, 415-626-1351.*** *Founded 1960 by Alan Howard; John Pasqualetti artistic director since 1974, shifting emphasis from classical to contemporary ballet. Faculty: Michael Bradshaw, Alyce Taylor, Kahz Amudd. Guest teachers: Larry Burgoon, Maria Vegh.*

*Three studios offer variety of traditional ballet for beg., inter., adv. and prof. with workshops.*

*Company has toured California extensively, as well as France, Italy and Israel. Past three years spent refocusing, expanding facilities and local performances with aim to increase enrollment so company can have larger selection of qualified dancers. Repertoire includes works by Pasqualetti and several full length ballets.*

*Studio space rented to groups and individuals for auditions, rehearsals, classes, etc.*

# Ballet

## *San Francisco Companies*

***SAN FRANCISCO BALLET School and Company, 378 18th Ave., SF 94121, 415-751-2141.*** *Est. 1933. Lew Christensen and Michael Smuin, artistic directors. Richard Cammack, school director. Faculty includes Christine Bering (SFB); Christine Busch (ABT, SFB); Zola Dishong (ABT, SFB); Larry Grenier (Joffrey Ballet, Twyla Tharp); Zelda Mortimer (SFB); Susan Parry (Ballet West); Mary Ruud (Ballet West); Sally Streets (NYCB, official company teacher); Anatole Vilzak (Maryinski, Diaghilev, Ballet Russe de Monte Carlo). Company teachers include Richard Gibson, Larry Grenier.*

*Academic, company and adult ballet division. Threshold division (Marlene Swendson, director) offers 13 progressive levels; children's basic (8-10, no audition); student division (audition required; eight levels divided by age). School includes apprentice program whereby selected students rehearse with the company, with performance possibilities in large productions. Advanced students take pointe, men's class, pas de deux, and male and female variations,, both contemporary and classical; no master classes or workshops offered. Parents may visit the last class each month.*

*Adult division classes are given mornings and evenings, beg. through adv. Class enrollment limited; registration is required, though single classes may be taken.*

*As the first company to have six resident choreographers (Lew Christensen, Michael Smuin, John McFall, Robert Gladstein, Tom Ruud and Jerome Weiss), the company has developed an active repertoire of 65 ballets performed in three local seasons (Nutcracker, winter/spring, and summer) and on tour in Alaska, Hawaii, the Pacific Northwest, the Southwest and Midwest.*

*For audition information, call the school's administrator, Caroline Krieger, 751-2141. Formal audition times are not held; those interested in joining may take company class with Smuin's permission. Members are sometimes taken from other states after SFB's tours and talent scouts.*

*The school functions in a building owned by the San Francisco Ballet Association, with four studios comprising 9,365 sq. ft. The company has received an NEA Challenge Grant to raise $1.4 million dollars to build new, expanded facilities near the Opera House.*

*The ballet maintains a free Speaker's Program, consisting of talks illustrated with slides, films and/or live demonstrations. For information call the Community Relations Department, 751-2141, ext. 220.*

***SAN FRANCISCO CONSERVATORY OF BALLET AND THEATER ARTS, 1929 Irving, SF 94122, 415-731-7755 or 731-4454.*** *Includes the Nova Academy, Ballet Celeste-International, professional dancers/teachers training course. Merriem Lanova, director. Range of classes for children and adults, pre-school through professional. Twelve grades of ballet available, jazz, tap, and private lessons, body awareness, grace and exercise.*

*The Nova Academy, established in 1955, is the only complete academic school operated by any ballet foundation in the U.S. It offers a professionally-recognized curriculum for grades 1-12, as well as a four year college program. A two year teacher's course is offered for post high school age people, culminating in a state-authorized diploma certifying proficiency as a professional dancer. Curriculum includes dance and art histories, choreography, dance notation, studio rhythm, harmony and practice teaching.*

*Ballet Celeste, the junior apprentice company of Pacific Dance Theater, is a training ground for the Theatre Ballet of San Francisco, with an annual workshop combining several weeks of classes and rehearsals. Tours have included Japan, Alaska and Europe. Ballet Celeste children fill ballets such as Nutcracker. Alexandra Danilova selected the first company in 1949; since then, auditions have been presided over by many notables, including Igor Youskevitch and Tamara Toumanova.*

# San Francisco Companies

*The Theatre Ballet of San Francisco was founded in 1973 with the Nutcracker season. It participates in the California segment of the NEA Dance Touring Program. It is an ensemble company of 12 dancers offering performances, residencies and master classes.*

***SAN FRANCISCO DANCE SPECTRUM, 3321 22nd St., SF 94110, 415-824-5044.*** *Carlos Carvajal, founder, artistic director and choreographer; Jean Mathis, school director. Ballet (beg. through adv./prof. and company, pointe), yoga, modern, jazz, flamenco, tap. Children's program includes tap, ballet, creative dance, pointe, with recitals. Adult classes: ballet (nine graded levels), movement dynamics, pas de deux, adagio and men's and women's variations, modern and yoga for dancers, Afro-Caribbean Brazilian dance. Faculty includes Maria Vegh, Howard Sayette, Bruce Bain, Henry Berg, Sharon Marks, Jim Piersall.*

*Company repertoire includes about 40 pieces danced by about 20 core members with ranks filled in larger pieces by students. To audition, take company classes with Carvajal. Regular performing seasons winter and spring.*

***SAN FRANCISCO DANCE THEATER, 1412 Van Ness Ave., SF 94109, 415-673-8101.*** *Penelope Lagios Johnson, artistic director; former principal with SFB and soloist with Alonso's National Ballet of Cuba. Non-profit, tax exempt, educational and charitable California corporation.*

*Junior division students are given individual instruction geared to maturity and physical abilities. Registration is continuous. Seven graded levels from pre-ballet (5-8) to advanced (audition only). The division features Chrysalis, a performing company whose dancers range in age from 12 to 18. For registration information call 673-8101; Jody White, junior division director. (She can also give performance information.)*

*Adult division offers classes in ballet, pointe, jazz, and modern. Faculty includes Wendy Ballard, Emily Keeler, Alan Scofield and about 15 others. Enrollment open at all times. Singles and class cards.*

*The San Francisco Dance Theater is a performing group with modern and classical repertoire. It performs at the Van Ness Studio and the Palace of Fine Arts. Johnson also offers studio workshop performances, lecture/demonstrations and concerts at Bay Area schools and colleges.*

***MARC WILDE BALLET, Fort Mason Center, Bldg. 312, Marina at Laguna, SF 94123, 415-441-0535.*** *A dance workshop group with classes in ballet, modern, jazz; beg. through adv., all ages.*

# Ballet

## *San Francisco Classes*

***ACADEMY OF BALLET, 2121 Market St., SF 94114, 415-552-1166.*** *Janet Sassoon, director (Grand Bal du Marquis de Cuevas, Berlin Ballet). Classical ballet for children and adults. Company classes for San Francisco Dance Spectrum.*

***BALLET ARTS OF SAN FRANCISCO, 3528 Washington St., SF 94118, 415-567-1887.*** *Established 1968. Roberta Meyer, director (SFB and NYCB). Ballet is foundation of program, which includes tap and gymnastics. Classes held at Burke's School, 195 32nd Ave., SF. Tuition paid by semester; deposit secures place in class. School year Sept. through June.*

***BALLET RUSSE-MUSIC AND DANCE, 2105 O'Farrell St., SF 94115, 415-567-5691, 922-5921.*** *Natalia Borisova, Marsha Wales, directresses; trained with Kirov and Bolshoi ballets, Vienna State Opera Ballet, Moiseyev Dance Company, Sadlers Wells Ballet, character with Anatole Joukovsky. Curriculum stresses strong technique in academic Russian traditions of music and dance, versatility and expressiveness through stage performances and exposure to other techniques such as Russian character dancing (ballet, music and art history).*

***CAROL BEALS SCHOOL OF DANCE, 2201 Clement St., SF 94121, 415-752-6699 or 346-6672.*** *Facutly: Carol Beals (Cecchetti graded ballet), Carole-Geneve (modern based on Charles Weidman); Alan Scofield (jazz blending modern, ethnic). Ballet curriculum includes fundamentals (6-8, 8-19), and grades I-VII, with V-VII including pointe. Ballet students may take Cecchetti exams when determined ready by instructors. Beals and Geneve are members of CCofA and are qualified to sponsor applicants for the CCofA teacher examination.*

*Children's classes in creative modern are divided into five age groups, from 3 to 16. Ages above 16 qualify for the adult schedule, which includes eight levels of Cecchetti graded ballet, pointe, jazz (American-African, Afro-Cuban, modern), rhythmic and daily exercise, body movement. Singles and class cards.*

***BUSH STREET STUDIO, 1438 Bush St., SF 94109, 415-731-6795 or 731-1602.*** *Ballet classes with John Garb. All levels; trouble-shooting style for adv. and prof. Privates available.*

***COMPANY IN FLIGHT, at Samuel Lewis Studios, 3316 24th St., SF 94110, 415-282-4020.*** *Ballet with Theresa Hill (Cecchetti), jazz, modern, Limon. Beg. through adult levels.*

***DANCE ARTS ACADEMY, 1 Washington, Daly City 94014, 415-992-6873.***

***DANCE CENTER, Central YMCA, 220 Golden Gate Ave., SF 94102, 415-885-0460.*** *Ballet, tap, modern, musical theater.*

***DANCE SOURCE.*** *See MODERN, SF.*

***EARTHLY STUDIOS.*** *See MODERN, SF.*

***LORNA FORDYCE DANCE STUDIO, 1926 Lawton St., SF 94122, 415-681-2150.*** *Established more than 26 years ago. Member DMofA and CCofA. Pre-school through prof., Cecchetti ballet, tap, jazz, Hawaiian, ballroom.*

***GOLDEN GATE BALLET CENTER, 3435 Army St., Suite 224, SF 94110, 415-626-1138.*** *Faculty: Sue Loyd and Henry Berg, directors, (SFB and Joffrey); Gay Wallstrom. Lower division: beg. children (8-12); inter. children (12-16); floor barre. Upper division: inter., pointe, adv., men, floor barre.*

## San Francisco Classes

**HYDE & GREEN COMPANY Studios, 1898 Hyde St., SF 94109, 415-441-2130.** James Howell (Joffrey Ballet; choreographic assistant, music consultant to Gerald Arpino) teaches daily classes for greater flexibility and coordination, increased awareness of balance and alignment of head, neck and back through use of classical ballet, hatha yoga and Alexander technique. Program for basic/beginning dancers, actors, atheletes,--anyone who lives inside a body, says Howell. May join class at any time; $5/class. Pre-ballet for ages 5-7, $3 per class on Sat. mornings.

Ward Smith teaches yoga/dance (ballet, yoga and tai chi ch'uan) to relieve tension, strengthen body, Monday evenings.

**KAY'S SCHOOL OF DANCE.** See TAP, SF.

**SAMUEL L. LEWIS STUDIOS, 3316 24th St., SF 94110, 415-282-4020.** Classes with Nancy Henderson (Pacific Ballet) emphasize centering and presence. Beg./inter. and inter./adv., pointe and floor barre.

**MASON-KAHN STUDIOS.** See TAP, SF.

**BETTY MAY SCHOOLS.** See TAP, SF.

**MODERN JAZZ WORKS.** See JAZZ, SF.

**ONE STEP AT A TIME STUDIO OF DANCE, 115 Manor Dr., Pacifica 94044, 415-355-0229.** Unda Blaine, director.

**AMY POWELL DANCE STUDIO.** See DISCO, SF.

**RECONSTELLATION, INC., 253 or 255 Leavenworth, SF 94102, 415-221-3333 (Mary Alice Mabee), ext. 434 or 441-2640.** 8-11 a.m. Ballet, pointe variations from classical repertoire, pointe *lab on balance in turns, contact improvisation based on ballet, modern jazz, other workshops. Center warmups, no barre. Sessions end in classical and modern duets for performances with new company. Private lessons by apointment. Rental contracts for non-company classes, rehearsals, performances.*

**RUTHIE'S SCHOOL OF DANCE.** *See TAP, SF.*

**SCHUMACHER'S SCHOOL OF DANCE, 222 Mosswood Way, South San Francisco 94080, 415-871-6913 or 871-4278.** *Established 1964. Dolly Schumacher James, director-choreographer. Performing arts center with classes for pre-school, teens and adults, private or group. Classical ballet (minimum age, 7), stylized tap, creative dance, acrobatics, modern jazz, technique (2½-4 yrs. old), disco, adult tap, adult ballet and adult creative jazz. Three classrooms, staff of eight. Parents may watch the last lesson each month.*

*A student performing group is available for bookings at clubs, schools, churches and other non-profit organizations. Yearly dance recital and musical production are held in June; every student has a chance to participate. Schumacher's is the official South San Francisco representative at the county fair each year at the end of July, with highlights from the major recital.*

**SMITH STUDIOS, 456 Post St., Second Floor, SF 94102, 415-397-3764.** *Pepper Smith, director; Tance Johnson, guest teacher. Richard Garcia, Marsha Pannone, Joan Potter. Ballet, modern and jazz. Choreography workshops, character classes. $5/single/class cards. Repertory group is Arabesque Concert Dance.*

**STAR DANCE STUDIO, 1883 10th Ave., SF 94122, 415-564-1200.** *Founded by Ruth Jevarian in 1951. Maxine Powell, director. Predominantly a children's school of dance (with more adult* *classes being added), classes are held Sept. through June. Most are filled by November, though there is no obligation to enroll for the full semester. Most students complete the course and perform in the June dance recital.*

*Pre-school (3½-5); beg. movements of tap, ballet and acrobatics; pre-school (4-6), adding combinations; beg. I (6-8) beg. II (9-12); beg.-inter. combination; beg. ballet (8-10, focus on posture, poise and grace); inter. ballet (11-15); beg. jazz and tap (13-18); adv. tap and beg. inter. jazz (13-18); adult tap, disco and jazz II. All classes last an hour; parents may visit class with permission from instructor. Monthly rates.*

**SUNDANCE STUDIO.** *See MODERN, SF.*

***THE SURF DANCE STUDIO, 4504 Irving St. at 46th Ave., SF 94122, 415-566-9122 or 359-2515.*** *Rosalie Bravo, Deirdre Carrigan, Janine Nolfi, instructors in ballet, jazz, tap for all ages.*

***TATIANA SVETLANOVA SCHOOL OF BALLET, 1944 Clement St., SF 94121, 415-752-1676.*** *Taught Margot Fonteyn in China; classes at all levels, all ages.*

***EVELYN WENGER BALLET SCHOOL, 3569 Sacramento St., SF 94118, 415-921-9777.*** *Same as Children's Ballet Theatre School.*

**XOREGOS STUDIO.** *See MODERN, SF.*

## San Jose Companies

***EUFRAZIA SCHOOL OF BALLET and Ballet Ensemble, 1461 Park Ave., SJ 95126, 408-241-1300.*** *Beverly Eufrazia Grant, director. Cater to children and those of college age who had some training when younger. Beg. through adv. ballet, graded for children. Annual studio performance for families.*

*The Eufrazia Ballet Ensemble is a small group of students who have progressed in skill through pointe to perform at local events. In five years the company has built a repertoire of 20 pieces, including one full-length, original ballet. It performs at the Sunnyvale Community Theater.*

***SAN JOSE BALLET SCHOOL and Dance Theatre, 157 N. Fourth St., SJ 95112, 408-297-6171.*** *Dimitri Romanoff. Classical ballet, all grades.*

***SANTA CLARA BALLET SCHOOL and Company, 2086 El Camino Real, Santa Clara 95051, 408-247-9178 or 248-3997.*** *Josepha Villanueva and Benjamin Reyes, directors. Reyes danced with SFB and SF Opera Ballet, and was choreographer, ballet master and premier danseur with the SF Conservatory of Ballet. He trained at the School of American Ballet, Ballet Russe de Monte Carlo school, and ABT school. Villanueva was with SFB, SF Opera Ballet, and SF Ballet Celeste. She trained in the Philippines, SFB, and ABT. Reyes has a degree from San Francisco State University, where he is on the faculty; Villanueva earned a degree in music and is a staff member of San Jose City College.*

*Highly classical and contemporary approaches to dance with emphasis on technique, whether the student plans a dance career or not. Pre-ballet (4½-6), children's ballet division, inter. and adv. ballet, character, men's class, adagio, ballet for adults and Afro-jazz. Classes paid singly or by the month.*

*Company repertoire includes Nutcracker and about a dozen other pieces. Dancers are auditioned in Jan., June and Sept., for spring, fall and winter seasons. The company performs locally, and has toured Oregon and Washington.*

# Ballet

## San Jose Classes

***ACADEMY OF BALLET, 2905 Park Ave., Santa Clara 95050, 408-295-5394 or 248-3567.*** *Established 1950. Janet Vertin, director.*

***ACADEMY OF DANCE ARTS, 988 W. El Camino Real, Sunnyvale 94087, 415-739-7182.*** *Dawn Sarto, director; RAD associate. Ballet, pointe, jazz, tap, belly, disco, yoga, exercise and production. Master classes, performances and recitals. Studio is 1,500 sq. ft. and rentable. Ehud Krauss teaches jazz focused on starting a touring company.*

***ACADEMY OF SPEECH AND DANCE, 1720 Hopkins Drive, SJ 95122, 408-923-9539.*** *Ballet, African (master classes), drama, disco, speech therapy, tap, charm course. Beg. through inter., ages 4 and above. Recitals at end of each session; voluntary participation in monthly local performances.*

***ALMADEN BALLET AND SCHOOL OF THEATRE ARTS, 1433 Branham Lane, SJ 95118, 408-264-5884.*** *Katherine Bartholomew, director; formerly with ABT, teaching in San Jose area since 1963. Seven graded ballet classes, including pre-ballet, beg. through adv. for juniors and adults. Creative dance for children under 5. Studio is 26 x 40 with oak hardwood floor. Tuition based on number of classes per week. Enrollment limited; registration required. Visitors by appointment only.*

***ALOHA'S STUDIO OF DANCE.*** *See TAP, SJ.*

***MARIAN ANDRES DANCE STUDIO.*** *See JAZZ, SJ.*

***ATLAS SCHOOL OF DANCE.*** *See TAP, SJ.*

***BALLET TODAY, 1984 Homestead Road, Santa Clara 95050, 408-984-6008.*** *Carol Tobkin, director. Children through advanced; Cecchetti graded method. Also modern, jazz, tap, Aida's Spanish dance with Aida Cabral.*

# Ballet

## *San Jose Classes*

***RUBY BARLEY SCHOOL OF DANCE.*** *See TAP, SJ.*

***GLORIA MOHR BUSLIK INTERNATIONAL BALLET SCHOOL, 236 W. Campbell Ave., Campbell 95008, 408-269-3079.*** *Buslik formerly with NYCB. Graded classical ballet from preschool through adv.; Spanish.*

***CALIFORNIA YOUNG WORLD.*** *Five studios; see TAP, SJ.*

***DANCE ART STUDIO, 1094 S. Second St., SJ 95112, 408-293-1930.*** *Glenna Bell Moenning, director; member DMofA, CCofA, Imperial Society of Teaching and Dancing, London. Cecchetti graded ballet; modern jazz, tap, Hawaiian and Spanish.*

***MICHAEL DAVID'S SCHOOL.*** *See JAZZ, SJ.*

***LIVIA DETRE SCHOOL OF CLASSICAL BALLET, 4173 Monet Circle, SJ 95136, 408-578-9520.*** *Detre was soloist in Hungary; classes stress Russian technique from age 5 through adult.*

***PAM EAST'S SCHOOL OF DANCE.*** *See JAZZ, SJ (Cupertino).*

***LORRAINE EVANS SCHOOL OF DANCE, 1045 S. Saratoga-Sunnyvale Road, SJ 95129, 408-996-8022.*** *Ballet, tap and jazz.*

***FRAZIER DANCE STUDIO, 4945 Manitoba Dr., SJ 95130, 408-379-4907.*** *Beg. through adv. ballet, jazz and tap.*

***LOS ALTOS BALLET SCHOOL, 1st and Whitney, Los Altos 94022, 408-948-9898.***

***LOS GATOS ACADEMY OF DANCE, 16 Lyndon Ave., Los Gatos 95030, 408-354-3930.*** *Paul Curtis, director; Shawn Stewart, associate director. Classical ballet, graded from pre-ballet through teens and adults. Modern jazz, modern and tap also offered.*

# Ballet

## San Jose Classes

***MARY ANN'S DANCE CENTER.*** *See TAP, SJ.*

***URSULA MILLETT SCHOOL OF BALLET, 38 Chabot Ave., Santa Clara, 408-247-3857.*** *Millett was formerly with National Ballet of Canada. Graded ballet for children and adults, from pre-ballet through adv. Therapeutic referrals and jazz classes also available.*

***DEAN NENA SCHOOL OF DANCE AND MUSIC.*** *See TAP, SJ.*

***REA SCHOOL OF DANCING.*** *See TAP, SJ.*

***CATHERINE REUTHER SCHOOL OF BALLET, Branham Lane and Pearl Ave., SJ 95136, 408-265-7368.*** *Member RAD. Classical ballet for children, teens and adults; modern jazz and modern.*

***SARATOGA DANCE SCHOOL, Studio Park Place, Saratoga 95070, 408-867-4210.*** *Ursula Gerlitz, director. Classes in ballet and jazz, pre-school through adv.*

***SARATOGA MUSIC AND FINE ARTS CENTER.*** *See MODERN, SJ.*

***SCHOOL OF BALLET ARTS, 240 N. Bascom Ave., SJ 95128, 408-286-6118 or 984-2320.*** *Lelia Parello, director; worked professionally with SFB, SF Opera Ballet, Pacific Ballet, Ballet San Jose and San Jose Dance Theatre; many teaching and choreographic credits. Ballet for beg. children, beg. adults, inter. adults, beg. pointe, inter.-adv. ballet, and ballet exercise for adults. Singles and cards for six to eight weeks.*

***SCHOOL OF RUSSIAN BALLET, 4188 Jarvis Ave., SJ 95118, 408-269-1210.*** *Mrs. Virgina Ernenwein, director; worked professionally with Ruth St. Denis; studied Russian ballet under Theodore Bekefi and trained with Nijinsky in Leningrad. Has taught for 30 years, 19 in San Jose. No yearly recital, but about every two years qualified students perform a complete ballet in concert.*

# Ballet

## *San Jose Classes*

***BENNY SMITH ACADEMY OF DANCE, 2047 Broadway, Redwood City 94063, 415-364-6141; 655 Grape Ave., Sunnyvale 94087, 408-739-5466; 527 Valley Way, Milipitas 95035, 408-262-7546; 1946-48 Camden Ave., San Jose 95124, 408-371-2170.*** *Ballet, tap, jazz; ages 3-prof. Home of Benny Smith Dancers (perform at Miss California and Miss America pagaents).*

***TUDE'S SCHOOL OF DANCE, 1593 Pomeroy Ave., Santa Clara 95051, 408-985-1087 or 736-3407.*** *Tude Della Maggiore, director; member NADAA. Ballet, tap, jazz.*

# Ballet

## *Summer Workshops Groups*

***BALLET WEST Summer Dance School at Aspen/Snowmass, P.O. Box 8745, Aspen, CO 81611, 801-364-4343.*** *Under direction of William Christensen, University of Utah Dance Department. Two, three-week sessions in teaching Bournonville technique; pointe, jazz, character, pas de deux, modern.*

***JACOB'S PILLOW DANCE FESTIVAL, Box 287, Lee, MA 02138, 413-637-1322.*** *Norman Walker, artistic director. A summer training and performing program that has produced multi-company concerts for many years. Ballet technique and repertory, variations, pointe, modern (Graham-based), modern repertory, composition, improvisation, Spanish technique, jazz, rhythmic analysis. Three meals a day, some 20 rustic cottages with complete baths, included. Three, six and nine week courses; full and partial scholarships available.*

## *Groups*

***NATIONAL ASSOCIATION FOR REGIONAL BALLET, Craft of Choreographers Conferences, c/o Doris Jenkins, Box 172, Mill Valley, CA 94941.*** *Choreography, technique, music.*

***NATIONAL ASSOCIATION FOR REGIONAL BALLET, 1860 Broadway, NYC 10023, 212-575-9540.*** *Doris Hering, executive director. Center of information, arranges workshops, job placement, exchange of choreographers, obtains performing outlets. Newsletter, Dance America.*

***CECCHETTI COUNCIL OF AMERICA, c/o Jane Caryl Miller, 770 Greenhills Drive, Ann Arbor, MI 48105.*** *Organized in 1939, incorporated 1951; devoted to serious ballet teachers who adhere to Cecchetti instruction or who wish to become acquainted with it. Cecchetti style is known for development of speed, elevation and attack. Monthly meetings and summer school for students, seminars for teachers. Membership: c/o 1964 Detroit St., Dearborn, MI 48124.*

# Ballet

## *Style References*

*STUDIOS WITH CECCHETTI EMPHASIS:*

***BALLET TODAY.*** *See BALLET, SJ.*

***CAROL BEALS.*** *See BALLET, SF.*

***BEAUDOIN'S SCHOOL OF DANCE.*** *See BALLET, Peninsula.*

***CONSERVATORY OF BALLET AND THEATRE ARTS.*** *See BALLET, Marin & Sonoma.*

***CONTRA COSTA ACADEMY OF DANCING ARTS.*** *See BALLET, CCC.*

***DANCE ART STUDIO.*** *See BALLET, SJ.*

***LORNA FORDYCE DANCE STUDIO.*** *See BALLET, SF.*

***STEVE & MICKI GRANGER'S DANCE THEATRE WORKSHOP.*** *See BALLET, Peninsula.*

***SAMUEL L. LEWIS STUDIOS.*** *See BALLET, SF.*

***MASON-KAHN STUDIO.*** *See TAP, SF.*

***ALEXANDRA SAWICKA SCHOOL OF BALLET.*** *See BALLET, EB.*

***SUGANO-JONSSON SCHOOL OF DANCE.*** *See BALLET, Peninsula.*

## Style References

**THE ROYAL ACADEMY OF DANCING (in America), Inc., 335 East 50th St., NYC 10022; c/o 8 College Ave., Upper Montclair, NJ 07043, 201-746-0184 (coordinating secretary).** *Established in 1969 to foster, support and improve the teaching of ballet. Trains teachers of classical ballet and examines students according to RAD syllabi (children's, and ages 12 and above).Many services to teachers, students and parents. After RAD, London.*

**STUDIOS WITH RAD EMPHASIS:**

**ACADEMY OF DANCE ARTS.** *See BALLET, SJ.*

**DANCER'S REPERTORY THEATRE.** *See BALLET, EB.*

**DAVLIN-LOWELL.** *See BALLET, EB.*

**EAST BAY BALLET CENTER.** *See BALLET, CCC.*

**McBRIDE DANCE STUDIO.** *See BALLET, CCC.*

**NELSON.** *See BALLET, Peninsula.*

**NISSEN'S SCHOOL OF DANCE.** *See BALLET, CCC.*

**CATHERINE REUTHER SCHOOL.** *See BALLET, SJ.*

**SAN JUAN SCHOOL OF DANCE.** *See BALLET, Peninsula.*

**ALEXANDRA SAWICKA SCHOOL OF BALLET.** *See BALLET, EB.*

# Ballet

## *Style References*

*STUDIOS WITH RUSSIAN-KIROV EMPHASIS:*

***BALLET RUSSE-MUSIC AND DANCE.*** *See BALLET, SF.*

***BALLET THEATRE WEST.*** *See BALLET, Marin & Sonoma.*

***CHILDREN'S CREATIVE DANCE THEATRE.*** *See OTHER DANCES/Creative.*

***CLASSICAL BALLET CENTER.*** *See BALLET, EB.*

***CONTRA COSTA ACADEMY OF DANCE ARTS.*** *See BALLET, CCC.*

***JANINA CYWINSKA.*** *See BALLET, SF.*

***GRACE MANN BALLET CENTER.*** *See BALLET, EB.*

***KIROV-CORDELLE SCHOOL OF CLASSICAL BALLET.*** *See BALLET, Peninsula.*

***ALEXANDRA SAWICKA SCHOOL OF BALLET.*** *See BALLET, EB.*

***SCHOOL OF RUSSIAN BALLET.*** *See BALLET, SJ.*

***SHAWL-ANDERSON MODERN DANCE CENTER.*** *See BALLET, EB.*

***SUGANO-JONSSON SCHOOL OF BALLET.*** *See BALLET, Peninsula.*

***TATIANA SVETLANOVA.*** *See BALLET, SF.*

***THE BALLET SCHOOL.*** *See BALLET, Peninsula.*

# Ballet

## *References*
## *Events*

**BALLET NEWS,** *The International Magazine of Dance, 1865 Broadway, NYC 10023, 212-582-7500. Began April 1, 1979; published by Metropolitan Opera Guild, Inc., publisher of Opera News. TV, stage, U.S. calendar, interviews. $21 for 12 issues; $18 by subscription.*

**BALLET REVIEW,** *Marcel Dekker, Inc., publisher, 270 Madison Ave., NYC 10016. Arlene Croce, editor. Student and professional rates; $12.50/yr. Published quarterly.*

**"DANCE AMERICA,"** *NATIONAL ASSOCIATION FOR REGIONAL BALLET (NARB) newsletter. See GROUPS.*

## *Events*

***MISSISSIPPI BALLET INTERNATIONAL, BOX 2467, Jackson, MS 39205, 601-944-1401.*** *Only U.S. sponsored world-wide ballet competition; two divisions, ages 13-18 and 19-25. First year July, 1979.*

***PACIFIC REGIONAL BALLET FESTIVAL. c/o Santa Barbara Ballet Theatre, 122 E. Arrellaga St., Santa Barbara 93101, 805-965-0121;*** *Festival's in May.*

# Ballroom

*Modern ballroom has its roots in the religious ritual, funerals, wooing and initiation rites of primitive times. Social dances with couples existed in 16th century Europe, though they weren't as filled out as today's forms. France, Germany and England developed dozens of dances through the 19th century, including the polka in the 1840s.*

*American pop music of the 20th century has created a new manner of ballroom dance, including the fox trot, cakewalk, Charleston and jitterbug and rock and roll. New dances are constantly being created and discarded, but the standbys dance on.*

*In addition to the studios listed here, YMCAs, senior citizens groups and city-sponsored recreation departments also offer occasional ballroom classes.*

# Ballroom

## *Contra Costa County*

**CONTRA COSTA ACADEMY.** *See BALLET, CCC.*

***DANCE CITY U.S.A. (DIABLO SCHOOL OF DANCE), 2026 Main St., Walnut Creek 94596, 415-933-6472; 3838 Grand Ave., Oakland, 415-451-8375.*** *Ballroom dance to Big Band Sounds; beg., adv., private and group. Fox trot, waltz, cha cha, swing, rhumba, disco and more.*

***DANCE MASTERS, No. 5 Country Club Plaza, Orinda 94563, 415-254-7272,*** *Mondays through Saturdays, 1 to 10 p.m. Steve Williams and Rita Bonel, owners. Touch, ballroom, social and disco, beg. through prof. Studio dance party every Friday night from 9 p.m. Newsletter.*

***RUTH H. PITTMAN, Lafayette, 415-284-5762;*** *ballroom and disco.*

***THE STUDIO OF DANCE, 1825 Mt. Diablo Blvd., Walnut Creek 94596, 415-939-0621.*** *Ballroom, disco, tap and jazz. Adv. and beg. disco includes both touch (couples) and freestyle. Standards of ballroom: bronze and silver social, exhibition and theater arts. Beginners ballroom and party practice sessions, monthly Saturday night dances open to guests.*

*Private membership studio. Lessons entitle you to use facilities, partipate in social events, travel and compete in dance events. Introductory offer: $10 to sample two half-hour private lessons, one hour class, 1½ hour party practice session.*

***VICTOR AND YVONNE BALLROOM INSTRUCTION, Concord, 415-798-5852.*** *Exhibitions and classes.*

# Ballroom

## *East Bay*
## *Marin*

***ALI BABA, 111 Grand Ave. at Webster, Oakland 94612, 415-451-7040.*** *With nearly 10,000 sq. ft. of floor space, the Ali Baba ranks as the West Coast's largest regularly used facility; and is one of the few "true ballrooms" still operating in the nation. Dances every Wednesday, Friday and Saturday with the latest steps; free instruction an hour before the social. Checkroom, food and beverage service available. Dress is formal. Big Band sounds, party nights, special Hawaiian dances, dinner and holiday dances. Instruction by Gene Evans and Leonard Carter.*

***ASHKENAZ FOLK DANCE COOPERATIVE.*** *See FOLK, EB.*

***DANCE CITY U.S.A.*** *See BALLROOM, CCC.*

***FASCINATING RHYTHM.*** *See DISCO, EB.*

***GRAND DANCE.*** *See DISCO, EB.*

***ARTHUR MURRAY DANCE STUDIO, 470 20th St., Oakland 94612, 415-836-0579.***

## *Marin*

***DANCE ARTS STUDIO,*** *See BALLET, Marin.*

***ARTHUR MURRAY DANCE STUDIO, 330 Sir Francis Drake Blvd., San Anselmo 94960, 415-454-6652.*** *Ballroom and disco.*

# Ballroom

## Peninsula San Francisco

**BEAUDOIN'S SCHOOL OF DANCE.** *See BALLET, Peninsula.*

**STEVE AND MICKI GRANGER'S DANCE THEATRE WORKSHOP.** *See BALLET, Peninsula.*

**SAN MATEO CITY PARKS DEPT.** *See GROUPS/SPONSORS --City.*

**IMOGENE WOODRUFF BALLROOM DANCE STUDIO, 1665 Fernside St., Redwood City 94061, 415-368-4187.** *Ballroom and disco, three levels each; fox trot, waltz, rhumba, cha cha, samba and tango.*

## San Francisco

**THE CHANGING TIMES, 1665 Market St., SF 94103, 415-863-2623 (TO-DANCE).** *Studio concentrates on adapting the tango, swing, cha-cha, rhumba, etc. to today's music. Classes and private instruction aimed at developing dancers who are strong on technique, style and footwork.*

**LORNA FORDYCE DANCE STUDIO.** *See BALLET, SF.*

**HINTON-PICK SCHOOL OF BALLROOM DANCING, 380 18th Ave. at Geary, SF 94121, 415-752-5658.** *Established 1961. Rhona Pick, proprietress. Roy Hinton and Rhona Pick, West Coast champions in ballroom and Latin American dancing; named to America's Dancing Hall of Fame in 1977.*

*International style ballroom and Latin American, American style social ballroom, disco, West Coast swing (beg., inter., adv.). Private lessons by appointment. Staff: Jenty Parkinson (fellow ISTD ballroom; associate ISTD Latin American); Gene Jennings (fellow ISTD ballroom and Latin American); Rex Lewis (associate ISTD Latin American). Dance party once a month with professional couple demonstrating.*

# Ballroom

## *San Francisco*

***TED AND KITTY LEE SCHOOL OF BALLROOM DANCING, 285 Ellis St., SF 94102, 415-474-0920.***

***MARIE'S DANCING STUDIO, 5316 Fulton St., SF 94121 415-751-5468.*** *Irene Weed, ballroom stylist. Ballroom, swing, Hawaiian, tap, disco, jazz; private and semi-private lessons. Party arrangements. See also GROUPS/SPONSORS--City (SF Park and Recreation Dept. 558-3601).*

***MASON-KAHN STUDIOS.*** *See TAP, SF.*

***AMY POWELL.*** *See DISCO, SF.*

***ARTHUR MURRAY DANCE STUDIO, 1226 Sutter St., SF 94109 415-885-4232.*** *Ballroom and disco. Sponsors West Coast Dance Olympics.*

***RENAISSANCE SCHOOL OF DANCE.*** *See DISCO, SF.*

***RUTHIE'S SCHOOL OF DANCE.*** *See TAP, SF.*

***RUVANO DANCE STUDIO, 1290 Sutter St., Second Floor, SF 94109, 415-474-5600.*** *Founded 1963 by Rudy Valle after being named top teacher of the year in Arthur Murray West Coast Dance Olympics. Gloria Meyer co-owner since 1968. Most classes now disco-oriented (six sessions weeknights). Friday nights ballroom and Latin dancing, followed by party (9-11). Private and semi-private lessons in disco, all levels of ballroom. Meyer teaches freestyle disco, including body, arms, hand and footwork styles; Valle and Meyer collaborate on touch disco. Both have performed professionally.*

# Ballroom

## San Jose

***PAT COSTELLO, SJ, 408-446-4411.*** *Ballroom, swing, Latin, rock.*

***THE DANCE CLUB, 152 South First St., SJ 95113, 408-998-3117.*** *Classes and private lessons in disco, social and ballroom. Three floors of about 5,000 sq. ft. each with actual dance areas on two of about 1,400 sq. ft., 3,000 sq. ft. on a third; all suspended wood. Two are equipped with band stand and bar. Largest is rentable for private functions, capacity 300. Rehearsal space available by appointment for $5/hr./couple.*

*Eight week class series for $28 per person or $50 per couple. Four levels of disco, specializing in New York style of all Hustle variations, plus freestyle disco and salsa. Imperial Society of Teachers of Dance ballroom curriculum; American style social ballroom in bronze, silver and gold and supreme gold levels. Theater arts movements also taught for exhibition and show work.*

*Annual student awards presentation ball held each June. Students attend several competitions a year and perform at many functions, including the local, annual Tapestry in Talent. Additional performances at private parties; disco dance party every Sunday, 7 to 10 p.m.*

***JOSETTA DANCE STUDIO, 3280 El Camino Real, Santa Clara 95051, 408-296-3245.*** *Josetta M. Buttitta; member DMofA. Ballroom, folk, disco, Latin American. Thursday night disco-ballroom taught at Community Center, 1305 Middlefield Rd., Palo Alto.*

***LOS ALTOS BALLET SCHOOL.*** *See BALLET, SJ.*

***ARTHUR MURRAY DANCE STUDIO, 938 The Alameda, SJ 95126, 408-297-3734.***

***SANTA CLARA DANCE STUDIO.*** *See TAP, SJ.*

***SARATOGA MUSIC AND FINE ARTS CENTER.*** *See MODERN, SJ.*

# Ballroom

## San Jose Events

*HELEN PABST WALSH BALLROOM DANCING, 20 Atlas Ave., SJ 95126, 408-295-5394.*

*WILLOW GLEN DANCE STUDIO, 1352 Lincoln Ave., SJ 95125, 408-275-8105. Ballroom and disco.*

## Events

*ARTHUR MURRAY WEST COAST DANCE OLYMPICS.* *See BALLROOM, SF.*

*SF BALLROOM DANCE FESTIVAL, INC., 760 Market, SF 94102, 415-362-8372.*

# Belly

*This ancient and functional dance began as a method of strengthening abdominal muscles prior to the birth of a child. It emphasizes isolating and controlling various parts of the body, in basic steps, to a variety of rhythms. It teaches body awareness, stamina, coordination, and strengthening muscles in the back, arms, belly, legs and neck. Though most women study it for exercise and grace, many have gone on to professional dancing and teaching with spiritual approaches.*

*This chapter is listed alphabetically rather than by area because of its brevity. Companies are listed separately from studios which only offer classes.*

# *Belly*

## *Companies A to Z*

***AMINA BELLY DANCE STUDIO, 829 Elizabeth St. (near Douglass), SF 94114, 415-282-7910.*** *Beg., inter./adv. Small classes include warmups, stomach and cymbal exercises, breakdown of steps, combinations, choreographed dances, guides for improvisational work, distinguishing musical changes. Small company, The Aswan Dancers, perform in the area.*

*Amina has performed at the Bagdad Cabaret since 1966. She has taught several workshop and master classes in Middle Eastern dance throughout California, and has taught and performed in Northern California colleges and universities. Style is mostly Egyptian cabaret with folkloric dances; the company performs mostly dance drama and folkloric works.*

***MAGAÑA BAPTISTE ROYAL ACADEMY OF BELLY DANCING and Magana and Walt Baptiste Centre of Dance and Yoga, 405 Arguello Blvd., SF 94118, 415-387-6833.*** *Beg. Greek dancing with Lorraine Garner; exercise/dance with Ellen Sandra; children's creative dance (belly, modern, yoga, stretches) with Devi Ananda Baptiste; Hindu temple and cosmic yoga dance with Magana Baptiste; Arabic dance for men and women, Magana Baptiste. Also beg. and inter. belly, interpretive/primitive/jazz/creative for men and women, Hindu-Indonesian temple dance, most taught by Magana. Fees based on number of classes per week.*

*Baptiste directs the Baptiste Royal/Belly Dancing and East Indian Troupe, with 40 dancers and musicians who perform Hindu-Afro jazz, ritual dances and professional routines. She trained with Devi Dja, performed with Ruth St. Denis. Baptiste is also available for choreography.*

***ILYANA'S STUDIO OF MID-EASTERN DANCE and Sciroccos Dance Theatre, Bay Area Mid-Eastern Dance Arts Association, 40 de la Guerra Road, San Rafael 94903, 415-479-1574.*** *Classes and private instruction for beg. through prof. students. She also choreographs routines and makes entertainment bookings. Rates based on 12 week sessions. Dance history, lectures on Jewish issues, and instructional rhythm tapes are also available. Students learn at their own rates through personalized instruction.*

*The association was formed to further the cultural appreciation of Middle Eastern dance as a concert art form. It recently received tax-exempt status as a non-profit group, the first such association to do so in the U.S. Ilyana is president.*

*Ilyana has performed in New York, Florida, Texas, California. She is artistic director of Sciroccos, which aims to unite Middle Eastern dance, music and ritual with contemporary dance, mime and psychology.*

***BELLY DANCE BY FARIDA KAROON, P.O. Box 2287, Menlo Park 94025, 415-325-6882.*** *Teaching emphasizes an accord with one's authenticity, femininity, creativity, and confidence, with costume design, make-up, show choreography and entertainment. Professional instruction for all ages, beg. through adv. Limited class sizes. Opportunities to join performing troupe. Rates depend on length of class and number of weeks.*

*Karoon studied modern, jazz, African dance, rock, Latin American and Middle Eastern dance, costuming, theatrical make-up and set design. She formed a curriculum in New York in dance therapy for troubled children. She has performed around the country, and gives benefit performances locally for private conventions and parties. The Farida Karoon Belly Dance Troupe has performed for hospitals, Crippled Children's Society of Santa Clara, etc.*

# Belly

## *Classes A to Z*

***ACADEMY OF DANCE ARTS.*** *See BALLET, SJ.*

***ASHKENAZ FOLK DANCE COOPERATIVE.*** *See FOLK, EB.*

***BELLY DANCE ARTS STUDIO, 1178 Solano Ave., Albany 94706, 415-525-0722.*** *Najia Marlyz, artistic director; staff columnist for Bellydancer Magazine. Authentic cabaret style belly dance for women only, beg. through prof. Studio specializes in recreational dancing with regular recitals held in San Francisco nightclubs. Several students have become professional dancers. Marlyz dances privately and does guest appearances at Bay Area nightclubs; she originated the independent dancer's performance contract.*

***BELROSE STUDIO THEATRE.*** *See BALLET, Marin.*

***BEA BLUM'S.*** *See TAP, Marin.*

***CENTRAL OAKLAND DANCE STUDIO.*** *See MODERN, EB.*

***CREATIVE BODYWORK CENTER.*** *See BODYWORK, Massage.*

***EVERYBODY'S DANCE CENTER.*** *See MODERN, EB.*

***FOOTHILL COMMUNITY COLLEGE DISTRICT.*** *See EDUCATION.*

***BELLY DANCING BY ZAHRA, 415-284-1487.***

***KHADIJA: GRACE, A DANCE CENTER, 159 Tamarack Road, San Geronimo 94963, 415-488-0942 (San Rafael).*** *Classes three times a week. Khadija Marcia Rand toured the U.S. (1970-72) with the Lucas Hoving Dance Co., taught at Cornell University, SF Dance Theater, School for Sufi Studies, was dance coordinator for the San Francisco Art Commission, and guest soloist with the Shawl-Anderson Dance Company and guest teacher at the Rotterdam Dans Academie, Holland.*

# Belly

## Classes A to Z

**KATARINE, 415-843-1572 (EB).** *Belly, folkloric, Egyptian, Moroccan Shikhatt, Guerda, Ahouach; Turkish. Cabaret, costume, makeup and music. Children's classes (8 years and up).*

**BELLY DANCE BY KHADIJA RABANNE, Sausalito, 415-332-9100.**

**JANIE MILLER, Walden Center, 2446 McKinley, Berkeley 94703, 415-841-6500, ext. 434 (messages).** *Beg.-adv. belly dance through yoga and alignment.*

**SAN MATEO CITY PARKS DEPT.** *See GROUPS/SPONSORS--City.*

**SANTA CLARA DANCE STUDIO.** *See TAP, SJ.*

**SARATOGA MUSIC AND FINE ARTS CENTER.** *See MODERN, SJ.*

**SULA'S BELLY DANCE WORLD, 1235 Boulevard Way, Walnut Creek 94596, 415-937-7852, 935-2826.** *Shop, studio and mail order. Beg., inter., adv./inter., and adv. belly dancing. Egypt catalogue available for $2; student and professional costumes, accessories, costume supplies, patterns, records, books and cymbals. Professional entertainment for parties.*

*Leea teaches small classes in Arabic style belly dances. Performances prepare students for professional dance. Annual Belly Dancer of the Year pageant is a showcase of outstanding performers and teachers held in spring ($250 first prize, trophy).*

**SAMRA YASSMEEN Arabic Belly Dancing, P.O. Box 321, Los Altos 94022, 415-494-3361.**

**SAN JUAN SCHOOL OF DANCE.** *See BALLET, Peninsula.*

**THEATRE FLAMENCO.** *See FOLK/Latin.*

# Belly

## Reference Supplies

**ARABESQUE, *Journal of Middle East Dance and Culture.*** *Irahim Farrah, Inc., One Sherman Square, Suite 22F, NYC 10023, 212-595-1677. Bi-monthly; annual, $8.50.*

## Supplies

**BAZAAR BOUTIQUE,** *See MAGAÑA BAPTISTE.*

**BELLY DANCE BAZAAR, 4898 El Camino Real, Los Altos, 415-969-3362.**

**COST LESS IMPORTS, 1710 University Ave., Berkeley, 94703, 415-548-2800.** *Catalog on custom designed belly dance belts, accessories. One year guarantee on any belts, bras and jewelry. Coin belts, Mideastern coins, ethnic belts, mirror belts, bra covers, jewelry, chain and material for do-it-yourself.*

**FARIDA KAROON BOUTIQUE, P.O. Box 2287, Menlo Park 94025, 415-325-6882**

**MOON GODDESS IMPORTS, P.O. Box 4916, Stanford 94305, 415-494-6083.** *Belly dance accessories.*

**THE SUN AND THE LION, 391 Miller Ave., Mill Valley, 415-383-6855.** *Belly dance accessories.*

# disco

*Is disco here to stay? Three years ago disco music was heard mainly by a few who turned the seldom frequented discotheques into after-hour shrines. But the fever is no longer limited to Saturday night. Billboard estimates 36 million boogied at 20,000 clubs in 1978. There are disco proms, weddings, caterers, cruises, clothes ad infinitum. Of 1978's top 100 songs, 20 percent were disco.*

*This chapter lists classes offered in studios. It is impossible to keep up with the clubs that provide disco entertainment and classes. You can find these listed weekly in Friday and Sunday newspaper entertainment sections, local entertainment and some underground-type tabloids, local magazines, etc. You can also call Shawl-Anderson Modern Dance Center (415-654-5921) for a copy of Crispin Hayes Pierce's guide (50¢). Other sources for classes and night spots: ballroom studios, Yellow Pages (Discotheques), and the Performing Arts Column in newspaper classifieds.*

## *Contra Costa County East Bay*

**CONTRA COSTA ACADEMY.** *See BALLET, CCC.*

**DANCE CITY, U.S.A.** *See BALLROOM, CCC.*

**DANCE MASTERS.** *See BALLROOM, CCC.*

**PITTMAN.** *See BALLROOM, CCC.*

**SAN RAMON VALLEY ACADEMY OF DANCE.** *See BALLROOM, CCC.*

**THE STUDIO OF DANCE.** *See BALLROOM, CCC.*

## *East Bay*

**ASHKENAZ FOLK DANCE COOPERATIVE.** *See FOLK, EB. NY rope hustle, NY Latin hustle. Partners not necessary.*

**ALAMEDA SCHOOL OF DANCE, 1402 Park, Alameda 94501, 415-635-3745.** *Pamm Drake and Arthur Stone.*

**DANCE REPERTORY THEATRE.** *See BALLET, EB.*

**FASCINATING RHYTHM—OUT OF THE BLUE, 5638 College Ave., Oakland 94618, 415-658-8035.** *Marge Gabbert and Mikel Blue. Specializing in social or touch dancing, with beg. through adv. classes in disco, ballroom, salsa and swing, jazz exercise, tap for children and adults.*

*They also own a mobile disco called Dial-A-Disco, which provides everything from disco environment with lights, music and dance sessions to breakfast in bed the following morning. Services brought to home, office or specified location.*

**FULL SPECTRUM STUDIO.** *See BALLET, EB.*

# *disco*

## *East Bay*
## *Marin*

**THE GRAND DANCE, 3501 Grand Ave., Oakland 94601, 415-835-9460.** *Jan Keshen, director. A relatively new studio, it is evolving into two departments, art dance and disco, including disco exhibitions for parties and promotions.*

*Jazz, ballet, modern, tap, creative movement for 4-9 year olds, salsa and fiesta. Disco levels, I-IV. Faculty: Crispin Pierce, Jan Keshen, Theresa Gensler, Marilyn Sandifur, Manuel Puertas, Michael James, Sandy O'Rourke, Michelle Jurika, Luisa Pierce, Patti Meagher, Edith White.*

*Ruby and the Diamonds is a tap performing company with members from the studio. Grand Dance Disco Club members get together to share routines, and go to discotheques together.*

**NEW DANCE WORKSHOP.** *Disco, partners and for women only. Messages, 415-841-6500, ext. 385. See TAP, EB.*

**THE DANCE WORKS, INC, 2212 Parker St., Berkeley 94704.** *(See also JAZZ, EB). Disco, line hustles, partnering, dips and lifts.*

**WEST COAST DANCE THEATRE.** *See JAZZ, EB.*

## *Marin*

**BEA BLUM'S.** *See TAP, Marin.*

**BELROSE STUDIOS.** *See BALLET, Marin.*

**CONSERVATORY OF BALLET AND THEATRE ARTS.** *See BALLET, Marin.*

**DANCE ARTS STUDIO.** *See BALLET, Marin.*

**MARIN CIVIC BALLET THEATRE.** *See BALLET, Marin.*

## *Peninsula San Francisco*

***BEAUDOIN'S.*** *See BALLET, Peninsula.*

***MAJOR DANCE STUDIO, 1261 E. Hillsdale Blvd., Foster City 94404, 415-527-8404.*** *Disco, tap, ballet and jazz.*

***SAN MATEO CITY PARKS DEPT.*** *See GROUPS/SPONSORS --City.*

***SAN CARLOS DANCE COLLECTIVE.*** *See BALLET, Peninsula.*

***IMOGENE WOODRUFF.*** *See BALLET, Peninsula.*

## *San Francisco*

***BROADWAY DANCE STUDIO, 1624 Franklin St., Room 520, SF 94109, 415-452-0639.*** *Disco and social ballroom classes; couples $3.*

***HINTON-PICK SCHOOL OF BALLROOM DANCING.*** *See BALLROOM, SF.*

***KAREN LUSTGARTEN, disco instructor, SF, 415-285-1138.*** *Author of The Complete Guide to Disco and The Complete Guide to Touch Dancing. Disco instruction and private party instruction, with occasional classes.*

***MARIE'S.*** *See BALLROOM, SF.*

***MASON-KAHN STUDIOS.*** *See TAP, SF.*

***BETTY MAY SCHOOL OF DANCING.*** *See TAP, SF.*

## *San Francisco*
## *San Jose*

**AMY POWELL DANCE STUDIO, 1940 Ocean Ave., SF 94127, 415-333-1011.** *Damara Powell-Reilly, DMofA. Disco, ballroom, salsa, ballet, tap, jazz, modern; pre-school through professional. Space available for rent.*

**RENAISSANCE SCHOOL OF DANCE, 285 Ellis, SF 94102, 415-474-0920.** *Disco, ballroom, salsa, class or private. All ages, six days a week.*

**SCHUMACHER'S SCHOOL OF DANCE.** *See TAP, SF.*

**THE SPIRIT, 628 Divisadero, SF 94117, 415-567-0660.** *New spiritual disco.*

**THEATRE FLAMENCO.** *See FOLK, SF.*

**ARTHUR MURRAY DANCE STUDIO.** *See BALLROOM, SF.*

**RUVANO DANCE STUDIO.** *See BALLROOM, SF.*

**STAR DANCE STUDIO.** *See BALLET, SF.*

## *San Jose*

**ACADEMY OF DANCE ARTS.** *See BALLET, SJ.*

**ACADEMY OF SPEECH AND DANCE.** *See BALLET, SJ.*

**THE DANCE CLUB.** *See BALLROOM, SJ.*

**JOSETTA DANCE STUDIO.** *See BALLROOM, SJ.*

**SARATOGA MUSIC AND FINE ARTS CENTER.** *See MODERN, SJ.*

**WILLOW GLEN.** *See BALLROOM, SJ.*

# disco

## *Addenda*
## *Mobile Disco for Hire*

***BAY AREA DISCO DJ ASSOCIATION, 2120 Market St., SF 94114, 415-431-6025.***

## *Mobile Disco for Hire*

***DIAL-A-DISCO.*** *See FASCINATING RHYTHM, DISCO, EB. For all occasions, full services.*

***DISCO DOWN'S MOBILE DISCO, Daly City, 415-755-4094.*** *Parties, weddings, dances, create-your-own.*

***DISCO TO GO, 408-926-9606.*** *Live DJ for events, all type music.*

***MISTER MASTER AND MS DISCO, Concord, 415-798-5852.***

***THE MUSIC MAN MOBILE DISCO, 1463 Rollins Rd., Burlingame, 415-342-0612.*** *Parties, fetes, receptions, reunions, fashion shows.*

***PROSOUND MOBILE DISCOTHEQUE, P.O. Box 12, Moraga, 415-376-0288.*** *DJ, lighting, music for weddings, parties, dances, fashion shows.*

***TWENTIETH CENTURY LIMITED, 55A Natoma St., SF 94103, 415-495-5780.*** *Cater to all occasions; complete lighting and sound systems, etc.*

# Ethnic Folk

*There is a fine distinction between ethnic and folk dancing today. When dance speaks for a race, we call it ethnic. Folk dance IS ethnic, but it usually is communal and participatory. Ethnic dance is more complex, more theatrical, and performed by gifted dancers incorporating arts and legends created over thousands of years of cultural heritage. At its essence ethnic dance reflects the instinctual, cosmic dance of early man, who moved to communicate, to control, to pray or to mirror the universe around him.*

*Folk dance in America is a massive phenomenon. There are hundreds of companies in Northern California, and any night in the Bay Area--in schoolrooms, studios, meeting rooms, city parks--there are classes and get-togethers for friendship, fun and happpiness.*

*This chapter is divided into the geographic areas where the folk dance originates rather than local geographic area. Companies and classes are listed together under folk style, and events, supplies, etc. are described at the end of the chapter.*

# Ethnic Folk

## *Afro American*

***AFRO-AMERICAN FRIENDS OF THE DANCE, c/o Community Art Resource, 137 B Steiner St., SF 94117.***

***AQUARIUS RISING DANCE THEATER, 354 21st St., Oakland 94612, 415-451-1230.*** *Ms. Halifu Osumare, director. Twelve member multi-racial company fusing modern jazz and Afro-Caribbean. "Total theater," with emphasis on dance with changing spiritual and social values. Perform for special events. See EVERYBODY'S DANCE STUDIO, MODERN, EB.*

***MAGAÑA BAPTISTE.*** *See BELLY, SF.*

***HELEN CARROLL SCHOOL OF THEATRE DANCE.*** *See BALLET, EB.*

***CENTRAL OAKLAND DANCE STUDIO.*** *See MODERN, EB.*

***DIMENSIONS DANCE THEATER.*** *Afro-Haitian classes. See MODERN, EB.*

***EVERYBODY'S DANCE STUDIO.*** *See MODERN, EB.*

***FULL SPECTRUM STUDIO.*** *See BALLET, EB.*

***HARAMBEE DANCE ENSEMBLE, c/o 3026 57th Ave., Oakland 94605.*** *Akili Denianke. Harambee is Swahili for "let's pull together." Twenty-two dancers and drummers with repertoire of voodoo ritual of Haiti, South African boot dance, American black bottom and boogie.*

***GWEN LEWIS DANCE EXPERIENCE, 2534 Grant St., Berkeley 94703.*** *Naima, artistic director. Her dances are a blend of African and American styles, including movements researched in Nigeria and Ghana. Naima began her part-time company in 1969 to record the black experience in dance. She obtained an M.A. in dance at Mills, danced with Ruth Beckford's Afro-Haitian*

Ethnic Folk

## Afro American

Company, and set up an innovative black dance program with the Oakland Recreation and Parks Department. She has choreographed a tribute to the late Josephine Baker, gospel pieces, a tribute to Black soldiers settling the West. She teaches jazz in Berkeley, is available for master classes and workshops for children and adults, in African (traditional), jazz and modern, or training courses for teachers. Solo performances, film and videotape rental (16mm b/w of the company in performance, teaching children, discussion of black dance, $10). Fees negotiable.

**LOTUS AFRICAN ENSEMBLE DANCE COMPANY, South San Francisco Opera House, 4705 Third St., SF 94124, 415-824-1283.**

**L.O. SLOAN'S JUBILEE MINSTRELS, 137 B Steiner St., SF 94117, 415-346-0168.** Combines African cultures, slaves and European cultures in a musical, acrobatic show for schools, etc. Tours widely; six minstrels.

**SWAHILI DANCERS AND DRUMMERS, 1625 Carroll Ave., SF 94124.** For bookings, call 415-822-3490, 8:30-4:30 Mondays through Fridays. Classes M, W and F afternoons at South San Francisco Opera House, 4705 Third St., SF (824-1283). Afro-Haitian with jazz and ballet. Performances in San Francisco and state, Nevada, Barbados West Indies. Qualifications: "youths that have the willingness and discipline to endure the training." The Temple Arts and Cultural formed the group in 1970, under director Julia Middleton.

**WAJUMBE CULTURAL ENSEMBLE, Western Addition Cultural Center, 762 Fulton St., SF; c/o Nonsizi Cayou, P.O. Box 12421, SF 94112, 415-922-5550.**

# Ethnic Folk

## Asian

***ASIAN-AMERICAN DANCE COLLECTIVE, c/o Yuki Shiroma, 829 North Pointe, SF 94109, 415-552-0467.*** *Indonesian, Japanese, Okinawan and Chinese dance. Group seeks a style that is uniquely Asian-American. Low cost to free dance classes; core performing group of about 10. Yearly membership about $5.*

***ASIAN AMERICAN DANCE COLLECTIVE, 1230 Grant Ave., Box 335, SF 94133.*** *Classes in Kyogen (Japan's first dance theater of social protest), taught by Yuriko Doi, and Okinawan dance, taught by Yuri Shiroma, as well as dancersize, at UJCS, 2012 Pine St., SF.*

***CHINESE FOLK DANCE ASSOCIATION, 178 Acacia St., Daly City 94104, 415-398-8212.*** *Diana Hong. Cooperative of about 50 dancers and musicians performing both traditional and contemporary (mainland) works, as well as martial arts.*

***CHINESE PERFORMING ARTS ENSEMBLE, c/o Virginia Wei-Lo Tsou, 2631 45th Ave., SF 94116.***

***CHINESE PERFORMING ARTS SOCIETY, c/o Intersection, 756 Union St., SF 94133, 415-397-6061.***

***CHUNG NGAI DANCE TROUPE, 1454 Taylor St., #5, SF 94133, 415-392-6320.*** *Jimmy Chan. Lion dancing, martial arts, classical dances. Performances at universities in Las Vegas, St. Louis and Taiwan. Thirty-five members with room for more. Practice is at Club House, 109 Waverly Place (Chinatown). Lion dances Friday nights; Chinese classical dance, Sunday afternoons.*

***ROKUSHIGE FUJIMA, 562 22nd Ave., SF 94121, 415-752-4480.*** *Japanese dance.*

***MICHIYA HANAYAGI JAPANESE DANCE STUDIO, c/o 435-432 63rd St., Oakland 94609, 415-652-0052.***

***SAN FRANCISCO TAIKO DOJO, c/o Seiichi Tanaka, 15 Western Shore Lane, #3, SF 94115, 415-921-5863.***

# Ethnic Folk

## Greek

*Note: More Greek dancing is listed under INTERNATIONAL.*

***AITOS FOLK DANCE TAVERNA, 1920 San Pablo Ave., Berkeley 94702, 415-841-7846.***

***AITOS GREEK DANCERS, c/o Ashkenaz Folk Dance Cooperative, 1317 San Pablo Ave., Berkeley, 415-525-5054, or Andy Saffas, 61 Corte Encanto, Danville 94526, 415-820-3693.*** *Nikie Saffas, artistic director; Andy Saffas, director. Aitos means "eagle," symbol of Byzantium. Specializes in dances, songs and customs learned first-hand from villagers in various regions of Greece. Meticulous reproductions supplement genuine local costumes from the 19th century. Dancers and musicians welcome at weekly rehearsals at Ashkenaz. (see INTERNATIONAL).*

*Aitos is available to present suites of dances and songs from: Crete (quick-stepped); Ipiros (stately); Macedonia (intricate); Pontos (fiery); Thrace (spirited). N. Saffas is available for workshops and seminars on dance, costumes and lore, with artifacts, slides and films.*

***ALKMINI GREEK DANCE ENSEMBLE, 16 Corte Los Sombras, Greenbrae 94904, 415-461-1174.*** *About 15 young people perform authentic dances from Greece at libraries, art centers, schools. Alkmini Bloom, director.*

***MAGAÑA BAPTISTE BELLY DANCE CENTER.*** *See BELLY, SF.*

***MANDALA FOLK DANCE TAVERNA.*** *See INTERNATIONAL.*

# Ethnic Folk

## *Indian*

***ASHKENAZ FOLK DANCE COOPERATIVE.*** *See INTERNATIONAL.*

***THE BALASARASWATI SCHOOL OF MUSIC AND DANCE, 2936 Domingo, Berkeley 94705, 415-843-8501.*** *Beg. and continuing classes at St. Clement's Church, 2837 Claremont Blvd. (corner of Ashby). Karen Elliott, instructor. Advanced students perform in Bay Area.*

*Balasaraswati, the great Indian Bharata Natyam dancer, first came to the USA in 1962. The impact of her performance and teaching inspired students to create a school in her name. In 1978 Asian Traditions offered for the first time the study of Yakshagana, a theater-dance form of South Indian folk tradition. Another first in the curriculum is the arrangement of several programs presented in the Bay Area by faculty and advanced students.*

*Bharata Natyam is probably the oldest of the four major dance styles of India, indigenous to the south. In the past it was a major part of temple rituals, combining music, literature and dance to express religious poetry to please the gods.*

***KALANJALI, dance of South India. Katherine Kunhiraman, 1929 Delaware St., Berkeley 94709, 415-548-3811, 234-5624.*** *Trained in Bharata Natyam and Kathakali at Kalakshetra, India for 11 years. Has performed for 10 years in Egypt, Lebanon, England and the U.S. Her husband, K.P. Kunhiraman, comes from a family of Indian dancers and trained at Kalakshetra Institute of Fine Arts in Madras from 1947-59.*

*Together they give beg. and inter. classes in Bharata Natyam for beginners at the East Bay Center for Performing Arts, 415-234-5624. Advanced classes are private. Both conduct intensive workshops in Berkeley in both dance styles as well as hatha yoga, dance theory and folk dance. Classes are small; students are urged to attend at least twice a week.*

*Kalanjali is a teaching and performing group formed in 1975 to preserve and popularize traditonal Indian art, the dance drama of South India. Kalanjali is a Sanskrit compound word meaning "salutation to art." The company of 2-6 dancers is available for performances, lecture/demonstrations and workshops for cultural and educational organizations, showing Kathakali, Bharata Natyam and Odissi dance styles with traditional costumes and jewelry. At present it is the only dance company in the country presenting fully costumed Kathakali dance dramas. Goals: to let the ancient culture of India reveal itself through art, and demonstrate that different people can achieve understanding through sharing art and culture. Company also sponsors dancers from out of town.*

***MIMI AND LESANDRE, Way of the Dance, 1043 Buchanan St., Albany 94705, 415-526-5346.*** *Specializing in classical eastern dance of South India (Bharata Natyam), Indonesian (Javanese court and Balinese ritual), Japanese, Chinese, and Korean; and creating works animating Tibetan and Japanese Buddhist art, Indian sculpture, ancient Egyptian art, mythology and religion of ancient cultures. Available for lecture/demonstrations, concerts and master classes. Regular classes in Bharata Natyam and Javanese court dance, beg. to adv., held at several studios in Berkeley and SF. Mimi and Lesandre began their dance careers in ballet, and completed their training at the Royal Ballet, London. Have performed and taught classical eastern dance for nine years.*

***THEATRE FLAMENCO.*** *See FOLK, Spanish.*

# Ethnic Folk

## *International /Folk*

***ASHKENAZ FOLK DANCE COOPERATIVE, studios and coffee house, 1317 San Pablo Ave., Berkeley 94702, 415-525-5054.*** *David Nadel, director. "Ashkenaz was built on a shoestring and unshakable convictions--high quality in art and low prices so that people can come and boogie." Daily classes in Israeli, Greek, Balkan, ballroom, square, modern, tai chi ch'uan, kung fu, Feldenkrais, Bharata Natyam, tap, dance exercise, disco-hustle, belly, Javanese court dance, ballet, Flamenco, salsa, hustle, freestyle; workshops in Swedish folk dance, Hungarian, Croatian, etc.*

*Lessons are generally $1.50 with $1 charge for the party following. Fridays: films, benefits, rock dances, performances, parties, square dancing. The Arkansas Sheiks play alternate Fridays 8 p.m. to late; $2.*

*Space for rent: $2/hr. or 40 cents per person, whichever is more. With Mandala, one of the Bay Area's two major folk dance centers.*

***BALLET ARTS OF SF.*** *See BALLET, SF.*

***BELROSE STUDIO.*** *See BALLET, Marin.*

***THE BERKELEY FOLK DANCERS, 415-530-2771.*** *Club president, Marilyn Sheehan. Classes week nights; dues $20/year or $1 per visit.*

***CALIFORNIA ACADEMY OF DANCE.*** *See BALLET, Peninsula.*

***CONTRA COSTA ACADEMY OF DANCE.*** *See BALLET, CCC.*

***DANCE ART STUDIO.*** *Ethnic Hawaiian, Spanish. See BALLET, SJ.*

***DANCE ARTS OF OAKLAND, 11468 Dillon Way, Dublin, 415-828-5976.*** *Sponsored by Oakland Recreation Department. (See GROUPS/SPONSORS--City.) Group of 10 performs Filipino, Russian, Ukranian, Hungarian dances. Millie Van Kionsky,* *director; also leads Junior Dancers Internationale, who perform at city functions.*

**EL CERRITO DANCE CENTER.** *See BALLET, EB.*

**ETHNIC DANCE ENSEMBLE, Dance Department, California State University, San Francisco, 1600 Holloway Ave., SF 94132.** *See EDUCATION, CSUSF.*

**THE GRAND DANCE.** *Salsa. See DISCO, EB.*

**JOSETTA DANCE STUDIO.** *Latin and folk dance. See BALLROOM, SJ.*

**KOPACHKA DANCERS, Dean and Nancy Linscott, 40 Glen Drive, Mill Valley 94941.** *Friday nights at Park School, 360 E. Blithedale, Mill Valley; international folk dancing $1.50. Dean Linscott (415-383-1014) teaches beg. class in international folk dance Wednesday nights, $1; Almonte Folk Dancers, Wednesday nights at Almonte Hall, 104 Almonte Blvd., Mill Valley, $1; Dolina Dancers, Monday nights at Mill Valley Recreation Center, 180 Camino Alto, Mill Valley, $1. Nancy Linscott also teaches inter. international folk. D. Linscott teaches beg. to adv. international folk at UCSF (666-1660). All classes meet year-round except in August.*

**LOS ALTOS BALLROOM SCHOOL.** *See BALLROOM, SJ.*

**MANDALA FOLK DANCE CENTER AND BALLROOM, 603 Taraval St., SF 94116, 415-731-9829, 552-4990 (2-7 p.m.).** *Neil Sandler, director. Folk, jitterbug (every Saturday 9 p.m. to 1 a.m.), cha-cha, western swing. Monday is Greek night; Tuesday, Israeli; Wednesday, Thursday and Friday, Balkan. Classes offered.*

# Ethnic Folk

## *International /Folk*

***SAN FRANCISCO STATE ETHNIC DANCE ENSEMBLE, c/o SFSU, 415-469-1815 or 469-2244.*** *International, beg. through adv. Performances under Department of Physical Education. Also classes in theory and practice of ethnic dance. Director is Jerry Duke, Dance-SFSU, 1600 Holloway Ave., SF 94132. Available for concerts, school assembly programs, lecture/demonstrations, workshops.*

***SAN MATEO CITY PARKS DEPT.*** *See GROUPS/SPONSORS--City.*

***SAN JUAN SCHOOL OF DANCE.*** *See BALLET, Peninsula.*

***STANFORD INTERNATIONAL FOLK DANCERS, Stanford Physical Education Department, 415-497-4895.*** *Troupe of about 12 student dancers who give exhibitions for community groups. Leanne Elliott, director. Dances include Israeli, Scandinavian, Ukranian and Russian.*

***TERPSICHOREAN INTERNATIONAL DANCE TROUPE COMPANY, 47 Belcher St., SF 94114.*** *Ten member group dancing since 1945; Russian, Polish, Spanish, Portuguese, Mexican. Rehearsals at 50 Scott St., SF.*

***UNIVERSITY OF CALIFORNIA, BERKELEY, FOLK DANCE CLUB. 415-642-3288.*** *Sunni Bloland.*

***IRENE WEED.*** *See TAP, SF.*

***WESTWIND INTERNATIONAL FOLK ENSEMBLE, 446 Campbell Ave., SF 94134, 415-468-5038.*** *Lori Sroka. With more than 33 dancers and musicians, this group is one of the Bay Area's largest. Dances from Norway, France, Bulgaria, Yugoslavia. Company noted for beauty of original costumes, many considered museum pieces.*

## Israeli

*AMI FOLK TROUPE, c/o Hillel Foundation, 2736 Bancroft Way, Berkeley 94720, 415-658-3465.* Suzanne Talmy, director and choreographer. Group has performed in folk festivals, celebrations and on television. Folk classes Tuesdays from 8-9 p.m., with request dancing 9-11 p.m. Sessions 50 cents each; year around.

**CAFE SHALOM, San Francisco Jewish Community Center, 3200 California St., SF 94118, 415-346-6040.** Folk dance and open requests. Gary Kirschner teaches Israeli, Greek and Balkan. Members $1.75; guests, $2.25, Wednesdays 8-10 p.m.

**GARY KIRSCHNER, First Unitarian Church, 1187 Franklin St., SF, 415-776-4580.** Lessons in Israeli and Balkan. Tuesdays 8-10:30 p.m. No prior dance experience needed. Requests; refreshment.

**EVE LANDSTRA, El Cerrito Community Center, 7007 Moeser Lane, El Cerrito 94530, 415-525-6747.** Balkan and Israeli.

**NIRKODA OF SAN FRANCISCO, Israeli folk dance group, 54 Alma St., SF 94117, 415-668-7740 or 922-3108.** Members express enthusiasm for Israeli folk dance through originally choreographed programs directed by Jim Horton. Nirkoda has performed at the SF Ethnic Dance Festival, Stern Grove Festival, Bay Area Jewish community centers, California Folk Dance Federation festivals. Folk singers and classes available.

"An expression of love and joy, to give thanks to God and to celebrate life." Included are the pioneering dance, Yemenite Jews dance (incorporating Arab elements); traditional blended with modern.

**MANDALA FOLK DANCE TAVERNA.** See INTERNATIONAL.

# *Israeli*

***RIKUDOM ISRAELI FOLK DANCE GROUP, meeting at the Mandala, 603 Taraval, SF 94116, 415-731-9829.*** *Twenty-six years in existence; open to public. Sundays 7:30 to 10:30 p.m., instruction by Yale Rosenblatt, 7:30-8:30; songs led by Koppel Bergen, 8:30-8:45; request dancing, 8:45-10 p.m. Adults, $1.25; children, $1.*

*Performance by invitation only; group has danced for the California Folk Dance Federation, senior citizens, convalescent homes, schools, weddings, etc. For more information call Karen Koppel Bergen, director, Rikudom Exhibition Group, 2426 Benjamin Drive, Mountain View 94043, 415-961-3389; or Ruth Bramell, secretary, 241 Mountain View Ave., Mill Valley 94941, 415-388-6176, before 9 p.m.*

## *Middle Eastern*

***ARAB CULTURE CENTER DABKEH GROUP, 2654 22nd Ave., SF 94116, 415-664-2200.***

***CHILDREN OF ISIS, Zahia Sorrells, 1115 Bancroft Way, Berkeley 94702.*** *Private lessons in Egyptian dancing; Zahia studied Banat dance in Luxor and Cairo. The Children of Isis troupe features live music and dances of Egypt, Turkey, Tunisia and Afghanistan (also veil, stick, sword, snake dances). Film and slides of Egypt and Eygptian dancers available.*

***MOLLY RODRIGUEZ, 1129 Folsom, SF 94103.*** *Studied with Baptiste, Alisha Ali, Bobby Farrar, Amina; former member of Masha Archer's Classical Dance Troupe. Now director of Ar'Rusala music and dance troupe that combines folk and cabaret, with specialty in Ghawazee.*

***ZAH'RAH, 711 Hyde St., #3 SF 94109, 415-441-1550.*** *A free form troupe with a core of three dancers with 7-10 years of training in Middle Eastern dance. Shows feature a variety of musicians and dancers; no classes. All are professional performers with cabaret training.*

## *Northern European*

***ENGLISH COUNTRY DANCE SOCIETY OF SAN FRANCISCO, c/o Brad and Jenny Foster, 1138 Francisco St., Berkeley 94702, 415-525-1931.***

***ANN HEALY IRISH DANCE STUDIO, 2036 Taraval St., SF 94116, 415-664-3247.***

***JOHN T. KENNELLY SCHOOL OF IRISH DANCE, 3827 17th St., SF 94107, 415-431-1610.***

***RED THISTLE DANCERS, John and Jennifer Kelly, 1227 Fulton St., Palo Alto 94307, 415-327-1350.*** *Sixteen dancers preserve centuries-old steps; formed about five years ago to perpetuate the traditional dance.*

***THE ROYAL SCOTTISH COUNTY DANCE SOCIETY, 417 27th St., SF, 415-826-0761, San Francisco Branch, Inc.; 233 Margarita Ave., Palo Alto 94306, 415-493-5349.*** *In its 23rd year. All classes held under auspices of the SF branch, a non-profit organization with membership now more than 200. Annual weekend workshop, annual Valentine's Ball and monthly dance parties in The City. Regular exhibition dance performance.*

*Membership is $5/year, which includes subscription to a bi-monthly newsletter. Classes at several levels; beginners welcome. Music is played by the Berkeley Scottish Players (with three albums). Lin Pettengill, branch secretary.*

*Classes in Berkeley, Fresno, Lafayette, Livermore, Mill Valley, Monterey, Oakland, Palo Alto, Petaluma, Sacramento, San Francisco, San Jose, Santa Cruz, weeknights. Dancers learned include the Eighth Reel, Hamilton Rant and Rakes of Glasgow.*

***SCOTTISH DANCE, 404 Clement St., SF 94118, 415-665-5710 or 752-4706.*** *More Scottish dance classes: Sheena West, 3360 Fernside Blvd., Alameda; Marjorie Kistemaker, 419 27th St., SF.*

## Northern European

**SWEDISH FOLK DANCE GROUP, c/o Dr. Kenneth Seeman, 599 College Ave., Suite 3, Palo Alto 94306, 415-327-3200.** *Primarily a recreational group, the dancers meet every Thursday from 7:30 to 10:30 p.m., for levels from beginners to advanced, at the auditorium of the Peninsula School on Peninsula Way at the Corner of Berkeley, Menlo Park. Dances are primarily choreographed for couples, though most people come as singles and find partners. "We do turning couple dances as well as sets; genuine folk dances from circumscribed regions of the country, as well as more choreographed and stylized dances. The dances are exclusively from Scandinavia. Estimate is 70% Sweden, 25% Norway and a scattering of Danish and Finnish." Newcomers welcome. Occasional performances for exhibitions or parties.*

## Pacific /Indonesian

**BAGONG DIWA DANCE COMPANY, 1101 Plymouth Ave., SF 94112, 415-333-7762.** *Leonard Luna. Begun as a workshop in 1974, "new spirit" is now a performing company featuring choreography based on Filipino legends and traditional movement, with western technique. Perform at local schools, museums, on TV.*

**RUCINA BALLINGER.** *Ancient Hawaiian hula and traditional Balinese, SF, 415-648-7032.*

**BEAUDOIN'S.** *Hawaiian. See BALLET, Peninsula.*

**THE FILIPINO DANCERS OF SAN FRANCISCO. 1500 Innes St., SF 94124, 415-557-1552.** *Small group performing ethnic dances of the islands for about five years. Rosalina Balla-White.*

**FORDYCE.** *Hawaiian. See BALLET, SF.*

**FRAZIER STUDIO.** *Hawaiian and Spanish; See BALLET, SJ..*

**MARIE'S.** *Hawaiian. See BALLROOM, SF.*

**MARY ANN'S.** *Hawaiian. See TAP, SJ.*

**McJUNKIN.** *Hawaiian. See TAP, SJ.*

**POMAIKAI POLYNESIAN DANCE COMPANY, 3656 Mission St., SF 94110, 415-282-7966, messages.** *Gayle Aquino. Hawaiian, Tahitian, Samoan.*

**REA STUDIO.** *Hawaiian. See TAP, SJ.*

**SAMOA ART WORKSHOP, 934 Brannan St., SF 94103.**

**SANTA CLARA DANCE STUDIO.** *Hula, Tahitian. See TAP, SJ.*

## *Pacific/Indonesian*

***SONS OF SAMOA, 2 Dublin St., SF 94112, 415-621-5555.*** *Tusipa Anoai. Dances from Tahiti, New Zealand, Hawaii and Samoa. Performances usually include the fire walk.*

***TIARE'S OTEA, c/o Julia Velete, 83 Carl St., SF 94103, 415-731-3233.*** *About 23 dancers, 10 drummers. Established 1971 by Hawaiian-born Tiare Clifford. Focus on Polynesian dances.*

***THEATRE FLAMENCO.*** *Polynesian. See SPANISH.*

***WEST JAVA ARTS, 900 ALABAMA St., SF 94110.***

# *Ethnic Folk*

## *Slavic*

***BALLET RUSSE.*** *Natalia Borisova; character dancing (ethnic-based with ballet technique), choir and orchestra. See also BALLET, SF.*

***CEYLON, c/o Ashkenaz*** *(see INTERNATIONAL) Turkish dance group of about 15 who started out by performing at Turkish parties. About half the members are not Turkish.*

***KHADRA ETHNIC MUSIC AND DANCE ENSEMBLE, P.O. Box 6800, SF 94101, 415-549-3444.*** *Non-profit corporation of 35 dancers and musicians dedicated to preservation of folk arts. Careful research in dance, music, folklore, costuming and interpretations of folk traditions and an understanding of each culture it represents.*

*Founded in 1971 by Graham Hempel, artistic director until 1978 when Susan Oaks and Leanne Elliott took over. Jan Sejda is director, professional dancer, choreographer, researcher.*

*Company has performed at schools, fairs, festivals, on TV and at many local and state cultural events. Repertoire includes suites from Russia, Ukraine, Caucasus, Poland, Hungary, Turkey, British Isles and U.S. Auditions for men and women dancers; previous dance training and performance experience preferred but not required. Call 821-7626 (SF), 383-0657 (Marin); East Bay 549-3444; San Jose 408-241-6698. Patron's organization accepts donations to help pay for choreographer's fees, etc. Newsletter available.*

***LOWICZANIE-POLISH FOLK DANCE ENSEMBLE, c/o 26 Whitney St., SF 94131.***

***MANDALA FOLK DANCE TAVERN.*** *Balkan. See INTERNATIONAL.*

***MATIJA GUBEC CROATIAN FOLKLORE ENSEMBLE, 4285 Coolidge Ave., Oakland 94602, 415-531-4285.*** *Formed in 1973 to preserve Croatian culture, enlighten and entertain, provide* *sociocultural outlets. Named after 16th century Croatian national hero. Singers, dancers, musicians; full membership open to those over 16 paying periodic dues. Company is about 90% Croatian (more than half born in Croatia). Practice Fridays, 7-10 p.m. in Hayward or in SF at Croatian Church Hall. Ten to 15 annual engagements at Croatian and non-Croatian functions. Workshops periodically offered to public at Ashkenaz. One hour video of live performances available for promotion or education.*

*Prospective members should be 18 and display some talent and understanding of Croatian culture; San Francisco 415-681-2543; San Jose, 408-249-3242. Dances from capital of Croatia, influences from Hungary, Turkey. Teacher is Leo Andres; 22 dancers, folk band of six musicians under direction of Tony Pavlovic.*

***RUSSIAN FOLK DANCE ENSEMBLE, Vladimir Perfiloff, 508 Cabrillo St., SF 94118, 415-386-8944.*** *Russian, Balkan, East European dances. Some spectacular dancing.*

***TROIKA BALALAIKAS, c/o 2389 30th Ave., SF 94116.***

# Spanish/Flamenco Mexican/Latin

**AIDA'S (BALLET TODAY).** *Spanish dance class. See BALLET, SJ.*

**ASHKENAZ.** *Flamenco. See INTERNATIONAL.*

**GLORIA MOHR BUSLIK STUDIO.** *Spanish dance. See BALLET, SJ.*

**CABADBARAN CULTURAL DANCE GROUP, 609 Madison St., Albany 94706, 415-525-1552.** *"Unity" is a parent cooperative of some 40 young people whose repertoire ranges from Spanish dance with castanets to Moslem dance and drum dances of mountain people. Rosita Arcol, founder.*

**DANZAS Y CANTOS DE MEXICO, 339 Madrid, SF 94112.**

**EL CUADRO FLAMENCO, 1880 Centro West, Tiburon 94920, 415-435-4398.** *Booking: Sandra Brewer, address above. Ensemble of Flamenco singers, dancers and guitarists who perform a varied repertoire of classical, Spanish, flamenco, traditional and regional music and dance. Company is 3-6 dancers, 1-2 singers, two guitarists. Agustin Quintero is musical director. Guest artists have included Isa Mura, Cruz Luna. Choreographers include Matilde Coral (Seville), Ciro (Madrid) and Rosa Montoya.*

*Company performances: two hour concerts of all phases of Spanish dance; lecture/demonstrations, master classes and workshops.*

**FRAZIER DANCE STUDIO.** *Spanish. See BALLET, SJ.*

**GRUPO UTRERA, c/o Roberto Zamora, 1412 Milvia St., Berkeley 94709.**

**GRAND DANCE, 3501 Grand Ave., Oakland 94610, 415-835-9460.** *Manuel Puertas, salsa. See also DISCO, EB.*

## Spanish/Flamenco
## Mexican/Latin

**MARIA HAYDEE DANCERS OF AMERICA AND SPAIN, 2 Mission Circle Drive, Daly City 94014.**

**HINTON-PICK SCHOOL OF BALLROOM DANCING.** *Latin.* *See BALLROOM, SF.*

**LOLITA AND JOSE'S SPANISH DANCE ACADEMY, 841 Jones St., SF 94109, 415-775-3805.** *Authentic Flamenco. Privates and classes.*

**LOS FLAMENCOS DE LA BODEGA, Old Spaghetti Factory, 478 Green St., SF 94133, 415-885-4588.** *Richard Whalen. Six dancers who do cabaret or cuadro-type Flamenco. Perform weekends and give private instruction.*

**LOS LUPEÑOS DE SAN JOSE, GRUPO DE DANZAS FOLKLORICAS MEXICANAS, Hotel de Anza, 2nd floor, 233 West Santa Clara St., San Jose 95113, 408-292-0443.** *Andrew S. Cohn, company manager. Studio is at 10 Notre Dame, San Jose 95113, 408-292-0443, 292-0473. Founded in 1969 to develop, promote and perform traditionally Mexican folk dance and music. Organized by Susan Cashion and Ramon Morones. Group now has a repertoire of several hundred dances from a dozen different states of Mexico. The range of influences--Spanish, Northern European, Indian and African reflect Mexico's enormous cultural variety.*

*Costumes meticulously detailed, dances researched at the source and presented as close to original as possible. Dances are linked in suites and cuadros, in original contexts, and form part of brief skits with audience involvement. Perform with live musicians about 100 times a year. Have toured through the West, elsewhere.*

**MARIN CIVIC BALLET SCHOOL.** *Flamenco.* *See BALLET, Marin.*

## *Spanish/Flamenco Mexican/Latin*

***MISA CRIOLLA, The Dancers Circle.*** *Argentine dance; workshops.* ***Gina Sungar, 415-254-3323.***

***ROSA MONTOYA BAILES FLAMENCOS, 1880 Centro West, Tiburon 94920, 415-435-4398.*** *Performs Flamenco, classical Spanish and regional dances of Spain in formal concerts, lecture/demonstrations and master classes. Booking through Sandra Brewer, manager.*

*Montoya comes from a Spanish gypsy family of famous Flamenco artists, including her uncles, guitarists Ramon and Carlos Montoya. She has performed all over the world, and now teaches beg. through adv. at Dance Spectrum (BALLET, SF; 824-5044 or 239-7510). Included in class are castanets, arms, footwork, choreography, classical technique.*

***POWELL-REILLY STUDIOS.*** *Salsa. See DISCO.*

***SF DANCE SPECTRUM.*** *Flamenco. See BALLET, SF.*

***TERESITA OSTA, 1975 Jefferson St., SF 94123, 415-567-7674.*** *Flamenco, Spanish, classical folk.*

***THEATRE FLAMENCO OF SAN FRANCISCO, 465 South Van Ness Ave., SF 94103, 415-431-6521.*** *Adela Clara, artistic director. Bay Area's only resident professional Spanish dance company, and the only Spanish dance company in U.S. offering full-scale productions and dances from other Spanish-speaking countries. Twelfth year. Company is active throughout the year with ethno-cultural school programs and newly-founded Ethnic Dance Center, a facility that brings together diverse forms of dance with commitment to quality in performance, educational programs and service to the community.*

*Company presents regular seasons in SF and tours the western states (under NEA dance touring program); participates in artists-in-school/dance component of NEA.*

## Spanish /Flamenco Mexican /Latin

*Residencies have been held in many schools, with focus on Hispanic culture. A 55-page teachers' guide, with the bilingual "Yo Soy" program (seen in over 500 schools), and cross cultural work of dance, music and art from India, Africa, Spain and the U.S., available.*

*Classes in Flamenco, classical and regional Spanish dance, Mexican folk, East Indian Bharata Natyam, disco, tap, belly, Polynesian, and karate. Scholarships, children's workshops and work/study opportunities given when possible to talented students. Three studios available to other performing groups at $2.50-$5/hr.*

*Singles, class cards (six weeks).*

**THE TRUJILLO DANCE COMPANY, 405 Serrano Dr., #C, SF 94132, 415-334-1555 or 666-6878.** *Lorenzo Trujillo, artistic director. The company formed in 1970; presents repertoire of Spanish, Mexican and American Indian songs and dances. Master classes, workshops, lectures and lecture/demonstrations in modern and children's dance, international folk dance, choreography, Spanish, Mexican and Southwest American dances. The company has performed on national television, in nightclubs, hotels and concert theaters throughout California, Wyoming and Colorado.*

*The company toured extensively in 1975-76 with a grant from NEA. Local programs have included SFSU dance faculty concert, SFSU's Music of the Whole Earth Festival.*

*Trujillo has studied and performed throughout the U.S. and Mexico. He received an M.A. in dance from the University of Colorado, and his doctoral degree in multi-cultural education from USF, where he is program associate/research assistant in multi-cultural education. He studied with Teo Morca, Jose Greco, Nana Lorca, Raul Valdez and Tizoc Fuentes, Rudy Perez and Blanche Evans.*

## *Spanish/Flamenco*
## *Mexican/Latin*

***ELOISA VASQUEZ Y SU CUADRO FLAMENCO (Eloisa Vasquez and her Flamenco Group), 1916 Pine St., #3, SF 94109, 415-922-8604.*** *Eloisa Vasquez, dancer; Carlos Volantes, guitarist; Antonio Sanchez, singer-dancer. Formed in 1974 after Vasquez and Volantes returned from performing in Spain. Vasquez feels that her most valuable instruction in Flamenco has come through living in Spain and watching and listening to other Flamenco artists, as well as intense private practice and personal exploration. Her dancing and teaching stress strong individual interpretation and spontaneity with high technical achievement. For teaching and performing information call the above number.*

## Unclassified

***CAPP STREET CENTER DANCE COMPANY, 362 Capp St., SF 94110.***

***CENTER FOR WORLD MUSIC, c/o Robert E. Brown, 397 Gravatt Drive, Berkeley 94709.***

***CHICANINDIA DANCE GROUP, 3572 18th St., SF 94110.***

***CHILI MEKAR, 259A Fair Oaks, SF 94110.***

***DANCE THEATER OF OM, 1441 Jones St., SF 94109, 415-474-6010.*** *Ishvani Hamilton. Dancers and musicians; highlight of performance is series of fables using the language of gesture. Special programs for schoolchildren.*

***GOLDEN STATE CLOGGERS, 446 Campbell Ave., SF, 415-468-5038.*** *An offshoot of Westwind (see INTERNATIONAL, above). Specializes in American Appalachian style known as clogging, done in a circle formation with a caller. Sixteen dancers. Lori Sroka.*

***KOS-KADAS, c/o Sharon Sawyer, 1412 Milvia St., Berkeley 94709.***

***THE RUCKERS IN FLIGHT, 1105 83rd Ave., Oakland 94621.***

***UNITED PROJECTS, INC., 137 Steiner St., SF 94117, 415-431-3969.*** *Dance program features folk.*

# *Ethnic Folk*

## *Events*

*AMERICAN FOLK ARTS FESTIVAL, Spring, SF, Brooks Hall, Civic Center.*

*ETHNIC DANCE FESTIVAL, Spring, SF.* *See FUNDING, Local.*

*INTERNATIONAL FOLK DANCE FESTIVAL, c/o International Concerts Exchange, 9015 Wilshire Blvd., Beverly Hills 90211, 213-272-5539. Annual, March, since 1947.*

*MENDOCINO FOLKLORE CAMP, c/o 40 Glen Drive, Mill Valley 94941, 415-383-1014.*

*STOCKTON FOLK DANCE CAMP, University of the Pacific, Stockton 95211. Jack McKay, director; teaching camp.*

*SCHEDULE OF SAN FRANCISCO BAY AREA FOLK DANCE EVENTS, San Francisco Parks and Recreation Department, Drama and Dance Division, Recreation Arts Building. 50 Scott St., SF 94117, 558-3601.*

*THE SHINDIG, traditional U.S. folk festival, P.O. Box 8, Novato 94947, 415-892-1688.*

# *Ethnic Fo...*

## *References*

***CHURCH OF PLANINA DIRECTORY (folk dance, Bay Area), 1256 College Ave., Palo Alto 94306, 415-327-8115.*** *Federated, non-federated clubs; updated annually.*

***COUNTRY DANCE AND SONG SOCIETY'S DIRECTORY, 55 Christopher St., NYC 10014, 212-555-8895.*** *National listing of groups and contact people.*

***FOLK DANCE CATALOG, 1306 Arcadia Ave., Austin, TX 78757.*** *Ron Houston. Dances by country, region, source, date.*

***FOLK DANCE FEDERATION OF CALIFORNIA, INC., 1275 A St., Room 111, Hayward 94541.*** *Encourages advancement of folk dancing and related arts. Consists of many clubs or groups of folk dancers cooperating with area councils to provide instruction and leadership. Largest single folk dance organization in U.S. The federation sponsors institutes where new dances are taught and older ones reviewed; assembly meetings to help solve problems; research on dance descriptions and costumes; participation in folk dance festivals; subscriptions to Let's Dance, which contains news events, articles on costumes and customs; promotion of folk dance as character and family-building; publicity on club activities; assistance in organizing new groups; festivals, costume design, lists and brochures on existing classes and party places.*

*The federation also sponsors teacher training programs, folk dance scholarships (University of the Pacific folk dance camp, San Diego State University folk dance conference, Feather River family camp, Mendocino folklore camp, Idyllwild folk dance conference), and teacher/dancer institutes where new material is taught at least five times a year. Membership is through a club or as an associate member. Dues $10 or $8, respectively. Publications available include federation director, steps and styling manual, records, magazines, etc.*

## References

***LET'S DANCE MAGAZINE, c/o Max Horn, 6200 Alhambra Ave., Martinez 94533, 415-228-8598.*** *News and folk dance events for Northern California. $5/10 issues.*

***THE FOUNDATION FOR ETHNIC DANCE, 17 W. 71st St., NYC 10023.*** *Research assistance, audio library, performance support.*

***PEOPLE'S FOLK DANCE DIRECTORY, P.O. Box 8575, Austin, TX 78712.*** *$1.75; lists where to dance by state, performing groups, supplies, national publications and directories, newsletters, teachers, orchestras, events, camps, workshops, weekends, travel tours for folk dancers.*

***A RESOURCE LIST OF ORGANIZATIONS OF ETHNIC GROUPS IN THE EAST BAY, International Institute of Alameda County, 297 Lee St., Oakland 94610, 415-451-2846.***

***ROYAL SCOTTISH COUNTRY DANCE SOCIETY bi-monthly newsletter.*** *See FOLK/NORTHERN EUROPE.*

***SF COUNCIL OF FOLK DANCE GROUPS.*** *See ASHKENAZ, INTERNATIONAL; KIRSCHNER, ISRAELI.*

# Ethnic Folk

## *Supplies*

***LAWTON HARN'S MEMORIAL LIBRARY OF FOLK DANCE MATERIALS, University of the Pacific, Stockton 95211.*** *8,000 folk dance records; extensive cross reference card file.*

***THE HULA SHOP, 1775 S. Winchester Blvd., Campbell 95008, 408-371-6202.*** *Polynesian supplies: Maori, Tahitian, Tongan, Samoan, modern Hawaiian.*

***LARK IN THE MORNING, 5080 Little Lake St., Mendocino 95460, 707-937-5824.*** *Folk instruments; medieval instruments. Books, records; French, Celtic, Balkan, Russian, African instruments. Catalog, $2.*

# jazz

*Whereas modern dance has been defined as distinct, studied movement originating from the torso, jazz is a more eclectic form of movement relying on music for its impetus, on the teacher for its individuality. It aims to entertain more than emote, though any expression is possible.*

*Jazz is still young in terms of Bay Area exposures. Its foundations include Broadway, show, Afro, modern, and ballet. It differs from modern in syncopation, music style, energy output and use of the body.*

# jazz

## Contra Costa County

**CERRITO DANCE ARTS CENTER.** *See BALLET, CCC.*

**CONCORD YOUNG WORLD OF DANCE.** *See BALLET, CCC.*

**CONTRA COSTA ACADEMY OF DANCING ARTS.** *See BALLET, CCC.*

**CONTRA COSTA BALLET CENTER.** *See BALLET, CCC.*

**DANSE BOUTIQUE.** *See BALLET, CCC.*

**ELEANORA'S SCHOOL OF DANCE.** *See BALLET, CCC.*

**ENCORE STUDIO OF DANCE.** *See BALLET, CCC.*

**PEARL KAY DANCE STUDIO.** *See BALLET, CCC.*

**McBRIDE DANCE STUDIO.** *See BALLET, CCC.*

**VERNON RUSSELL.** *See TAP, CCC.*

**SAN RAMON VALLEY DANCE ACADEMY.** *See BALLET, CCC.*

**THE STUDIO OF DANCE.** *See BALLROOM, CCC.*

jazz

## *East Bay Companies*

***THE BERKELEY DANCE COMPANY, THE DANCE WORKS, INC., 2212 Parker St., Berkeley 94704.*** *Jazz, ballet, modern. Space for performance. Justin Asher Zitler, director. Jazz I-III. Class cards good for two months; reduced rates for Danceworks members. Faculty: Zitler, Donna Frenna, Craig Voelkert, Susan Strasburger.*

***WEST COAST DANCE THEATRE, 2323A Santa Clara Ave., Alameda 94501, 415-865-3833.*** *Norine E. Xavier, artistic director. Classes in jazz, tap, ballet, disco, Mondays through Saturdays. Beg. to adv. professional, with performing company. Faculty: Norine Xavier, jazz; Marnell Xavier, tap (Mason-Kahn methods); Donna Krasnow, ballet. Home of West Coast Dancers and West Coast Junior Dancers.*

# Jazz

## East Bay Classes

***ALAMEDA SCHOOL OF DANCE.*** *See BALLET, EB.*

***ANDRE'S SCHOOL OF DANCE.*** *See BALLET, EB.*

***BALLET ARTS CENTER.*** *See BALLET, EB.*

***HELEN CARROLL SCHOOL OF THEATRE DANCE.*** *See BALLET, EB.*

***CENTRAL OAKLAND DANCE STUDIO.*** *See MODERN, EB.*

***THE CLASSICAL BALLET CENTER.*** *See BALLET, EB.*

***DANCE REPERTORY THEATRE.*** *See BALLET, EB.*

***EAST BAY CENTER FOR THE PERFORMING ARTS.*** *See BALLET, EB.*

***FASCINATING RHYTHM.*** *See DISCO, EB.*

***FULL SPECTRUM STUDIO.*** *See BALLET, EB.*

***THE GRAND DANCE.*** *See DISCO, EB.*

***NEW DANCE STUDIO, East Bay, 415-549-1613 or 843-3973.*** *Shara teaches Jazz I, II, show jazz, lyrical jazz, character jazz classes, workshops. Private classes available. Preregistration only.*

***NEW DANCE WORKSHOP.*** *See TAP, EB.*

***SHAWL-ANDERSON MODERN DANCE CENTER.*** *See BALLET, EB.*

***THE STARR DANCE STUDIO.*** *See BALLET, EB.*

*jazz*

# *Marin Companies*

***AQUARIUS DANCE THEATER, 330 Sir Frances Drake Blvd., San Anselmo 94960, 415-457-7618 or 456-9592.*** *Richard Browne and Kathy Fregulia, directors. Classes in jazz, ballet, modern, tap. Under auspices of The New Theater Company of Marin, Inc., a non-profit performing company, Aquarius has sponsored a series of choreographer's showcases, "an opportunity for Bay Area dancers to have their works performed in a warm and casual setting."*

***REC RUSSEL DANCE CENTER and Theatre of Marin, 740 Adrian Way, San Rafael 94903, 415-472-3355.*** *Jazz (I-III), ballet, kinesiology, alignment. Jazz repertory group; studio performances by students in both ballet and jazz. Int. and adv. dancers audition for professional training program, a performing company and school including adv. jazz, ballet, modern, stage performance technique and kinesiology five hours daily.*

*Rec Russel, artistic director, jazz; Jody White, ballet mistress; Karen Clippinger, kinesiology lectures/body alignment; Lee Hudson, jazz teacher and resident choreographer; Alan Scofield, jazz teacher and choreographer; Carlos Carvajal, guest artist and choreographer.*

*Also summer workshops in Mendocino, San Rafael, Santa Rosa. San Rafael studio is 40 x 56, with new performance/theater space.*

*jazz*

# *Marin Classes*

**BALLET THEATRE WEST.** *See BALLET, Marin.*

**BELROSE STUDIO THEATRE.** *See BALLET, Marin.*

**CONSERVATORY OF BALLET AND THEATRE ARTS.** *See BALLET, Marin.*

**DANCE ACADEMY OF MARIN.** *See BALLET, Marin.*

**DANCE ARTS OF MARIN.** *See BALLET, Marin.*

**DANCE ARTS STUDIO.** *See BALLET, Marin.*

**MARIN CIVIC BALLET THEATRE.** *See BALLET, Marin.*

**MARVELEEN DANCE STUDIO.** *See TAP, Marin.*

**TAMALPAIS DANCE CENTER.** *See BALLET, Marin.*

# jazz

## *Peninsula Companies*

***DANCE ARTS CENTER AT MARLIN COVE.*** *(See BALLET, Peninsula). The Jazz Set, directed by Berle Davis; auditions from inter. and adv. classes.*

***THE SAN CARLOS DANCE COLLECTIVE.*** *(See BALLET, Peninsula). Line dancers, "The Collectibles," dance for beauty pageants, etc.*

# *jazz*

## *Peninsula Classes*

***BALLET ARTS CENTER OF PALO ALTO.*** *See BALLET, Peninsula.*

***BEAUDOIN'S SCHOOL OF DANCE.*** *See BALLET, Peninsula.*

***CALIFORNIA ACADEMY OF BALLET.*** *See BALLET, Peninsula.*

***CONSERVATOIRE DE BALLET.*** *See BALLET, Peninsula.*

***SONIA IVANOVA ACADEMY OF CLASSICAL BALLET.*** *See BALLET, Peninsula.*

***ROBERT KIRKPATRICKS'.*** *See BALLET, Peninsula.*

***LEE LANE DANCE STUDIO.*** *See BALLET, Peninsula.*

***MAJOR DANCE STUDIO.*** *See DISCO, Peninsula.*

***MARIE'S.*** *See BALLROOM, Peninsula.*

***MENLO PARK ACADEMY OF DANCE.*** *See BALLET, Peninsula.*

***NANCY'S DANCE STUDIO.*** *See TAP, Peninsula.*

***SHEILA NELSON SCHOOL.*** *See BALLET, Peninsula.*

***SAN JUAN SCHOOL OF DANCE.*** *See BALLET, Peninsula.*

***SAN MATEO CITY OF PARKS AND RECREATION.*** *See GROUPS/SPONSORS--City.*

***BENNY SMITH STUDIOS.*** *See BALLET, Peninsula.*

***MARLENE THERKELSEN.*** *See MODERN, Peninsula.*

# jazz

## San Francisco Companies

**ELINOR COLEMAN DANCE ENSEMBLE, Samuel L. Lewis Dance Studios, 3316 24th St. at Mission, SF 94110, 415-648-0936.** *Jazz, beg., inter. and modern, master classes, dance composition workshops, residencies, performance workshops. Kids classes in modern jazz dance and music at The Farm, 1499 Potrero, SF. $4 single; $14/four classes. For more information: 394 Elizabeth St., SF 94114, 648-0936.*

**COMPANY IN FLIGHT, Samuel B. Lewis Studios, 3316 24th St., SF 94110, 415-282-4020, 648-5365.** *Laura Dudell, instructor.* *See BALLET, SF.*

**THE DANCERS' SYNECTICS GROUP, 564 Monterey Blvd., SF 94127, 415-585-8405, 333-4386.** *Ann Marie Garvin, coordinator; performing credits in Mitzi Gaynor, Steve Allen and Pearl Bailey shows, choreography/directing credits including Pointer Sisters, Earl "Fatha" Hines. Also: Lisa Mariea Altamirano, disco-jazz. Pre-jazz through jazz IV, tap (pre through IV), gymnastics, beginning ballet and disco. Singles and monthly cards. Pre-registration required in pre-jazz and pre-tap.*

**BAYAN JAMAY, Women's Bldg., Dovre Hall, 3543 18th Ave., SF 94110.** *Jazz I-II, Horton warmup; jazz, blues and gospel with Ailey repertoire.*

**ED MOCK DANCE STUDIO (West Coast Dance Works), 32 Page St., SF 94102, 415-861-8583 (10 a.m. to 7:30 p.m. daily).** *Ed Mock, director. One large studio with new hardwood floor. Space used for teaching and performances. Classes: ballet, jazz, modern-jazz and Afro-jazz. Overall goal is to develop curriculum into dance-theater. Currently offer composition class focusing on character presentations through dance, mime, voice, etc. Pre-jazz workshop each month. Christmas holiday workshops, and at other times during the year. Faculty: Mock, Linda Heine, Douglas Caldwell, Cecilia Marta, Raymond Johnson, Sulpicio Wagner, Carmen, Alleluia Panis, Pam Carrara, Kathy Sanson. Singles and monthly cards.*

Jazz

## San Francisco Companies

**MODERN JAZZ WORKS, American Industrial Center, 2325 3rd St. (at 20th St), Suite 336, SF 94107, 415-332-9100 (ans. serv.).** *Cecelia-Marie Bowman has M.A. in professional choreography from UCLA; has taught in Northern California since 1974, now on faculty at USF. Classes in jazz, beg.-adv., and Feldenkrais movement. Cecilia-Marie Bowman and Company established to promote modern jazz idiom on a structured as well as an improvisation basis, incorporating musicians. Dancers interested in participating in company classes and performing with junior company, leave message with 332-9100.*

*School aims "to teach people to function well, a non-competitive atmosphere where you can concentrate on becoming strong and centered, finding own style; strong bodies that can function in all dance forms." Technique is gentle method of developing body and alignment through isolation of muscle groups using body parts as a supporting force; also called anti-gravity isokinetic floorwork. Combinations use elements from Afro, ballet, jazz and modern.*

*Bowman is available for master classes, workshops, residencies, etc., professional choreography. Company is available for teaching and choreography residencies.*

*Studio rented for teaching, rehearsing and concerts. Environment is appropriate for non-proscenium dance concerts. Space is 30 x 60, plus brick office with suspended dance floor and mirrors, 6 x 25.*

# jazz

## San Francisco Classes

**MAGAÑA BAPTISTE SCHOOL OF BELLY DANCING.** *See BELLY, SF.*

**CAROL BEALS SCHOOL OF DANCE.** *See BALLET, SF.*

**DANCE SOURCE.** *See MODERN, SF.*

**EPICENTER.** *See BALLET, SF.*

**FORDYCE.** *See BALLET, SF.*

**KAY'S STUDIO OF DANCE.** *See TAP, SF.*

**SAMUEL B. LEWIS STUDIOS.** *See BALLET, SF. Laura Dudell, 415-647-8979.*

**MARIE'S.** *See BALLROOM, SF.*

**MASON-KAHN STUDIOS.** *See TAP, SF.*

**BETTY MAY STUDIO.** *See TAP, SF.*

**NEW DANCE WORKSHOP, 1438 Bush St., SF 94109, 415-824-3824.**

**AMY POWELL DANCE STUDIO.** *See DISCO, SF.*

**RECONSTELLATION.** *See BALLET, SF.*

**RUTHIE'S.** *See TAP, SF.*

**SAN FRANCISCO CONSERVATORY OF BALLET.** *See BALLET, SF.*

**SAN FRANCISCO DANCE THEATER.** *See BALLET, SF.*

# San Francisco Classes

**SAN FRANCISCO DANCE SPECTRUM.** *See BALLET, SF.*

**SCHUMACHER'S.** *See BALLET, SF.*

**SMITH STUDIOS.** *See BALLET, SF.*

**STAR DANCE STUDIO.** *See BALLET, SF.*

**NADINE STUDER, Mercury Athletic Club, 404 Clement St., SF 94118, 415-668-3308.** *Hot Energy Dance Troupe, teaching seminars, beg. and inter. jazz.*

**SUNDANCE STUDIO.** *See MODERN, SF.*

**XOREGOS.** *See MODERN, SF.*

# jazz

## San Jose Classes

**ACADEMY OF DANCE ARTS.** *See BALLET, SJ.*

**ACADEMY OF SPEECH AND DANCE.** *Afro-jazz. See BALLET, SJ.*

**ALOHA'S.** *See TAP, SJ.*

**MARIAN ANDRES DANCE STUDIO, 1501 Blossom Hill Rd., San Jose 94518, 408-269-1363, 371-4424.** *Jazz, tap, ballet, ages four through adults.*

**ATLAS SCHOOL OF DANCE.** *See TAP, SJ.*

**BALLET TODAY.** *See BALLET, SJ.*

**RUBY BARLEY STUDIO.** *See TAP, SJ.*

**DANCE ART STUDIO.** *See BALLET, SJ. Modern jazz.*

**MICHAEL DAVID'S SCHOOL, 6922-C Almaden Expressway (at Via Valiente), San Jose 95120, 408-268-6453, and at 1168 Lincoln Ave. (in Willow Glen), San Jose 95125, 408-293-7800.** *Jazz, tap, ballet and disco; 55 minute classes. Regular attendance, dress standards required. Parents may watch first week of each month; prospective students may watch any time. Students encouraged to enter pageants and talent competitions. Studio develops routines for solos, duets and groups for contests. Students who want professional training are encouraged to take at least three classes weekly (ballet, jazz and tap). From these students the studio selects dancers for lines and tour groups, then requires them to take a production class each week.*

*Also: ballroom dancing (including Latin), body development and conditioning, belly dancing--on basis of sign-up sheets. Yearly recitals, usually in June. Dance for schools, churches, clubs, fairs, retirement centers, hospitals, parties.*

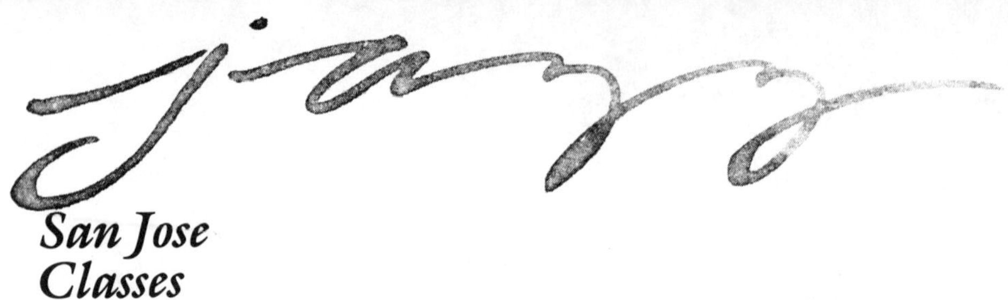


# *San Jose Classes*

***PAM EAST'S SCHOOL OF DANCE, 10080 N. Blaney, Cupertino 95014, 408-257-4523.*** *Jazz, tap and ballet, ages 4 through adults.*

***LORRAINE EVANS SCHOOL OF DANCE.*** *See BALLET, SJ.*

***FRAZIER DANCE STUDIO.*** *See BALLET, SJ.*

***KAISER DANCE STUDIO.*** *See TAP, SJ.*

***LOS GATOS ACADEMY.*** *See BALLET, SJ.*

***MARY ANN'S.*** *See TAP, SJ.*

***JUDY McJUNKIN STUDIO.*** *See TAP, SJ.*

***URSULA MILLETT.*** *See BALLET, SJ.*

***REA SCHOOL OF DANCING.*** *See TAP, SJ.*

***CATHERINE REUTHER SCHOOL OF BALLET.*** *See BALLET, SJ.*

***SANTA CLARA BALLET SCHOOL.*** *See BALLET, SJ. Afro-jazz.*

***SANTA CLARA DANCE STUDIO.*** *See TAP, SJ.*

***SARATOGA DANCE SCHOOL.*** *See BALLET, SJ.*

***SARATOGA MUSIC AND FINE ARTS CENTER.*** *See MODERN, SJ.*

***SCHOOL OF RUSSIAN BALLET.*** *See BALLET, SJ.*

***MARIE STINNETT STUDIO, 5108 Forest View Dr., San Jose 95129, 408-253-6657.***

***TUDE'S SCHOOL OF DANCE.*** *See BALLET, SJ.*

# modern

*In modern dance, born to be free of the restraints and structures of classical ballet, movement grew to speak for an individual, a race, a world--through satire, humor, abstraction, rhythm, form, or any adventure a choreographer would create. The focus of modern is the torso, from which all movement emanates to express emotional, intellectual, spiritual and physical being. The most widely taught techniques are Graham (contraction and release began here), Humphrey-Weidman (fall and recovery, natural equilibrium), Limón (angular, rhythmic), Cunningham (time/space interplay), Hawkins (sculptural, scientific), and Horton (fortified body, responsive to all techniques).*

*A quick reference of styles and studios is included at the end of this chapter.*

# modern

## *Contra Costa County*

***DANSE BOUTIQUE.*** *See BALLET, CCC.*

***ORINDA BALLET.*** *See BALLET, CCC.*

# theater

## East Bay Companies

**BAY AREA REPERTORY DANCE THEATER.** *See EDUCATION, UC Berkeley. Concerts and lecture/demonstrations in schools since 1969. David Wood, director; soloist, danced 15 years with Graham. Performances at UC Berkeley, Hearst gym.*

**BLAKE STREET HAWKEYES, 2019 Blake St., Berkeley 94704, 415-843-7043.** *Non-linear theater for four years. Robert Ernst, Cynthia Moore, John O'Keefe, David Schein. Theater company, dance ensemble, dramatic choir all in one; combination of writing, acting, directing, dancing and composing talents.*

**CENTRAL OAKLAND DANCE STUDIO, YMCA, Third Floor, 2101 Telegraph Ave., Oakland 94612. Right Angle Left Dance Ensemble, Cinnamon Young, 415-839-5584.** *Classes in modern, ballet, jazz, belly, aerobics, African from pre-school through adults. Faculty includes Sharon Arslanian, Ferolyn Angell, Linda Ray, Frances Welter.*

**CHOREOGRAPHICS, INC., Wendy Rogers Dance Company, 1187 Shattuck Ave., Berkeley 94707, 415-524-6737 or 525-8256.** *The company consists of five dancers (Wendy Rogers, Carol Murota, Donna Yamagata, Janice Blalock and Betty Claassen). One major performance a year, with five or so secondary ones. Rogers began dancing with Ruth Hatfield in 1957, and continued with David Wood at UCB and Margaret Jenkins. She studied and performed in NY for five years. The company is a participant in the California Dance Touring Program of the NEA. After 10 years of choreography, 1978 NEA choreographic fellowship recipient. The company works from a strong modern technical basis incorporating movement shaped by rhythmic structures, weight, dynamic changes and invsible concepts, which give the dancing a wide spectrum of appearances, from formal line to frantic blur. Also give lecture/demonstrations, master classes, workshops. For booking contact Warren Franklin, company manager, 415-524-7476, address above.*

## Bay Companies

*Classes with Carol Murota (former modern dance director at Live Oak Park); now directs Choreographics program at 1000 Oaks Baptist Church, Colusa at Catalina, Berkeley. Member dance faculty UCB. Also with Janice Blalock (Lewitsky, Cunningham, Newman techniques and jazz).*

**CONSORT DANCE THEATRE, 2125 Channing Way, Berkeley 94704, 415-841-6500, ext. 415.** *Formed July, 1978. Directors: Lenore Kelley, trained in NYC, B.F.A. in dance from Denison University, Ohio; Diane McKallip, trained with Pennyslvania Ballet, worked in NYC with Louis Falco; Mary Christine O'Connor, B.A. in dance from Denison, interests in liturgical dance, theater.*

*CDT performs major works about six times a year, and is available for residencies, workshops and master classes. Work is more theatrical than abstract, demanding a high level of technical proficiency and dramatic quality. Each member has a commitment to kinesiology and anatomy and in proper training. Modern/improvisation classes available.*

**DANCER'S REPERTORY THEATRE.** *See BALLET, EB.*

**DIMENSIONS DANCE THEATRE, INC., 2352 Broadway St., Third Floor, Oakland 94612.** *Deborah Vaughan, director. Founded 1972. Theater and school promote understanding of the evolution of Afro-American and other African cultures to foster cultural awareness through dance, music and poetry. Represented western U.S. at second World Black and African Festival of Arts and Culture in Nigeria. Co-founder Elendar Barnes-Harrison; directors have traveled to Haiti and Africa to research history and cultural heritages out of which flow the movements that portray the legends that influence current lifestyles, "with dignity and integrity."*

*The company can provide dance residencies, concerts, seminars in black dance, lecture/demonstrations, master classes (African, Caribbean, modern jazz), choreography, drumming. Perform for the disabled, elderly, etc.*

Group tours colleges and universities. Harrison heads dance department at Laney College; Vaughan heads dance department at Contra Costa College. Each majored in dance at Mills and studied on east and west coasts with the renowned.

**EAST BAY DANCE PERSPECTIVES, 4101 Randolph Ave., #3, Oakland 94602, 415-482-4193 or 841-6500.** Now in its fifth season, EBDP is a modern and modern jazz dance collective originally formed as the company for the East Bay Center for the Performing Arts. The group has participated in the Dance Coalition's Gumption series and at many local theaters, public schools and colleges. Core members are Pamm Drake, Karen Soroca, Frances Welter and Mae Welter. Other dancers are included in the concert series.

Drake trained in modern dance and choreography at UCLA and earned an M.A. in dance at Mills College; extensive performing and choreography credits. Soroca is a New York trained dancer and singer with an M.A. and directs The Planet of Dance, children's dance theater piece. F. Welter has been active in studying, performing and teaching dance in the area for six years; degrees from SFSU and Merritt Junior College. with dance emphasis, and teaches annual master classes at the city-wide High School Dance Workshop at SFSU. M. Welter has a degree in dance from SFSU, and has taught ballet, modern and tap for four years.

Each year the company adds new works to its repertoire, which now numbers 18 pieces. EBDP is available for performances, lecture/demonstrations and master classes. For Planet of Dance information, call 415-548-3811, 482-4193 or 841-6500. Planet of Dance is a children's theater piece that includes one dance from each local ethnic group.

# modern

## *East Bay Companies*

***EVERYBODY'S CREATIVE ARTS CENTER, 354 21st St., Oakland 94512, 415-451-1230.*** *Halifu Osumare, artistic director of school and resident Aquarius Rising Dance Theater; former soloist with Rod Rodgers in NYC. Everybody's changed hands in 1977 with a goal to promote multi-cultural exchanges in western and international forms of dance, drama and music. Partially funded by a grant from the SF Foundation, the program includes modern, ballet, jazz, tap, tai chi, lighting design, African, Latin social, Middle Eastern belly and classical Indian dance. Children's classes include ballet, folk, tap, jazz and South African songs and dances, and summer workshop with concert. Ensemble courses in drumming and music include West African, Middle Eastern, Congolese and Afro-Cuban. Individual classes available. Drama workshops include improvisational acting and children's drama (under 13 years).*

*Robert Antonio teaches Limón technique (Limón, with whom he studied, is his uncle) and gives master classes, including Afro-Cuban emphasis, based on training with Alonso's National Ballet School of Cuba. Other faculty: Edith White, Cinnamon Young, Cecelia Marta, Michelle Stanbrough, Linda Jones, Nancy Moreo.*

*Student performances offered periodically to the public. Teaching staff has access to Everybody's large studio to present their works. Artists from the Bay Area may rent facilities for performances. The Aquarius Rising Dance Theater, 12 member multi-racial company with emphasis on total theater that speaks of changing spiritual and social values, the dawn of the age of Aquarius, premiered works in summer of 1978.*

*Everybody's also offers community outreach programs, periodic opening of entire day's classes free to the public, social and alternative entertainment events, productions for schools, churches, prisons and community groups, work-study scholarships and child care. Memberships and sponsorships are available. Members receive discounts on master classes, concerts, workshops and social events. Organizational members receive discounts on outreach programs and free use of facilities.*

# *East Bay Companies*

***MOVING PARTS DANCE COMPANY, 6205 Laird Ave., Oakland 94605, 415-636-0959.*** *Formed in fall, 1977, by four dancers who met at Mills College: Kathleen Dooley, Kasandra Green, Jan Johnson, and Jane Manson. First concert season spring 1978 at Hearst Gym, UCB, Shawl-Anderson and Project Artaud (SF). Premiered two new works in Jan., 1979. Four core members choreograph for company, and welcome guest choreographers. Dancers selected by open audition or by invitation. Any dancer is required to give a year's commitment as a guest artist; after a year, may become permanent company member.*

*Based in Oakland and rents rehearsal space in Alameda. Available for master classes, workshops, and lecture/demonstrations. Background includes Graham, Cunningham, Limón and Nikolais, as well as ballet and improv. training. At times a classical modern dance style is used; accompaniment ranges from Stravinsky to experimental instrumentation, recitation or silence. Company manager Cheryl Silva, 415-652-6577.*

***MOVING SPACE, 2051 San Pablo Ave., Berkeley 94702, 415-548-9605.*** *Marcia Sakamoto, director. Non-profit, tax-exempt corp. Beg. modern: emphasis on kinetic awareness through the enjoyment of moving. Inter.: formal technique, movement sequences, space time elements. Adv.: technique for professionally oriented dancer, broader dynamic range, kinetic sensitivity and means to clarify and enrich the personal movement style. Kinetic alignment clinic with Ruth Hatfield to change body alignment patterns, increase body awareness, etc. Faculty: Sakamoto and Kim Tritt.*

*Sakamoto choreographs and directs all company repertoire. She has an M.A. from Mills, has performed across the country in colleges and universities. Her work has been characterized as a juxtaposition of images to create a mood or statement, rather than a direct narrative. The company draws its dancers from the Bay Area and includes men and women with varied dance backgrounds. Concerts at SF Dance Coalition Awards Performance, CSUH, Jenkins, College of Marin.*

# modern

## *East Bay Companies*

***THE NUBA DANCE THEATER, c/o 263 Athol Ave., Oakland 94606.*** *Evelyn Thomas, artistic director. A new company, currently gives class Saturdays 11 a.m. to 1 p.m. at YMCA Oakland, 21st at Telegraph. Performed at Laney College, Everybody's Creative Arts Center, and Oakland Auditorium. Rehearsals Tues. and Fri., 7 to 10 p.m. Thomas was former lead dancer, The Wiz National Company.*

***ROBERTS AND BLANK DANCE THEATER, 415-525-2113.*** *Classes for all ages.*

***SHAWL-ANDERSON MODERN DANCE CENTER.*** *See BALLET, EB. Advanced modern students are selected to perform repertoire from the company. The style of dance and vocabulary has evolved over the years.*

***WENDY ROGERS DANCE COMPANY.*** *See CHOREOGRAPHICS, INC.*

***TEMPLE OF THE WINGS, Quitzow Studio, 2800 Buena Vista Way, Berkeley 94708, 415-843-5775.*** *Classes, children and adults. Teen Temple of the Wings repertory group (choreography of Vol Quitzow, Charles Weidman, Jose Limón, Duncan tradition). Faculty: Sulgwyn, OEloel, Ann Quitzow. Guest faculty: Ruth Beames, Elin Sowle, others. Temple of the Wings was featured in the 1978 SF Dance Film Festival at SF Museum of Modern Art and KPIX Evening magazine. Concerts include Palace of Fine Arts, dances from the Isadora Duncan centennial celebration (Oeleol, artistic director); Interfaith Unity of Life. Company includes 11 dancers and 10 apprentice dancers. More information, Margaretta Mitchell, 415-655-4920.*

*The studio is located on a hillside amidst columns with a courtyard where young dancers flow among fluted columns, 20 feet high, festooned with garlands and wildflowers. It is a realization of the dreams of Florence Treadwell Boynton, a friend and sister spirit of Isadora Duncan. Dance, "not for performance, but for life" as part of a program for physical and spiritual well-being that includes sleep in the open air, fresh fruits and vegetables, loose clothing. Dedicated to the freedom of women.*

# modern

## East Bay Classes

***ALAMEDA SCHOOL OF DANCE AND GYMNASTICS.*** *See BALLET, EB.*

***ASHKENAZ FOLK DANCE COOPERATIVE.*** *See FOLK/INTERNATIONAL. Marti Zuckrow, instructor, 415-524-4831 or 525-5054.*

***BALLET ARTS.*** *See BALLET, EB.*

***BERKELEY DANCE COMPANY.*** *See JAZZ, EB.*

***CLASSICAL BALLET CENTER.*** *See BALLET, EB.*

***EAST BAY CENTER FOR THE PERFORMING ARTS.*** *See BALLET, EB.*

***FULL SPECTRUM STUDIO.*** *See BALLET, EB.*

***BETSY KAGAN, 734 Creston Road, Berkeley 94708, 415-524-7798.*** *Modern, choreography, improvisation, Effort/Shape, basic alignment and creative movement for adult non-dancers. Predominant stylistic elements of modern technique are Limón and Cunningham, with emphasis on breath and flow of energy, spatial clarity and attention to placement problems. Certified reconstructor and teacher of Labanotation.*

*Kagan has performed with Jean Erdman Theatre of Dance, the New Haven Dance Ensemble, and in pieces under personal director of Charles Weidman, Merce Cunningham, Viola Farber, Paul Taylor and Dan Wagoner. She has taught in East Coast and Bay Area colleges and universities, and has performed her own works in NYC and in SF Dance Coalition-sponsored concerts.*

***LIVE OAK PARK THEATER, 1301 Shattuck Ave., Berkeley 94709, 415-841-5580.*** *Ballet, modern, tap.*

## *Marin /Sonoma Companies Classes*

**MERCURY MOVING COMPANY, Cinnabar Theater, 3333 Petaluma Blvd., Petaluma 94952, 707-763-8920.** *Sebastopol Summer Dance Workshop, 2836 Bloomfield Road, Sebastopol 95472, 707-823-1142. Ann Woodhead, director. Since 1973. "Committed to discovery and rediscovery in dancing. Together the members explore new ways of dancing, feeling and being." All choreography is by company members, with improvisation as well as composed pieces. Original music is performed live for each event. Six major productions since Red Dreams in 1974. Solo performances have featured Carol Friedman, Ann Krantz and Ann Woodhead. Master classes are offered in technique, improvisation, choreography. There are presently five company members. Lighting designer and technical director is Michael Jayson.*

**MOTION COLLECTIVE, 141 Pine St., San Anselmo 94969.** *Nina Wise. See OTHER DANCES, Creative.*

## *Classes*

**AQUARIUS DANCE THEATER.** *See JAZZ, Marin.*

**DANCE ARTS STUDIO.** *See BALLET, Marin.*

**MARIN CIVIC BALLET.** *See BALLET, Marin.*

**TAMALPAIS DANCE CENTER.** *See BALLET, Marin.*

# Peninsula Companies Classes

**MARLENE THERKELSEN DANCE COMPANY and Studio, 237 Broadway, Millbrae 94030, 415-697-9422.** *Marlene Therkelsen, artistic director and choreographer. Company incorporated Jan. 1976. Ballet, jazz and modern, for children, young dance students and adults. Therkelsen has M.F.A. and B.F.A. in dance from UCLA; Rockefeller foundation fellowship for two years; choreographer and dancer with Dance LA. Has taught master classes for CDEA at Mills, SJSU, SFSU, Cabrillo College (Santa Cruz).*

*Company performances throughout the Peninsula, for SF Dance Coalition, Channel 14/live TV-video, at shopping centers, senior citizen centers. Dancers: Irene Gondai, Nina Hovermale, Melinda Martin, Robin Walin and Marlene Therkelsen. Memberships: San Mateo Dance Development Center, Mid Peninsula Center for Dance Development, CDEA, Council for The Arts/Palo Alto; Art Rise, San Bruno; NEA, SF Dance Coalition.*

## Classes

**THE BALLET SCHOOL.** *See BALLET, Peninsula.*

**PACIFIC DANCE THEATER.** *See BALLET, Peninsula.*

# San Francisco Companies

**CHRISTOPHER BECK & COMPANY: DANCE/THEATER, Centerspace, 2840 Mariposa St., SF 94110, 415-771-8316.** *Christopher Beck, artistic director and founder. Company is an activity of Centerspace Dance Foundation, Inc., a non-profit corporation formed in 1977 to solicit support from individuals and organizations. The company is available for performances, residencies, lecture/demonstrations, workshops and master classes. Workshops and classes include all levels of modern dance, ballet, dance for children, partnering, improvisation, composition, dance therapy, alignment and correctives, massage for dancers, and production techniques. Beck is available to stage existing works or create new ones.*

*The company, organized in 1975, is composed of nine dancers and emerged as a development of Beck's earlier solo work in New York City. "The company performs an extensive repertoire which explores the realms of dreams, myths and visions as fresh impulses. These dramatic dances of the psyche use movement as a catalyst for the audience to experience feelings which contribute to their own inner search."*

*Beck leads creative movement workshops throughout the country, with Jungian, Gestalt, Quaker and Epsicopal groups, among others. His works have been performed throughout the U.S. Local summer intensive experience in community living, using movement for integration and growth. For more information call 415-861-9759.*

**NANCY CARP & DANCERS, SF, 415-482-1419.**

**DANSFRANCISCO, 2560 B Pine St., SF 94115, 415-567-6329.** *Carol Thaler, Sharonjean Leeds, artistic directors. Thaler worked with Graham, Pearl Lang, Dan Wagoner and others, choreographed and performed with SF Dance Theater; Leeds has B.A. and M.A. in dance, trained with Jose Limón, Mia Slavenska, Murray Lewis, and teaches at USF and SF Dance Theater. Guest performances and choreographers.*

# Modern

## San Francisco Companies

***ISADORA DUNCAN HERITAGE SOCIETY, INC., 625 Polk St., SF 94102, 415-863-7365.*** *Mignon Garland, director; Nika Newcomb, instructor. High artistic standards in the heritage of Duncan's artistry.*

***EPICENTER DANCE WORKS, 3030 Ingalls, SF 94124, 415-467-6867.*** *Founded in 1978 by Arnette de Mille; focus on performance and choreography. First performance, 1978, five new works by de Mille. Any company member wishing to present choreography is supported by other members. No regular classes offered, but workshops given. Modern/contemporary and jazz techniques are presented with live and/or taped music. Anyone interested in auditioning may call de Mille at 467-6867, or Marla Percal, 468-4714.*

***EARTHLY STUDIOS, and Company, 223 Mississippi St., SF 94107, 415-626-4622.*** *Sheri Gaia, artistic director; former soloist with Nederlands Dans Theater. Ballet and contemporary technique classes; choreography of Gaia is basis for advanced technique classes. Yoga taught by Robert Amacker, musical director. Earthly Co. is a modern repertory group featuring Gaia's choreography. Members: Gaia, Steve Cates, Phylles Holt, Amacker, Tai Louie.*

***JOHN EFFING DANCE CO., 3995 17th St., SF 94114.*** *Workshops, classes, auditions (male and female).*

***FOOTLOOSE, 2325 Third St., SF 94107, 415-863-8588; or 1730 Carleton St., Berkeley 94703, 415-548-6116.*** *Irini Nadel, artistic director; background combines classical with contemporary training in New York and London with improvisation and theater influence from the West Coast. She has been teaching, choreographing and performing for almost 20 years. Her work synthesizes modern, improvisation and voice. She is also trained in constructive rest and massage.*

## San Francisco Companies

*Formerly a modern dance repertory ensemble, now a producing and sponsoring organization for new and experimental works. Provides solo performances or works created by Nadel and guest artists; ensemble works in collaboration with other artists; many workshops and classes in new forms of dance theater to expand vocabulary of creative expression without rejecting traditional forms.*

*Collaborators and guest artists are invited to contribute to the collective vision. Visual artists, musicians and theater people are integral part.*

*Workshops taught by Nadel train dancer/performance artists in a combination of technique, voice training, theater techniques, improvisation skills, movement theater, repertory workshops to create new works. Programs offer solo performances or ensemble work. Lecture/demonstration and master classes given in technique, improvisation and the creative process. Footloose is available for one day, half week and full week residencies--or for performances only.*

***MARGARET JENKINS DANCE COMMUNITY PERFORMING SPACE and Company, 1590 15th St. at Mission, SF 94103, 415-863-7580.*** *Jenkins, a native San Franciscan, studied locally and at Juilliard and UCLA. She taught at the Cunningham studio and on her own while performing with Gus Solomons, Twyla Tharp, Cunningham and Viola Farber. Her teaching goal is to develop strong technical facility so that a personal style can emerge with clarity and definition.*

*Adult classes: modern (continuing), gymnastics. Children's (ages 5-7 and 8-12): combining modern and gymnastics. Teens: special Saturday modern technique and improv. class; open enrollment. All adult classes taught by Jenkins and company members. Faculty: John Henry, Andrea Hicks, Judy Lazaroff, Virginia Matthews, Colleen Mulvihill, Larry McQueen, Dan Silver, Elin Sowle, Lucinda Weaver and Lonna Wilkinson. Ballet: Larry Grenier. Singles, cards and professional rates.*

*There are also Christmas workshops including repertory composition and kinesiology/technique.*

# *San Francisco Companies*

*Members of the company not only perform the work but participate in its development according to their ways of moving. Repertoire includes Interferences II, Equal Time, Story, Videosongs, Copy, About the Space in Between, and Intro Three. The company was formed in 1970. It is available for master classes, performances and lecture/demonstrations. For booking, call Susan Stowens, 1590 15th St., SF 94103, 415-683-7580.*

**LYNDA KNAPP, TERRY MEYERS AND DANCERS.** *See EDUCATION, USF.*

**MOBIUS, directed by Donna Krasnow.** *See MODERN, SF.*

**OBERLIN DANCE COLLECTIVE, SF Performance Gallery, 3153 17th St., SF 94110, 415-863-6606.** *Faculty: Brenda Way, (director), Doug Winter, Kimi Okada, Pam Quinn, Eric Barsness, Bill Chetel, Katie Nelson, Hannah Schwarzchild, Julie Lifton. Curriculum: I & II modern, inter. modern, choreography, tap, improvisation, aesthetics, company class (ballet and improv.). Singles, six weeks of choreography or aesthetics, technique or improv.; work-study.*

*Formed in 1972 by Brenda Way in Oberlin, Ohio as a professional outlet at Oberlin College. In 1976 moved to SF. Aesthetic is technical proficiency and commitment to strong ensemble with individual excellence, artistic and personal growth in the classroom, emphasizing intellectual as well as physical discipline.*

*Sponsors the Performing Arts Forum (series of nine performances by experimental artists in a variety of media) and publishes a quarterly, New Performance. Sponsors three week performance workshop intensives (technique, music, vocal, dance and music composition). Seminars on contemporary aesthetics, dance photography, technical theatre, dance management. Lecture/demonstrations, open rehearsals and concerts.*

*San Francisco Companies*

*ODC produces three area seasons each year, in addition to guest appearances around California. Tours major U.S. cities and has received NEA, CAC, and private foundation support.*

**PERFORMING ARTS WORKSHOP, 340 Presidio Ave., SF 94115, 415-931-9228.** *Gloria Unti, founder and artistic director; "dance and theater as ways of self-discovery and growth." PAW began in 1965 at the Buchanan Street YMCA as a dance/theater school with strong community ties. Classes, seminars and workshops in the performing arts with performances during the year open to all throughout the semester; scholarships and work-study. For adults: modern, jazz, ballet and men's; also children and teen classes, and morning exercise class.*

*An adult performing group is composed of PAW staff and advanced students. Year-round rehearsals, and performances in community theaters, festivals and schools are provided. Children's workshops emphasize dance elements through music, movement games and story telling, class demonstrations and public performances. Teen workshops stress dance and theater arts fundamentals, collective work on original performance pieces.*

*PAW also sponsors a community outreach program, with classes and performances in SF public schools; Mission Arts Complex dance program; contracted instruction to local private schools and children's centers; teaching seminars and lecture/ demonstrations to PAW's approach to dance education; artists exchange program where outside dance/theater groups perform at the studio each month.*

**THE SAN FRANCISCO MOVING COMPANY, Modern Dance Inc., 1519 Mission St., SF 94103, 415-863-4406.** *Rhonda Martyn, artistic director; Matthew Stowell, company manager. Nearly three years old, its goal is to facilitate the enjoyment and understanding of modern dance as an accessible art form. The company produces low cost, quality modern dance concerts and educational dance activities. The company seeks to present artistically intriguing dance pieces from a variety of choreo-*

*graphers, to communicate joy in the art of dance. ("Rainmaker" by Emily Keeler was restaged in 1979 for Joffrey II dancers.) It maintains an ensemble of trained modern dancers devoted to "performing excellence and creativity." Company now tours out of state under CAC Dance Touring Program.*

*Company has presented spring and fall seasons, lecture/ demonstrations at local colleges and universities, artists in residence at De Anza College in Cupertino, taught workshops seasonally. Classes have been offered in modern, jazz, ballet, contact, improvisation. Seasonal workshops, intensives, master classes, concert tours, expanded dance education activities, touring are current activities after a winter season studying in New York. Workshop guest teachers have included Betsy Kagan, Kathleen McClintock and Karen Steele; classes include technique, repertory, choreography, individual body work and alignment, and culminate in workshop performance. The technique classes (two levels) are designed for maximum technical and aesthetic mastery of modern dance. Class size limited; early enrollment guarantees acceptance.*

***THE PAUL SCARDINA DANCE STUDIO and Company, 1052 Geary St. (between Polk and Van Ness), SF 94109, 415-626-8973. Office: 340 Corbett Ave., SF 94114.*** *For adults: modern dance workshop for "absolute beginners" emphasizing conditioning, body awareness and appreciation of dance as an art form. Sessions run eight weeks: advanced registration is required. Beg. through adv. classes meet on a continuous basis; no pre-registration required. Workshops for children ages 5 through 12 are available. The company performs around the Bay Area, including Flint Center in Cupertino and Hertz Hall on the UCB campus. Singles, three-month cards, professional rates, work-study and scholarships.*

## *San Francisco Companies*

***SUNDANCE STUDIO SAN FRANCISCO, Studio and Company, 301 Eighth St. at Folsom St., SF 94103.*** *Robert Stuart Murphy, director and teacher. "The studio has been created to develop a wider range of dance theater. All performance projects are undertaken with purpose, and content with integrity is the absolute rule. The core of this work is the wilderness project, a theater presentation undertaken to reunite urban Americans with their wilderness heritage, and to provoke realistic relationships with the environment. A serious place for serious people who work." Classes nightly Mondays through Thursdays, and Saturday afternoons, with rehearsals after classes. Beg. through adv. with elements of modern, ballet and jazz combined to create correct placement, clean strong line and shape, and the ability to move. Size: 30 x 50 feet. Second floor.*

***SYNERGIC THEATER, 545 Haight St., SF 94117, 415-431-1171, 552-2742.*** *Suzanne Manning, artistic director. Classes in modern, movement fluency, creative movement. Auditions for resident company.*

***TUMBLEWEED/The Farm, 1499 Potrero St., SF 94110, 415-282-3271, 824-6292.*** *Local and out of state performances. Theresa Dickinson, director.*

***XOREGOS DANCE STUDIO and Company, 70 Union St., SF 94111, 415-989-3617.*** *Shela Xoregos, director. Modern, Beg., jazz and ballet. Faculty members are professional dancers. Classes are continuous throughout the year. Adv. modern classes given when the company's in rehearsal. Singles and monthly cards, professional rates. Ballet and jazz rates for consecutive four week periods. $5 charge for observing class if not enrolled. Registrar is Libby Brahms, 873-0823, days.*

# modern

## *San Francisco Classes*

***ARABESQUE CONCERT DANCE.*** *See BALLET, SF.*

***CAROL BEALS.*** *See BALLET, SF.*

***BRAND X STUDIO, 855 Folsom St., SF 94107, 415-957-1633.*** *Barbara Roesch, director. Modern classes. Space available for bookings for weekend performances, rehearsals and teaching.*

***COMPANY IN FLIGHT.*** *See BALLET, SF.*

***DANCE CENTER.*** *See BALLET, SF.*

***DANCE SOURCE, 3316 24th St., SF 94110, 415-282-4020 between 10 a.m. and 2 p.m.*** *Donna Krasnow, director; trained at UCB with David Wood, performed with Footloose, sponsored and performed in own concerts. Taught at UCB for three years. Faculty Aron Osborne, (Limón), Liz Rosner, (Falko-Horton), Toni Silver. Modern, beg. ballet, jazz, kinesiology, floor barre, hatha yoga stretches. Most modern classes based on Graham with a few Cunningham style. Some studio performances; students occasionally asked to perform in director's large annual concert. Workshop in contact improvisation, jazz, kinesiology, composition. More than 1,350 sq. ft. of space, hardwood floors, video equipment, showers.*

***MODERN JAZZ WORKS.*** *See JAZZ, SF.*

***AMY POWELL DANCE STUDIO.*** *See DISCO, SF.*

***POWELL-REILLY.*** *See DISCO, SF. Int. Horton/modern classes by Sharon Marks.*

# modern

## San Francisco Classes

**RUTH ST. DENIS--DENISHAWN DANCE, SF, 415-775-6874.** *Klarna Pinska (who danced with Denishawn) and Dixie Mahy (who is learning first-hand from Pinska). Pinska reconstructs her performances with Denishawn dancers. Classes and performances in Denishawn technique and choreography; children and teens, in SF and Mill Valley. "Students think of it as ballet," Mahy says, "though in its day the form was revolutionary." Pinska has costumes and photographs from the original dances.*

**SAN FRANCISCO CONSERVATORY.** *See BALLET, SF.*

**SAN FRANCISCO DANCE SPECTRUM.** *See BALLET, SF.*

**SMITH STUDIOS.** *See BALLET, SF.*

**SAN FRANCISCO DANCE THEATER.** *See BALLET, SF.*

**SAN FRANCISCO DANCERS FORUM.** *See GROUPS/SPONSORS.*

**STUDIO 210, 3534 Army St., SF 94110, 415-626-4929.** *Michelle Larsson, beg. and inter. modern. Also teaches at Women's Bldg. of the Bay Area, 3543 18th St., SF, 415-626-4929.*

**TALLER COREOGRAFICO, 339 Madrid, SF 94112.** *Robert Antonio del Pino. Trained in classical ballet (Alonso's National Ballet of Cuba school), modern dance (with uncle Jose Limon), and Afro-Cuban salsa forms. Toured as a child professional with Alonso, principal roles with the Ballet Internacionale de Caracas, Ballet Clasico de Mexico, Chicago Opera Ballet. His choreography is featured in several U.S. dance companies as well as in Mexico, Central and South America, and Australia. New pas de deux dedicated to the late Harvey Milk. Teaching at Everybody's Creative Dance Center (see MODERN, EB).*

**TRUJILLO DANCE COMPANY.** *See FOLK/SPANISH.*

## San Jose and Beyond Companies

***ASSORTMENT DANCE THEATRE COMPANY.*** *See EDUCATION, De Anza College.*

***TANDY BEAL & COMPANY, 2-1601 East Cliff Drive, Santa Cruz 95062.*** *Tandy Beal and Jonathan Scoville, artistic directors. Beal trained in NYC (Alwin Nikolais, Murray Louis, Gladys Bailin and Phyllis Lamhut). She performed with Nikolais Dance Theatre. She is on the faculties of Cabrillo College, UC Santa Cruz and University of Utah. She is a movement specialist for the NEA Artists-in-Schools program. In 1978 she received an NEA grant for choreography. Scoville composes much of the music for the company (electronic, jazz and percussion). He has designed and built many of the instruments he uses, and has co-authored a book on the subject.*

*Senior members include Ron Taylor, soloist; Donna McConnell, Kathleen McClintock, Brett Larson and Mark Lowdermilk. Other members include Kite Tail Mime, Letitia Bartlett and Rob List. Evan Parker is lighting designer.*

*Administrative director, Alan Savat; 408-462-0303 for booking/touring information. Single performances, master classes in technique, improvisation or composition, mime performances and classes in lighting design and other technical aspects of theater are offered. Tandy Beal and Company is under the auspices of Friends of Olympic Station, Inc., a non-profit organization. Full company available January-June 1980; Ms. Beal, open. Last winter season the company toured both coasts, giving 22 performances.*

***JANLYN DANCE COMPANY, ACADEMY OF BALLET AND MODERN DANCE, 2905 Park Ave., Santa Clara 95050, 415-968-0921 or 408-295-5394.*** *Janet Lynn Shaw, artistic director. Faculty includes Phyllis Bugglin. For men and women over 16; enrollment open. Beg.-adv. modern, master classes and workshops in care and prevention of dance injuries. Auditions: contact Janet Shaw. Inter.-adv. modern technique combined with company class on Mon. and Fri. evenings. Studio 24 x 70, wood floor, windows. Singles and monthly cards.*

*Shaw, who earned an M.A. in modern dance at the University of Utah, formed the company in fall 1977. Shaw on faculty at University of Santa Clara, choreographs for Assortment Dance/Theatre Co. of Cupertino. Has performed and choreographed since 1972. Company: Kathleen Hill, Phyllis Bugglin, Susan Morton, Leilani Tome, Cynthia Harrison.*

*"The company is a pool of unusual talent working to provide a complete spectrum of dance experience for local community of dancers: modern dance technique classes, concerts, arts for children, performances in school; the company is a platform for professional performances by trained dancers who want to maintain involvement in other areas of dance. Local touring program schedule allows members freedom to pursue other interests. Choreography is an interplay of creative lighting, sets, sound and movement. I want the audience to leave our concerts feeling broadened and satisfied by the experience, not baffled or unfulfilled."*

***PORTABLE DANCE TROUPE, Resident Dance Company, California State University, Fresno.*** *Mona Reed, manager. Guest artist Ronnit Land in 1979 season, new works by Land, Ruth Griffin (co-director with Madeline Perrone), Debra DeRosa, Kathe Copperman (LA). Has performed in SF, Fresno. Umbrella performing organization for all dance students enrolled at CSUF: sponsors studio concerts of new student work, coordinates performances by independent choreographers and out of town dancers.*

# modern

## *San Jose and Beyond Classes*

***BALLET TODAY.*** *See BALLET, SJ.*

***JUDY McJUNKIN.*** *See TAP, SJ.*

***CATHERINE REUTHER SCHOOL.*** *See BALLET, SJ.*

***SARATOGA MUSIC AND FINE ARTS CENTER, 18755 Cox Ave., Saratoga 95070, 408-379-5514.*** *Modern, jazz, tap, ballet, ballroom, disco and belly.*

***WILLOW GLEN DANCE CENTER, 1567 Callecita, San Jose 95125, 408-264-0181.*** *Jo Ann Blach, director.*

## Style References

*STUDIOS WITH AFRO EMPHASIS:*

***CENTRAL OAKLAND DANCE STUDIO.*** *See MODERN, EB.*
***DIMENSIONS DANCE THEATRE, INC.*** *See MODERN, EB.*
***EVERYBODY'S CREATIVE ARTS CENTER.*** *See MODERN, EB.*

*STUDIOS WITH CUNNINGHAM EMPHASIS:*

***MARGARET JENKINS DANCE STUDIO, INC.*** *See MODERN, SF.*
***DANCE SOURCE.*** *See MODERN, SF.*
***USF.*** *See EDUCATION.*

*STUDIOS WITH DENISHAWN TECHIQUE:*

***RUTH ST. DENIS—DENISHAWN DANCE.*** *See MODERN, SF.*

*STUDIOS WITH DUNCAN TRADITION:*

***CHOREIA STUDIO.*** *See OTHER DANCES/Creative.*
***ISADORA DUNCAN HERITAGE SOCIETY.***
***TEMPLE OF THE WINGS/QUITZOW STUDIO.*** *See MODERN, EB*

*STUDIOS WITH GRAHAM EMPHASIS:*

***BAY AREA REPERTORY DANCE THEATER (UC BERKELEY).***
***DANCE SOURCE.*** *See MODERN, EB.*
***PURE WINE DANCE COMPANY.*** *See OTHER DANCES/ Creative.*

*Style References*

***STUDIOS WITH HAWKINS EMPHASIS:***

**USF.** *See EDUCATION.*

***STUDIOS WITH HORTON EMPHASIS:***

**POWELL-REILLY.** *See DISCO, SF.*

***STUDIOS WITH LIMÓN TECHNIQUE:***

**DANCE SOURCE.** *See MODERN, SF.*
**EVERYBODY'S CREATIVE DANCE CENTER.** *See MODERN, EB.*
**TALLER COREOGRAFICO.** *See MODERN, SF.*
**USF.** *See EDUCATION.*

# tap

*The history of American Black dance began in the mid-1700's when slaves were forbidden to beat drums for fear this would incite them to rebellion. So they turned to other forms of percussion—most importantly, footbeats. Without the drum, they were left with only their bodies to express movement and sound. Combined with the white man's clog dancing, the tap dance was born--the first American art dance other than those of the Indians.*

*There are comparatively few studios in the Bay Area focusing primarily on tap; it is found most often in curricula of ballroom and theater-related studios. Therefore, all the entries in this section list classes, though some offer performances.*

## *Contra Costa County*

**CERRITO DANCE ARTS.** *See BALLET, CCC.*

**CONCORD YOUNG WORLD.** *See BALLET, CCC.*

**CONTRA COSTA ACADEMY.** *See BALLET, CCC.*

**CONTRA COSTA BALLET CENTER.** *See BALLET, CCC.*

**ENCORE STUDIO OF DANCE AND GYMNASTICS.** *See BALLET, CCC.*

**HAMILTON STUDIOS OF DANCE AND MUSIC, 500 Alcosta Mall, San Ramon 94583, 415-828-1890.** *Patsy and Bud Hamilton, directors. Tap, jazz, ballet; tots to adults.*

**PEARL KAY STUDIO.** *See BALLET, CCC.*

**NISSEN'S.** *See BALLET, CCC.*

**OAK PARK ACADEMY.** *See BALLET, CCC.*

**ORINDA BALLET ACADEMY.** *See BALLET, CCC.*

**VERNON RUSSELL DANCE STUDIO, P.O. Box 858, Danville 94526, 415-837-6178.** *Since 1963; tap, jazz, ballet, gymnastics, morning exercise. Performances every other year. Russell is former president of DMofC, Chapter 13. Two studios: 35 x 25 and 45 x 50.*

**SAN RAMON VALLEY ACADEMY.** *See BALLET, CCC.*

**THE STUDIO OF DANCE.** *See BALLROOM, CCC.*

# Tap

## *East Bay*

***ACT ONE STUDIO.*** *See BALLET, EB.*

***ALAMEDA SCHOOL OF DANCE.*** *See BALLET, EB.*

***ANDRE'S.*** *See BALLET, EB.*

***CARROLL.*** *See BALLET, EB.*

***DAVLIN-LOWELL.*** *See BALLET, EB.*

***EAST BAY CENTER FOR THE PERFORMING ARTS.*** *See BALLET, EB.*

***EVERYBODY'S CREATIVE ARTS CENTER.*** *See MODERN, EB.*

***FASCINATING RHYTHM.*** *See DISCO, EB.*

***THE GRAND DANCE.*** *See DISCO, EB.*

***LIVE OAK PARK, 1305 Shattuck, Berkeley 94709, 415-482-5820; 845-1718.*** *Mae Welter.*

***NEW DANCE WORKSHOP, 6371 Telegraph Ave., Oakland 94609, 415-843-3973.*** *Joan Flint, instructor; all levels. Intensive workshops.*

***STARR DANCE STUDIO.*** *See BALLET, EB.*

## *Marin*

***AQUARIUS DANCE THEATRE.*** *See JAZZ, Marin.*

***BALLET THEATRE WEST.*** *See BALLET, Marin.*

***BELROSE STUDIO.*** *See BALLET, Marin.*

***BEA BLUM'S DANCERS STUDIO, 765 E. Central Blvd., Fairfax 94930, 415-454-8447.*** *Opened Sept. 1, 1978. Tap, ballet, disco, modern, choreography, belly, staging, vocal, acrobatics, etc., with others provided on demand. Singles, cards and family rates.*

*Blum's premise is development of the total performer. She was a professional tap dancer with Dean Martin, Frank Sinatra, Ernie Ford, etc., shows. "You must do everything to become professional. I'm grateful to know that many of my students are now in shows and making their living as dancers."*

***CONSERVATORY OF BALLET.*** *See BALLET, Marin.*

***DANCE ACADEMY OF MARIN.*** *See BALLET, Marin.*

***DANCE ARTS OF MARIN.*** *See BALLET, Marin.*

***MARIN CIVIC BALLET.*** *See BALLET, Marin.*

***MARVELEEN DANCE STUDIO, 710 Adrian Way, Santa Venetia, 415-479-9575.*** *Eileen Dubs, instructor. Tap, ballet, jazz for ages 3 through adult. Special family rates; limited class size.*

***SAN ANSELMO PARKS AND RECREATION DEPT., 415-453-9055.*** *Tap for children and adults, beg. and inter.*

***SANTA ROSA BALLET SCHOOL.*** *See BALLET, Marin and Sonoma.*

# tap

## *Peninsula*

**BEAUDOIN'S.** *See BALLET, Peninsula.*

**DANCE ARTS CENTER AT MARLIN COVE.** *See BALLET, Peninsula.*

**GRANGER'S.** *See BALLET, Peninsula.*

**LEE LANE.** *See BALLET, Peninsula.*

**MAJOR DANCE STUDIO.** *See DISCO, Peninsula.*

**MENLO PARK ACADEMY.** *See BALLET, Peninsula.*

**NANCY'S DANCE STUDIO, 1662 Broadway, Redwoood City 94063, 415-366-2581.** *Tap, ballet and jazz.*

**SAN CARLOS DANCE COLLECTIVE.** *See BALLET, Peninsula.*

**SAN JUAN SCHOOL.** *See BALLET, Peninsula.*

**SAN MATEO PARKS DEPT.** *See GROUPS/SPONSORS--City.*

**GLEN SHIPLEY SCHOOL OF THE DANSE, 1490 El Camino Real, San Bruno 94066, 415-583-1801.** *Tap, jazz and ballet; tots to professionals.*

**BENNY SMITH ACADEMY.** *See BALLET, Peninsula.*

## San Francisco

**ANDERSON SISTERS SCHOOL OF DANCING, 276 Sixth Ave., SF 94118, 415-751-6629.**

**BALLET ARTS OF SF.** *See BALLET, SF.*

**DANCER'S SYNECTICS.** *See JAZZ, SF.*

**FORDYCE.** *See BALLET, SF.*

**KAY'S SCHOOL OF DANCE, 21 San Pedro Rd., Daly City 94014, 415-755-2121.**

**MARIE'S.** *See BALLROOM, SF.*

**MASON-KAHN STUDIO, 1125 Market St., SF 94103, 415-861-2110.** *Est. 1945. Pat Mason-Kahn, principal of the school, teaches all grades of ballet, Cecchetti method. Member of Imperial Society of Teachers of Dancing, London; former assistant dance director of Ice Follies. Stanley Kahn teaches tap, has staged vocal and dance acts for many noted performers; current president of board of directors of youth of America "On Stage." 32 years with Ice Follies.*

*Tap for teens and adults, ballet for beg. adults, acrobatics (beg. and elem.), modern jazz, general movement (elements of ballet and jazz.).*

*Tap includes instruction in use of "k" symbols (Kahnotation), the only existing method for accurately annotating tap rhythms and movement.*

*Performances by adult students mostly limited to senior citizens and lodge meetings. Major performing group is youth of America "On Stage," a variety revue including a 30 piece orchestra, 20 voice chorus and dance group of 12 teenagers.*

*Youth of America, Inc., is a non-profit corp. dedicated to providing talented young entertainers with opportunities to perform under as nearly professional conditions as possible. Auditions, membership open to all teens with appropriate training. Applicants may audition at rehearsals or by appointment. Stanley Kahn, 415-861-2110 (SF); Ray Barker in San Leandro (577-3033) may be telephoned for orchestral auditions.*

***BETTY MAY SCHOOL OF DANCING, 1052 Guerrero, SF 94110, 415-824-6057; 1524 Geneva Ave., 415-334-5416.*** *Tap, ballet, jazz, disco for adults and children, day and evening.*

***ED MOCK STUDIO.*** *See JAZZ, SF.*

***OBERLIN DANCE COLLECTIVE.*** *See MODERN, SF.*

***AMY POWELL.*** *See DISCO, SF.*

***RUTHIE'S SCHOOL OF DANCE, 2229 Taraval, SF 94116, 415-681-5226.*** *Tap, ballet, modern jazz, ballroom for adults, beg. through prof., class or private. DMofA and PDTA member.*

***SF CONSERVATORY OF BALLET.*** *See BALLET, SF.*

***SF DANCE SPECTRUM.*** *See BALLET, SF.*

***SF JEWISH COMMUNITY CENTER.*** *See GROUPS/SPONSORS--Community.*

***SCHUMACHER'S.*** *See BALLET, SF.*

***STAR DANCE STUDIO.*** *See BALLET, SF.*

***TAP DANCE CENTER, 540 Alabama, SF 94110, 415-621-8277.*** *Performance training.*

***THEATRE FLAMENCO.*** *See FOLK, Spanish.*

# tap

## *San Francisco*

**IRENE WEED, SF Parks and Rec. Dept., Rec. Arts Bldg., 50 Scott St., SF 94117, 415-558-3601.** *Graduate of SF State, studied ballet, Spanish, tap, jazz, etc. Member Dance Masters of Chicago and California, Folk Dance Federation of California. Teaching over 25 years. Beg. and inter. tap, including steps, terminology and routines in waltz, clog, soft shoe and rhythm. Sponsored by SF City Drama and Dance Advisory Committee. Weed also teaches ballet, exercise, jazz, ballroom, disco, ballroom swing, Latin. Some classes free. Classes for singles, groups. Weed also teaches disco and ballroom at SF City College, private instruction or group tap, jazz, Hawaiian, at home studio (751-5468).*

*Ballroom has been taught at 50 Scott St. for 20 years, with 40-50 in a class. Twice a year formal disco-ballroom party for all ages. Last Christmas a group went on a Mediterranean fly/cruise to look at ethnic folk dance.*

**TONY WING DANCE STUDIO, 447 Stockton St., SF 94108, 415-986-1649.** *Wing has danced for 40 years, taught for 30. Children and adults, beg., inter., adv. and prof.*

# tap

## San Jose

***ACADEMY OF DANCE ARTS.*** *See BALLET, SJ.*

***ACADEMY OF SPEECH AND DANCE.*** *See BALLET, SJ.*

***ALOHA'S STUDIO OF DANCE, 305 McCovey Lane, San Jose 95127, 408-251-6199.*** *Tap, ballet and jazz from tots to teens.*

***MARIAN ANDRES.*** *See JAZZ, SJ.*

***ATLAS SCHOOL OF DANCE, 2982 Almaden Expressway, San Jose 95118, 408-267-2520.*** *Fran Atlas, director. Tap, jazz, ballet, rock.*

***BALLET TODAY.*** *See BALLET, SJ.*

***RUBY BARLEY SCHOOL OF DANCE, 5455 Camden Ave., San Jose 95120, 408-264-3380.*** *Since 1936. Tap, ballet, modern, jazz; for children, teens and adults.*

***CALIFORNIA YOUNG WORLD, 1472 Saratoga Ave., San Jose 95129; 5410 Taft Drive, San Jose 95124, 408-266-1504; 3530 Lochinvar Ave., Homestead Shopping Center, 408-244-5555; 22330 Homestead Road, Cupertino 95014, 408-736-2261; 438 N. White Road, East San Jose 95127, 408-251-3931.***

***DANCE ART STUDIO.*** *See BALLET, SJ.*

***MICHAEL DAVID'S.*** *See JAZZ, SF.*

***PAM EAST'S.*** *See JAZZ, SJ.*

***LORRAINE EVANS.*** *See BALLET, SJ.*

***FRAZIER DANCE STUDIO.*** *See BALLET, SJ.*

# tap

## San Jose

***KAISER DANCE STUDIO, 2391 Kenwood Ave., San Jose 95128; 2925 Park Ave., Santa Clara 95050, 408-243-4834.*** *Janie Stanley, director. Member DMofA. Tap and jazz, for children and adults, day and evening.*

***LOS GATOS ACADEMY.*** *See BALLET, SJ.*

***MARY ANN'S DANCE CENTER, 1487 Franklin, Santa Clara 95050, 408-247-5550.*** *Tap, jazz, ballet, Hawaiian, ballroom.*

***JUDY McJUNKIN DANCE STUDIO, 2927 Cherry Ave., San Jose 95125, 408-267-5525.*** *DMofA member. Tap, jazz and Hawaiian for pre-school through adults.*

***DEAN NENA SCHOOL OF DANCE AND MUSIC, 1029 Blossom Hill Road, San Jose 95123, 408-268-1303.*** *Tap, ballet and supply store.*

***REA SCHOOL OF DANCING, 1095 Malone Rd., San Jose 95125, 408-269-2530.*** *DMofA member. Tap, ballet, modern jazz and Hawaiian classes.*

***SARATOGA MUSIC CENTER.*** *See MODERN, SJ.*

***TUDE'S.*** *See BALLET, SJ.*

# Other dances

*The search for inner purpose and more expansive ways of being has infused dance with many new forms of movement contained in verbal cages. This chapter provides a place to explore these Other Dances. They include, but are not limited to: aerobic, creative, exercise, sacred, square and unspecified.*

# Other dance

## *Aerobic*

***AEROBIC DANCING, Jackie Sorensen, SF, 415-474-4173.***

***CENTRAL OAKLAND DANCE STUDIO.*** *See MODERN, EB.*

***SAN MATEO CITY PARKS DEPT.*** *See GROUPS/SPONSORS--City.*

# Other Dance

## *Creative Companies*

*Companies and classes listed in this section are called "creative" because of their new and varied appproaches to dance. They can be improvisational, classical, modern or just different.*

***JANE BROWN FOUNDATION FOR DANCE AND RELATED STUDIES, The Lesser Oakland Dance Theatre, 4226 Park Blvd., Oakland 94602, 415-530-6611.*** *"Our approach to dance and all human motion is fundamentally different from all other theories of motion known to us. We say that people are erect because of gravity, not in spite of it. Therefore, we teach classic dance with the understanding that 'turnout' is natural, as is erectness, and that gravity impels us to dance, opening to us step by step as our bodies release their tensions, the marvels of the vast language of classic dance. This enables us to emerge into the essence of creative dance and an understanding of motion that encompasses our living processes. On these we build our dance theatre.*

*"We challenge the myth that dancers must begin to dance when three and finish at 40, or earlier, with injuries. If you are a dancer, it is of the utmost importance that you study through relaxation, not tension." From 3-7 yrs. children learn to understand and enjoy their bodies in motion. For 8-12ers, basics of classic dance as a communicating art.*

*The Lesser Oakland Dance Theatre is a repertory company presenting original works based on an understanding of the evolution of human motion and what it reveals of the human character and experience. Its standards are professional. The only qualification for participation is a commitment to the work. It is neither modern nor ballet, though classic technique, including pointe, is used in exposition of ideas. "It is simply 'dance,' performed to all manner of music--Bach, street sounds, classic poetry, jazz blues."*

*School also offers classes for pregnant women and fathers, adult classes (men as well as women study pointe to learn the erect nature of people), history of how and why we move as we do today, creative floor work, relaxation, dance composition,* music theory. Private lessons and consultations available. Faculty includes Jane Brown, director (studied with Graham, Sokolow, Horton and Mundstock, Muriel Stuart); Vicki Gunter; Cheryl Johnson.

Studios are 34 x 42 and 15 x 42, available for rent. No master classes, no auditions. Plans for company tours in progress.

**CHILDREN'S CREATIVE DANCE THEATRE, 1406 Euclid St., Berkeley 94708, 415-843-4270; CREATIVE DANCE THEATRE, 659 Arlington, North Berkeley, 94704, 415-526-9783.** Founded in 1976 by Katy McGuire who has performed since age 5; MFA specializing in dance movement; consultant for NEA since 1972. Instructors: Jo Indovina (beg. ballet, Kirov), Leni Seigel, Cathy Heinrich. Growth through creative expression, improvisation and composition in dance and theater. General performance skills emphasized with costumes, props, music and related arts, movement techniques to develop correct body alignment. First class free. For ages 3-5, 4-6, 5-7, 7-10 (beg.), 7-10 (performing group), 11-15 (teens and adults). Sliding fees cover art materials, props, costumes, music, etc. Family discounts, scholarships.

Studio rental $6/hr., 40 x 60 space in Berkeley Hills, Bay view, dressing room, for classes, workshops, rehearsals.

**MANGROVE, 499 Alabama St., #120, SF 94110 (Project Artaud), 415-415-552-4190 or 626-5052.** Improvisation performance collective of seven men, developed in San Francisco about three years ago. U.S. tours; intensive improvisation workshops including related theater and vocal arts. Videotapes of performances have been aired on TV. Members: John LeFan, Byron Brown, Bob Rease, Charles Campbell, Ernie Adams. James Tyler, former member, now teaches at the studio. Drop-in classes and privates available. Dynamics give birth to physical communication and personal and group rapport.

# Other dances

## *Creative Companies*

***MOSTLY WOMEN MOVING, 415-863-8462 (studio).*** *SF-based women's improvisational dance group.*

***ROBERT MURPHY STREET DANCE COMPANY, South of Market Cultural Center, 934 Brannan at Eighth Street., SF 94103, 415-664-5051.*** *Improvisation.*

***PURE WINE DANCE COMPANY, Samuel L. Lewis Dance Studio, 3316 24th St. at Mission, SF 94110, 415-282-4020.*** *Formed in June, 1977, as a performing company whose members are "united in the experience that dance can enhance and balance the whole being." Teachers: Ana Perez, Devi Rudman, Vasheest, Zuleikha, Ayat Cate. Classes in spirit of eastern classical dance, yoga, Graham technique, language of movement, caravan dances of India and Afghanistan, acting and music for dancers and mime. Singles, cards and work/study.*

***SAN FRANCISCO DANCERS' WORKSHOP, 321 Divisadero St., SF 94117, 415-626-0414.*** *Anna Halprin, artistic director. A unique approach which brings dance to the people as a participatory form. Includes a natural approach to the movement of the body, feelings and mind to release artificial patterns and tensions. Theater becomes the creation of rites, rituals and ceremonies out of life experiences; the use of this whole process as a way to transform life. Friday night dances, special events. Matching grant from NEA, Arts Expansion Program, with Reachout program for Third World scholarship leadership training through the arts and dance. Write for application.*

*Movement ritual and dance exploration are taught in SF and Berkeley. For information call 415-863-5802, or write Soto, 4343 19th St., SF 94114. Also: performance techniques, dance explorations, kinesiology and Feldenkrais awareness through movement, contemporary American black dance, creating and performing scores, intensives, training and advanced programs.*

Other dances

## *Creative Companies*

***SYNERGIC THEATER, 545 Haight St., SF 94117, 415-552-2742. or 431-1171.*** *Suzanne Manning, technique and improvisation, feedback, basics, fluency.*

***THE WOMEN'S PERFORMANCE CONNEXION, c/o Joya Cory, 141 Pine St., San Anselmo 94960, 415-456-8165.*** *Originally a performance group, now a coalition of women in performing arts (dancers, actors, music, filmmakers, performance artists, visual). Have about 20 members; coalition since Jan. 1978. Nina Wise, 1148 High Court, Berkeley 94708, 415-527-5693. Improvisational dance from natural movement; body work for women. Movement for self-discovery with psychic implications.*

## *Creative Classes*

***LUCIA AUGUST, 760 14th St. #9, SF 94114, 415-853-6529.*** *Create with Dance Seminars. Dance seminars and individual consultation in using dance body movement and games to express the child within and natural aliveness, experience emotions, relate to body--all to create an experience of self through dance processes. August has danced more than 20 years; training with Gertrude Knight, Joan Smallwood, Bella Lewitsky, Margaret Jenkins, Ed Mock and others. She is a Motivation Management Seminars-trained consultant.*

***MAGAÑA BAPTISTE.*** *See BELLY, SF. Children's creative movement.*

***THE BERKELEY ART CENTER, 1275 Walnut Ave., Berkeley 94709, 415-849-4120.*** *Carl Worth, director; Richard Sargent, curator. "Moving with art;" participation in happenings through movement.*

***MIRIAM BORNE'S DANCE AND YOGA STUDIO, 425 14th St., SF 94114, 415-431-6182.*** *Dance of the self.*

***CENTERSPACE, 2840 Mariposa, SF 94110, 415-861-5059 or 826-5379.*** *Freddie Long, classes in technique and improvisation. Long studied Limón, Nikolais, Cunningham, has many teaching and performing credits.*

***CHINA BASIN DANCE THEATRE, 2325 Third St., SF 94107, 415-864-4485.*** *Dreams and dance workshops, contact improvisation, ballet for athletes and much more.*

***CHOREIA, Studio 336, 2325 Third St. at 20th, SF 94107, 415-626-3131 (messages).*** *Nika Newcomb-Quirk. Classes in Duncan style, technique, movement theory and choreography, with energy awareness, meditation and visualizations.*

Other dances

## *Creative Classes*

***CLASSICAL BALLET CENTER.*** *See BALLET, EB.*

***CONSERVATORY OF BALLET.*** *See BALLET, MARIN.*

***JOYA CORY, 141 Pine St., San Anselmo 94960, 415-456-8165.*** *With Women's Performance Connexion. Teaching for eight years, performing for 10. Work is physical theater (narrative, theatrical). Often teach people with some dance training and who want theater skills. Workshops to free the body and imagination and voice; performance technique, natural movement and dance, improvisation, voice skills, postural alignment, stretching, ensemble movement.*

***MARIA CURTIS, 2345 Channing Way, Berkeley 94704, 415-524-9649.*** *Rhythmical movement for grace, flexibility, relaxation, posture, joy of movement. Since 1972.*

***DANSE BOUTIQUE.*** *See BALLET, CCC. Children's creative movement.*

***DANSPHERES with Carol Soleau, 1037 Waverly, Palo Alto 94301.***

***THERESA DICKINSON, Dovre Hall, 3543 18th St., SF 94110, 415-282-3271.*** *Classes in movement improvement with centering and stretching. Dickinson danced with Twyla Tharp; currently performs with Tumbleweed Dancing, Inc.*

***EAST BAY CENTER FOR THE PERFORMING ARTS, 1819 Tenth St., Berkeley 94710.*** *Dance meditation. See also BALLET, EB.*

***EVERYBODY'S CREATIVE ARTS CENTER, 354 21st St., Oakland 94612, 415-451-1230.*** *Dance and meditation. See MODERN, EB.*

# Other dances

## *Creative Classes*

***RICHARD HAISMA, the Art of Motion, Samuel Lewis Dance Studios, 3316 24th St. at Mission, SF 94110, 415-552-7069 or 282-4020.*** *Classes as sentient bodily answers to the questions of where is art and what is motion. Beg., inter. eight week sessions.*

***HEALING OURSELVES CENTER, 2547 Eighth St., Berkeley 94710, 415-841-6911.*** *Dance jams, introductory workshops in movement and improvisation, bioenergetics, dance therapy, massage.*

***KERIAC, 415-552-0911.*** *Contact improvisation for beginners, movement for dancers, therapists, groups, etc. "Earn trust, giving, taking weight, interpersonal sensitivity, greater movement range, release of muscle tension."*

***VANESSA KINGSTON, 415-626-8765.*** *Dance from the spirit, classes explore moving from the inside. Wholistic approach stressing awareness of body and spirit. Energy balancing. Blocked areas are taught to breathe and experience life.*

***BRYNAR MEHL, 415-933-2623.*** *Athletic workshops to produce greater performance through centering and economy of motion. Classical ballet fundamentals; children through adults; separate boys classes. For boys: to develop positive physical awareness, discipline, confidence and respect. For girls: elements of harmony, line and form. Adults: all this for stronger physical body. Child's prep: bring forth child's inner world and integrate it with external through games of rhythm and imagination in atmosphere of caring and sharing. Sessions in Lafayette, Walnut Creek.*

*Formerly of Manhattan Festival Ballet, Merce Cunningham, New York City Opera, Maine State Athletic Workshops.*

## *Creative Classes*

***PACIFIC BALLET CENTER, 1519 Mission St., SF 94103, 415-626-1357.*** *Mary Alice Mabee, contact improvisation with emphasis on levitation techniques.*

***PERFORMING ARTS WORKSHOP.*** *See MODERN, SF.*

***ALAN PTASHEK, 415-661-9204.*** *All levels of contact improvisation.*

***RECONSTELLATION. 415-221-3333, ext. 434, or 441-2640.*** *See BALLET, SF. Improvisation workshops.*

***ROBERTS AND BLANK DANCE WORKSHOP,*** *Carla Blank and Jody Roberts, directors. Modern, folk, ballet, vaudeville, yoga. See MODERN, EB.*

***SAFE SPACE YOUNIVERSITY.*** *See GROUPS/GENERAL. Movement and meditation; movement for children.*

***SAN FRANCISCO DANCE SPECTRUM.*** *See BALLET, SF.*

***SCHUMACHER'S.*** *See BALLET, SF.*

***SHAWL-ANDERSON MODERN DANCE CENTER.*** *See BALLET, EB.*

***SHOOTING STAR STUDIO, 578 Folsom St., SF 94105, 415-495-0260.*** *Improvisation; Boko-maru.*

***JOHN WILSON, Berkeley Moving Arts, 2200 Parker St., Berkeley 94704, 415-841-6676.*** *Posture class using ballet and yoga; placement improvement for dancers, constructive exercise.*

# *Other dances*

## *Dance Exercise*

***CONTRA COSTA COUNTY:***

***SAN RAMON VALLEY DANCE ACADEMY.*** *See BALLET, CCC. Body conditioning dance exercise.*

***EAST BAY:***

***THE BALLET SCHOOL.*** *See BALLET, EB. Dancersize classes.*

***BERKELEY MOVING ARTS.*** *John Wilson, 415-841-6676.*

***FULL SPECTRUM STUDIO.*** *See BALLET, EB. Dance exercise.*

***MARIN:***

***DANCE ARTS STUDIO.*** *See BALLET, Marin. Body conditioning through dance exercise.*

***SAN FRANCISCO:***

***MAGANA BAPTISTE.*** *See BELLY, SF. Dance exercise.*

***CAROL BEALS.*** *See BALLET, SF. Body conditioning dance.*

***EMBARCADERO YMCA.*** *See GROUPS/SPONSORS--Community. Levels I and II.*

***SF JEWISH COMMUNITY CENTER.*** *See GROUPS/SPONSORS--Community.*

***SAN JOSE:***

***ACADEMY OF DANCE ARTS.*** *See BALLET, SJ. Exercise/dance.*

# Other dancing

## *Religious / Sacred*

*Sacred dance is as old as primitive man's expression of natural religious feeling. With some groups such movement is an integral part of their expression of divine impression. Devotees throughout history have believed that the body is a channel for religious expression; why not, then, develop movement to show in public, the private state of the soul. In defending dance against those who saw it as pagan, one early Christian thinker urged the people to think of their feet as given to them by God to dance with the angels.*

*Visual aids and a newsletter on sacred dance in the U.S. are available from The Sharing Company, P.O. Box 190, North Aurora, IL 60542. Membership in the guild is $5/yr; $3 students. Back issues of the Sacred Dance newsletters are on file at the Pacific School of Religion library in Berkeley (The Margaret Taylor Dance Book Collection.)*

*Also Resources in Sacred Dance lists books, periodicals, unpublished manuscripts, audio-visual materials and other sources on dance as an art form in religious worship and education. Write Mrs. Charles Wolbers, 111 S. Green St., East Stroudsburg, PA 18301.*

**MAGAÑA BAPTISTE.** *See BELLY, SF.*

**BODY AND SOUL DANCE COMPANY, Residence Company of St. John's Presbyterian Church, College Avenue at Forest, Berkeley 94705, 415-254-5094.** *Modern and liturgical; members available for performances, classes and workshops in children's dance, liturgical and modern.*

**ISHTAR SCHOOl OF CREATIVE ARTS, P.O. Box 6365, Albany 94706, 415-524-1192.** *Dance of religious experiences. "A space for the meeting of the arts and the spirit."*

# Other dance

## Religious/Sacred

**PACIFIC SCHOOL OF RELIGION, 1798 Scenic Ave., Berkeley 94709, 415-848-0528.** *Doug Adams, director of Ph.D., M.A. and M. Div. programs in Religion and Dance. Judith Rock, program assistant and lecturer in theology and dance. Degree programs offered with major works each quarter. Dancers and companies welcome at quarterly workshops and performances.*

*M.A. and M.Div. degrees with major in sacred dance are available at Pacific School of Religion, Ph.D. and Th.D. with major in sacred dance are available at the Graduate Theological Union with residence at PSR. Students specialize in one of five areas; liturgical; performance dance and theology; dance therapy; dance in religious education; and religious dance history. Some require outside study at Mills College and UC Berkeley through an exchange program. Regular modern technique offered.*

*Quarterly dance workshops and summer school courses have brought dance leaders such as Christopher Beck and Anna Halprin to the students. Body and Soul Dance Company is the performing group in residence at Pacific School of Religion, led by Judith Rock.*

*Theology and the arts courses include: dance towards wholeness/healing (handicapped work); dance in western religions; sacred dance in India; dance in Black religions; humor and faith; craft and creation of dance images. The school is fully accredited by the Association of Theological Schools and Western Association of Schools and Colleges. General requirements for all graduate students are observed by M.A. and M.Div. students in sacred dance.*

*Religion and the arts graduate program requires observing the general rules for doctoral students. Workshops include humor in dance and arts; dance improvisation, Jewish folk humor; humor and healing; storytelling and dance in worship education; the dance of death as prophetic humor. Two studios: 25 x 30, and 30 x 60.*

## Religious/Sacred
## Square/Swing

**THEOSOPHICAL SEMINARS, 258 Kathleen Dr., Pleasant Hill 94523, 415-687-3649.** *Metaphysics of dance seminars in cooperation with S.F. Bay Area Dance Coalition.*

**UNIVERSITY OF SANTA CLARA.** *See EDUCATION. Liturgical dance workshop, a one quarter course.*

## Square/Swing

*The dancing may be square, but for more than 1,500 square dancers in the Bay Area, it's the greatest fun around. The Northern California Square Dance Association lists more than 100 clubs on its rosters, divided into districts geographically. For more information call or write Alan and Lois Conroy, 124 Marin Valley Dr., Novato 94947, 415-883-6057.*

**OTHER LISTINGS:**

**ASHKENAZ FOLK DANCE COOPERATIVE.** *See FOLK/INTERNATIONAL.*

**LAKESHORE SCHOOL, Middlefield and Eucalyptus Streets;** *Beg. and inter., Tuesdays 7:30-10:30 p.m., 415-775-1309, 878-9771.*

**MENLO PARK ACADEMY.** *See BALLET, Peninsula.*

**SWING:**

**CALIFORNIA SWING CLUB, meets at the Jolly Friars, 950 Clement St., SF 94118, 415-752-4094,** *Sundays.*

**CARDINAL LOUNGE, 101 Parrott 94577, San Leandro, 415-357-7333.** *Free lessons Mondays.*

## *Square/Swing References*

***TOP OF BEARDSLEY'S, Broadway at El Camino Real, Burlingame.*** *Swing/western dancing Wednesdays.*

## *References*

***AMERICAN SQUARE DANCE, Box 788, Sandusky, OH 77870.*** *Annual, $7; monthly publication.*

***FIESTA DE LA CUADRILLA, Square Dance Assn. of San Diego County, P.O. Box 81573, San Diego 92138.*** *Annual since 1950; first weekend in September.*

***NATIONAL SQUARE DANCE CONVENTION, c/o G. Ken Parker, 427 Phillips Way, Vista, CA 92038.*** *Annual, late June, since 1952.*

# Other dances

## *Unclassified*

*This list includes all studios and companies not specifying styles of dance taught and/or performed.*

***RAYNA ALLEN SCHOOL OF DANCING, 2787 California St., SF 94115, 415-346-1233.***

***CATHY ARBA SCHOOL OF DANCE AND GYMNASTICS, 2050 El Camino Real, Santa Clara 95051, 408-984-2391.***

***COMMUNITY MUSIC CENTER, SF, 415-647-6015.*** *Music and dance.*

***DANCE FOR THE DEAF, California School for the Deaf, D'Estrella Auditorium, 2601 Warring St., Berkeley 94704, 415-841-8431.*** *Sign language with live drums; warmup and disco. For those who are hearing-impaired, but open to all on drop-in basis.*

***DEL ORO CONSERVATORY, 2352 Broadway, Oakland 94618.***

***GEORGE DIXON DANCE COMPANY, 2 Dakota St., SF 94107.***

***FILLMORE STREET STUDIO, 3142 Fillmore St., SF 94123.***

***I. GAILANI SCHOOL OF DANCING, 3951 Balboa St., SF 94121, 415-387-2434.***

***KATIE'S SCHOOL OF ACROBATICS AND DANCE, 445 Colusa Ave., Kensington 94707, 415-524-1310 or 799-1535.***

***LOCOMOTION, 27 Hartford St., SF 94114.***

***LOTUS COMPANY, 1556 Quesada Ave., SF 94124.***

***PHOENIX SPRING ENSEMBLE, 1224A Stockton St., SF 94133.***

# Other dances

## *Unclassified*

***GLEN SHIPLEY SCHOOL OF THE DANSE, 1490 El Camino Real, San Bruno 94068, 415-583-1801.***

***SHOOTING STAR STUDIO, 578 Folsom St., SF 94105.*** *See also JOYA CORY.*

***MICHAEL SOKOLOFF DANCE ENSEMBLE, P.O. Box 610, SF 94101.***

***STUDIO II, 2325 Third ST., SF 94107.***

# *dance Fields*

*Bodywork*

*Education*

*Funding/Booking*

*Groups/Sponsors*

*Spaces*

*Resources*

*Supplies*

*Appendices*

# Bodywork

*Some people would say that injuries go hand in hand with dance. Whether dancers believe that pessimistic statement or not, there is a growing trend toward making a conscious, daily commitment to health. This chapter focuses on alternative methods of health and healing, not in denial of traditional forms, but as a supplement to them. Medical centers are not listed because they can be found in telephone books.*

*The chapter is divided by type of treatment, with brief explanations of many of the less known forms of healing. No endorsement is made for any listing, as injuries--and healings--have personal, unique causes. A more complete list of centers and individual therapists can be found in COMMON GROUND (see MEDIA), and in the Yellow Pages under Physicians.*

# Bodywork

## Acupuncture

*Acupuncture is a natural healing therapy to maintain health or prevent disease. It entails the insertion of fine needles into specific points (there are about 70,000 charted) on the surface of the skin to balance the flow of energy along certain established meridians. It is used to stimulate or awaken the body's natural healing powers.*

**ACADEMY OF EASTERN MEDICINE, 1414 Maria Lane, Walnut Creek 94596, 415-937-3344.** *A holistic organization dedicated to self-development and harmony of physical, emotional, mental and spiritual bodies. Dr. Alan Charles, director, trained in neurology and preventive medicine. Treatment includes acupuncture, nutrition, homeopathy, individual counseling, kinesiology. Classes and individual sessions.*

**THE ACUPUNCTURE CLINIC, 1811 Francisco St., Berkeley 94703, 415-841-4730.**

**ACUPRESSURE WORKSHOP, 1533 Shattuck Ave., Berkeley 94709, 415-845-1059.** *Michael Reed Gach, director. Acupressure and acupuncture used here, based on same meridians. Acupressure works on key blocks of tension by applying pressure with the hand. Practitioner training, shiatsu, fundamentals (release of shoulder, neck tension), yoga and acupressure massage, diet and individual sessions.*

**CHAKPORI-LING FOUNDATION, INC., College of Oriental Medicine, 890 Grove St., SF 94117, 415-922-4100.**

**COLLEGE OF ORIENTAL MEDICINE, 890 Grove, SF 94117, 415-922-4100.** *Acupuncture and Tibetan healing arts.*

**GREENBRAE ACUPUNCTURE AND ACUPRESSURE and moxibustion, 3043 Clement St., SF 94121, 415-221-0025.** *Peter S.K. Chou, certified acupuncturist.*

Bodywork

## *Acupuncture*

***THE HERING FAMILY HEALTH CLINIC, 2340 Ward St., Berkeley 94705, 415-548-1992.*** *Acupuncture and homeopathy, individual treatments.*

# Bodywork

## *Biofeedback*

*Biofeedback is a scientific process that reads brain waves and other body elements to give information on stress areas. Focus is on learning to regulate activity and relaxation for optimum health.*

***BIOFEEDBACK CENTER OF BERKELEY, 2510 Webster St., Berkeley 94705, 415-841-4333.***

***CLEARING, P.O. Box 621 Larkspur 94939, 415-924-6611.*** *Stanley Russell, director of the Association of Professional Clearing Consultants. Based on Dianetics, Scientology and Eductivism with biofeedback meter. Idea is that success can be limited by self-defeating attitudes.*

***COMPLETE BIOFEEDBACK SERVICES, 20 Lomita (at Lawton), SF 94122, 415-731-5576.*** *Michele Martin Llamas, M.A. biofeedback trainer; Ron Smothermon, M.A. neuropsychiatry. Established 1976. Stress management, creating and maintaining good health. Individual programs focus on complex interaction between body and mind. Center works on relief of chronic pain, anxiety, insomnia, neuro-muscular disorders. Clients take responsibility for recreating and maintaining maximum health. Hypnosis and relaxation used to gain control of tension-induced habits.*

***HOLISTIC HEALTH PROGRAM, Women's Community Clinic, 696 East Santa Clara St., San Jose 95112.*** *Individual sessions include biofeedback, relaxation training, visualization, time management, exercise planning, lifestyle health assessment and visit with staff physician. Programs for achieving personal well-being. Fees on sliding scale.*

***INTERNATIONAL SCHOOL OF MASSAGE.*** *See MASSAGE.*

***THE PSYCHOSOMATIC MEDICINE CLINIC, 2510 Webster St., Berkeley 94705, 415-548-1115.*** *Dr. Kenneth R. Pelletier, director (author Mind as Healer/Slayer.) Intensive training in biofeedback with faculty versed in medicine and physical therapy.*

# Bodywork

## Alexander Technique

*The following groups specialize in manipulating the body's structure and redirecting the mind to relieve tension and energy blocks for optimum energy and health.*

***THE AMERICAN CENTER FOR THE ALEXANDER TECHNIQUE (ACAT), 931 Elizabeth St., SF 94114, 415-282-8967.*** *Correction of back pain, fatigue, poor posture, physical tension caused by improper use of body.*

***ARICA SAN FRANCISCO ASSOCIATION, INC., 785 Market St., Room 1401, SF 94103, 415-546-1331.*** *School for self-realization and clarification of consciousness. Offerings: training, short programs and products for health and balance of body, emotions, mind and spirit. Breathing, meditation, physical movement, group work.*

***ASTON PATTERNING, Steven Feinberg, 415-654-7078; John McConnell, 841-6500.*** *Judith Aston, founder, created movement education to reduce unnecessary stress in the body. Individually tailored programs work with structural or functional patterns.*

***AUTOGENIC HEALTH CENTER, 2510 Webster St., Berkeley 94705, 415-547-3403.*** *Vera Fryling, M.D. Stress reduction and creativity training for relaxed psycho-physiological states, greater physical well-being and energy economy. Used to control pain, balance autonomic nervous system, correct sleep disorders and weight control, promote greater athletic performance and broaden creative expression.*

***AUTOGENIC TRAINING, 6401 Broadway Terrace, Oakland 94618, 415-526-3551.*** *Larry Jablon. Relaxation techniques to improve performance; meditation, visualization.*

***BAY AREA KI RESEARCH INSTITUTE, 135 Austin St., SF 94109, 415-928-4713 (evenings).*** *Focus on achieving harmony with the universe by achieving balance within. Breathing, meditation,* *exercise and massage to acquire calmness, relaxation, clear concentration. Introductory workshops, classes.*

***BIOTONICS INSTITUTE, P.O. Box 342, Corte Madera 94925, 415-924-6431.*** *System of exercises for people who hate to exercise to build strength and stamina. Developed by surgeon Dr. Rex Wideranders to keep joints supple.*

***BODYMIND SEMINARS, training with Ken Dychtwald (author Bodymind). 143 Dolores St., SF 94103, 415-552-5045.*** *Brochures; seminars on health care, physical fitness, body work.*

***CENTER FOR CONSCIOUS HEALTH, 1718 Taraval St., SF 94116, 415-664-7075.*** *Center for the synthesis of body movement, awareness and meditation. Founder: Meir Schneider, who healed himself of cataracts at age 27, offers classes which increase human functional potential and correct use of bodies. Classes include body relaxation through movement and correct breathing. Regulate body to full capacity and rebuild damaged parts.*

***GETTING IN TOUCH, Box 1225, Los Gatos, 95030, 408-353-3770.*** *Body-oriented educational center and mountain retreat. "We believe that our bodies are a vehicle for being in this world. Developing greater awareness with acceptance and enjoyment of our own bodies is one path to personal growth." All activities, body awareness and wholistic massage workshops aimed at more joyful and peaceful living. Northern California Center for Trager psychological integration and Mentastics training. On 30 acres in secluded valley in Santa Cruz mountains.*

***HEALING CENTER OF SAN FRANCISCO, 465 Brussels St., SF 94142.*** *Focus on joy through movement.*

***INTEGRAL BODY WORK, SF, 415-863-9366.*** *Steven J. Fox, Ph.D. Release of energy blocks through deep connective tissue work, massage, breathing, energy movement, psychic reading. Certified in massage and postural integration.*

# Bodywork

## *Alexander Technique*

***THE SONOMA INSTITUTE, 17500 Bodega Lane, Bodega Bay 94922, 707-876-3116.*** *Two year program in Lomi body work, time management.*

***WELL-SPRINGS, 11667 Alba Rd., Ben Lomond 95055, 408-336-8594 or 336-8177.*** *Alignment through music. Body attunes through massage and music, relieves the blocked energy that causes tensions.*

# Bodywork

## *Alexander Technique*
## *Individuals*

***AASE WILDE, Berkeley Central YMCA, 2001 Allston Way, Berkeley 94704.*** *Alexander technique.*

***WOMEN'S FITNESS CENTER, Oakland Central YMCA, 2101 Telegraph Ave., Oakland 94612, 415-451-5711, 465-4375.*** *Exercise, sauna, jacuzzi, weight room, pool.*

***THERAPY FOR ACTORS AND ARTISTS, Julie Henderson, 415-233-3292.*** *Body work, dreams, transactional analysis, drama.*

***ANATOMY THROUGH EVOLUTION, Frank Wildman, 1048 Sierra St., Berkeley 94707, 415-527-7198.*** *Recreation for dance instructors to observe and understand bodies more clearly, relationship between gravity and body alignment. Alexander technique classes. See also SOMATAXIS INSTITUTE, Feldenkrais.*

***ELEANOR ROSENTHAL, 415-771-5270.*** *Certified by American Center for the Alexander Technique, a 75-year-old method of working with posture and body mechanics to improve mental functioning. Work with body awareness, stress, relief from chronic tension and pain caused by poor use of body.*

***PAULA ROSS, 415-841-6500, ext. 575.*** *ACAT certified teacher.*

***SYDNEY LAUREL FONAROFF, 415-552-2243.*** *ACAT certified.*

# Bodywork

## *Chiropractics*

*Chiropractics uses physical manipulations to relieve stress at its source, the nervous system along the spine. Treatment styles vary from spine cracking to deep tissue palpitations that break patterns of muscular tension and pain.*

***CALIFORNIA CHIROPRACTIC ASSOCIATION.*** *Listed by geographic area in Yellow Pages under Chiropractic; the group gives names of chiropractors who meet their standards.*

***AFFILIATED AMERICAN ASSOCIATION OF DOCTORS OF CHIROPRACTIC, SAN FRANCISCO CHIROPRACTIC ASSOCIATION, 2535 Mission St., SF 94110, 415-826-0999.***

***SAN FRANCISCO CHIROPRACTIC INFORMATION BUREAU, 450 Post St., SF 94102, 415-392-4203.***

***SAN FRANCISCO CHIROPRACTIC SOCIETY, 595 Buckingham Way, SF 94132, 415-392-4524.***

## *Feldenkrais*

***ASHKENAZ FOLK DANCE COOPERATIVE.*** *See FOLK, EB.*

***BERKELEY MOVING ARTS, Parker at Fulton Sts., Berkeley. Cheryl Reinhardt 834-9578; David Bersin, 841-5613.***

***FORT MASON.*** *See GROUPS/SPONSORS.*

***INSTITUTE FOR ADVANCED SOMATIC STUDIES, 312 Morningsun Ave., Mill Valley 94941, 415-288-0329.*** *Founded 1978, to develop and protect wholistic techniques, including Feldenkrais, rolfing, orthomolecular medicine, physical therapy. Includes orthosomatics, systematic normalization of structure, movement, respiration and expression to restore physiological potential. Based on deep muscle manipulation, joint movement, awareness exercises. Training program.*

***MODERN JAZZ WORKS.*** *See JAZZ, SF.*

***MOVEMENT EDUCATION AND RESEARCH FOUNDATION (MER CENTER), a center for the study of Feldenkrais' work, c/o 4 Anchor Dr. #445, Emeryville 94608, 415-652-1869.*** *Awareness through movement exercises that reduce muscular stress and open realms of energy available. Functional integration, relief from muscular stress that reduces emotional and intellectual capabilities. Bill Callison, founder. Will Schutz and Ed Jackson, staff. Classes at Marin School of Yoga, 5627-C Paradise Dr., Corte Madera; Diablo Valley Yoga Institute, 3369 Mt. Diablo Blvd., Lafayette; Berkeley Fellowship of Unitarians, 1606 Bonita, Berkeley. More classes and workshops in San Francisco.*

***SOMATAXIS INSTITUTE FOR MOVEMENT EDUCATION AND RESEARCH, 1048 Sierra St., Berkeley 94707, 415-527-7198.*** *Frank Wildman, movement educator and therapist. Classes, workshops and lectures devoted to the study of organization of body in time and space. Courses year round in anatomy, Feldenkrais* *and body reading. Classes in Berkeley, San Francisco and Walnut Creek in correct body alignment, stress relief, improved coordination and efficiency, expanded body awareness.*

***UCSF.*** *See EDUCATION.*

***FELDENKRAIS method, 2644 Etna, Berkeley 94704, 415-848-1719, 388-0560.***

Bodywork

## General Centers

***BERKELEY HOLISTIC HEALTH CENTER, 2640 College Ave., (Epic West), Berkeley 94704, 415-845-4330.*** *Instruction in more conscious ways to create better health. Classes include body care, stress reduction, nutrition, burnout prevention, massage, metaphysics. Free quarterly newsletter listing classes, seminars, events. Health education and referrals in the healing arts; information bureau. Healing circle, physical conditioning and counseling. Classroom space available for $5/hr.*

***CENTER FOR CONSCIOUS HEALTH, 1718 Taraval St., SF 94116, 415-664-7075.*** *Body awareness classes; rebuild damaged parts and regulate body to full capacity.*

***EAST-WEST ACADEMY OF HEALING ARTS, 210 Spear St., SF 94105, 415-564-6446.***

***FELLOWSHIP OF THE AWAKENING, 1701 Spruce St., Berkeley 94709, 415-849-2699.***

***HEALING CENTER OF SAN FRANCISCO, 465 Brussels St., SF 94134.*** *Holistic training for nurse consultants and health counselors.*

***HEALTH AWARENESS INSTITUTE, 1114B Mendocino Ave., Santa Rosa 94501.*** *Workshops and lectures, stress management.*

***HEALTH EDUCATION SEMINARS, P.O. Box 14472, SF 94114, 415-282-7999.*** *Classes and workshops and counseling for health professionals. Workshops in dance therapy with Lisa Sohr, 2764 McAllister, SF 94118, 415-752-5196, and Rachel Kraushar, certified Touch for Health instructor, 196 Arguello, SF 94122, 415-221-1429.*

***HEARTSONG School of Clairvoyant Reading, 1512 Grove St., Berkeley 94709, 415-527-4833.*** *Classes in body-mind work supplement those in psychic healing. Open healing circle and readings by appointment for individuals and couples.*

# Bodywork

## General Centers

**HEARTSONG HOLISTIC HEALING CENTER, 610 University Ave., Los Gatos 95030, 408-354-4563.** Mark Kramer, M.D., director. Focus is on integrating body, mind and soul.

**HOLISTIC LIFE UNIVERSITY, 1627 10th Ave., SF 94122, 415-665-3200.** Health education.

**HOLISTIC LOVING TOUCH, 20541 Canyon View Dr., Saratoga 95070, 408-867-4011.**

**MISSION CITY HOLISTIC HEALTH, 3242 McKinley, Santa Clara 95050, 408-241-2112.**

**NEUROPSYCHIC ASSOCIATION, 5521 Begonia Dr., San Jose 95124, 408-264-7560; 266-6183.**

**NEW AGE AWARENESS CENTER, 2239 Powell St., SF 94133.**

**PRAXIS CENTER FOR HOLISTIC LIVING, 1612 Sullivan, Daly City 94015, 415-994-9994.** Low cost therapy for self-healing and riddance of habits; self-hypnosis and hypnosis.

**PSYCHOSOMATIC MEDICAL CLINIC, 2510 Webster St., Berkeley 94705, 415-548-1115.** Biofeedback, stress education and relaxation training, holistic medicine, Alexander technique, Feldenkrais, acupuncture, nutritional counseling, autogenic training.

**SAFE SPACE YOUNIVERSITY, P.O. Box 31327, SF 94131, 415-285-7251 or 441-2677.** Individual counseling in body work, psychic readings, masssage for women, movement and meditation, homeopathy, healings. Healing circle.

**SAN ANDREAS HEALTH COUNCIL, 531 Cowper St., Palo Alto 94301, 415-324-9350.** Blend of eastern and western approaches to health to reduce stress, integrate mind/body/emotions/spirit. Yoga, expressive arts, rolfing, biofeedback, acupressure, bioenergetics.

# Bodywork

## General Centers

***STRESS EDUCATION CENTER, 315 E. Cotati Ave. #F, Cotati 94928, 707-795-2228, c/o Box 1213 Rohnert Park 94928.*** *Collective of health practitioners using biofeedback, hypnosis, therapeutic massage, body work. Emphasis on self-education and prevention of stress-related disorders. Includes movement exercise and breathing, progressive relaxations. Medical referrals. Classes, workshops, lectures throughout California.*

***THETA SEMINARS, 301 Lyon St., SF 94117.***

***TOOLS FOR HEALTH, P.O. Box 11071, Oakland 94611, 415-547-9833.***

***WHOLE LIFE CENTER, 3437 Alma St. #28, Palo Alto 94306, 415-493-0561.***

***WHOLLY WELL, 600 San Pablo Ave., Albany 94706, 415-526-9112.*** *Vitalism emphasized.*

# Bodywork

## *Heat Therapy*

*See also Yellow Pages, Baths.*

***ALBANY SAUNA, 1002 Solano Avenue, Albany, 415-525-6262.*** *Finnish rock sauna, Japanese redwood hot tubs, Swedish massage, health food juice bar.*

***AMERICAN FAMILY SAUNA AND TUB, 5496 College Ave., Oakland 94618, 415-654-8483; 242 25th St., Richmond, 415-234-1012.*** *Private saunas in Finnish tradition. Private tubs in California tradition. Noon-10 p.m. Closed Tuesdays.*

***THE BALANCE POINT, 1502B Walnut St, Berkeley 94707, 415-843-7741.*** *10 a.m. to 8:30 p.m. Esalen style massage and sauna by professionals. Free sauna with massage; buy six get seventh free.*

***THE BERKELEY SAUNA, 1947 Milvia St., Berkeley 94704, 415-845-8595.*** *Open daily noon-11 p.m., massage by appointment.*

***FAMILY SAUNA SHOP, 1214 20th Ave., SF 94122, 415-681-3600; 2308 Clement St., SF 94121, 415-221-2208.***

***GRAND CENTRAL SAUNA AND HOT TUB CO., 15 Fell St., SF 94102, 415-431-1370.*** *Private suites, saunas and hot tubs.*

***GRAND CENTRAL SAUNA AND HOT TUB, 1915 University Ave. near Grove St., Berkeley 94704, 415-843-4343. 10 a.m. to 12 a.m. Sundays through Thursdays, until 2 a.m. Fridays and Saturdays.*** *Sixteen private suites, each with sauna and hot tub. Singles, couples, families.*

***KABUKI HOT SPRING, Japan Center, 1750 Geary Blvd., SF 94115, 415-922-6000.*** *Massage by shiatsu experts daily. Japnese baths, saunas and steam cabinets. Validated parking.*

***ORR SPRINGS COMMUNITY, Star Route 1, Box 27, Ukiah 95482, 707-462-6277.***

## Heat Therapy
## Kinesiology

**REDWOOD CITY SAUNA BATHS, 797 Arguello, SF 94118, 415-365-5240.** *Massage by appointment; whirlpool baths.*

**SAN FRANCISCO HEALTH CLUB, 229 Ellis St., SF 94102, 415-775-8013.** *Men only, memberships not required. Turkish baths since 1911. 70 private rooms, sauna, live steam room, pool, gym, sun deck, coffee shop.*

**TASSAJARA HOT SPRINGS ZEN MOUNTAIN CENTER, Carmel Valley 93924; 300 Page St., SF 94102, 415-863-3136.**

**WILBUR HOT SPRINGS, Wilbur Springs 95987, 916-473-2306.** *Hot springs and health sanctuary for overnight or day use. Reservations required; free brochure on request.*

## Kinesiology

**CALIFORNIA STATE UNIVERSITY, HAYWARD.** *See EDUCATION.*

**DANCE CENTER.** *See BALLET, SF.*

**DANCE SOURCE.** *See MODERN, SF.*

**INTERNATIONAL SCHOOL OF MASSAGE.** *See MASSAGE.*

**DONNA KRASNOW, Kinesiology Workshop.** *See MODERN, SF.*

**SONOMA STATE COLLEGE.** *See EDUCATION.*

**THE STUDIO.** *See BALLET, SF.*

**UNIVERSITY OF SAN FRANCISCO.** *See EDUCATION.*

# Bodywork

## *Massage*

*See also Yellow Pages, Massage.*

***ALPHA HEALTH CENTER, 442 Peninsula Ave., San Mateo, 415-343-3840.*** *Corrective massage, Shiatsu, acupressure, baths.*

***AU-MAKUA SCHOOL OF PRACTICAL MASSAGE, 677 Portola Dr., SF 94127, 415-655-7233; 200 Jefferson St., Monterey 93940, 408-373-0701, 649-4841.*** *Principles of anatomy and massage for specific ailments, body movement and aliveness, relaxation and breathing. Maureen Barber, founder/director. Open house first Sunday of each month with refreshments.*

***THE BALANCE POINT.*** *See HEAT.*

***CAPTAIN CARROT CARESSERS, Dennis and Ruth Mayer, P.O. Box 32885, San Jose 95152, 408-354-8209.***

***CREATIVE BODYWORK CENTER, 4338 California St., SF 94118, 415-221-2683.*** *Massage, yoga, belly dance, tai chi'uan.*

***DEAN ASSOCIATES, 396 Euclid Ave., Oakland 94610, 415-835-5018.*** *Massage therapy and instruction.*

***DEVTA, 122 Ward St., Larkspur 94939, 415-924-0406.*** *Massage, yoga, rolfing, with classes.*

***GETTING IN TOUCH, P.O. Box 1225, Los Gatos 95030, 408-353-3770.*** *Massage, body awareness. Workshops, individual work.*

***GEFION SCHOOL, Gunver Ingeborg, c/o Charlene Gray, P.O. Box 9418, Berkeley 94709, 415-530-3819.***

***GUILD OF HANDS, 2126 Pine St., SF 94115.***

***INTEGRAL BODY WORK, SF 415-863-9366.***

# Bodywork

## *Massage*

***INTERNATIONAL SCHOOL OF MASSAGE, 2872 Folsom St., SF 94110, 415-285-5537.*** *Courses in massage, phsyiology, holistic health, anatomy, acupressure and Shiatsu, polarity therapy, kinesiology, nutrition, meditation, reflexology. Registration hours 10 a.m. to 8 p.m., 415-648-9584.*

***THE MASSAGE CENTER, 300 Bryant St., Palo Alto 94301, 415-321-7133.*** *Therapeutic massage to promote relaxation and body awareness. Swedish, Esalen and Shiatsu with work in movement, breathing and meditation.*

***MASSAGE INSTITUTE OF CALIFORNIA, 3119 Clement St., SF 94121, 415-668-0550.*** *State-approved school with professional course in massage certification. Lectures in anatomy, kinesiology, physiology. Day or evening classes. Margaret Elke, Carole Truman, co-directors.*

***THE McKINNON SCHOOL OF PROFESSIONAL MASSAGE, 3798 Grand Ave., Suite #1, Oakland 94610, 415-465-3488.*** *Judith McKinnon. Day and evening work with free demonstrations, question and answer periods. Various styles of massage with exercises for releasing tension, deep back massage, body reading, breathing.*

***THE MEDIUM IS THE MASSAGE, 6622 Tremont St., Oakland 95609, 415-658-4760.*** *Massage and body work instruction, hot tubs, Esalen massage, massage for women, stress reduction massage.*

***MEDSERVICES, Wholly Well Center, 600 San Pablo Ave., Albany 94706, 415-526-9112.*** *Open daily, for relaxation and concentration work.*

***MEDITATIVE MASSAGE THERAPY, Marin, 415-479-4138.***

# Bodywork

## *Massage*

***TOM CALHOON-MEYER AND MELANIE CALHOON-MEYER, massage and healing, 415-658-2506 (East Bay).*** *Experienced work with dancers; state-certified combining Swedish and Esalen massage. Monthly workshops. Ministers of the Healing Church of Golden Light; laying on of hands, channel energy to facilitate natural healing. Open healing group Monday mornings.*

***NANCY, LTD. Exercise Studio, 1836 Union St., SF 94123, 415-567-2262.*** *Total fitness; Swedish and Esalen massage, Kounosky method.*

***NEW SCHOOL OF MASSAGE, P.O. Box 958, Sebastopol 95472, 707-829-1295.*** *State-approved courses in eastern and western massage. Anatomy, physiology, dance therapy, kinesiology and applied anatomy. In Mill Valley and Sonoma.*

***SOLARIS FOUNDATION, P.O. Box 2103, San Jose 95103.*** *Spine, heat, foot, thorax body massage.*

***THE CELEBRATION, P.O. Box 67, Larkspur 94939, 415-924-5742.***

***UCSF.*** *Shiatsu. See EDUCATION.*

***BERKELEY YMCA, 2001 Allston Way, Berkeley 94705, 415-848-6800, ext. 34, women's fitness center; ext. 27, men's fitness center.***

# Bodywork

## *Massage Individuals*

***LAUREL ADAM, CMP, SF, 415-221-3333;*** *wholistic health practitioner with wholistic massage, Trager psychophysical integration, energy balancing, body/mind work for dancers by a dancer. State-certified.*

***CHRISTINA BRYAN, 1379 5th Ave., SF 94122, 415-731-3461.*** *Certified massage, shiatsu and Reiki healing.*

***IRENI NADEL, East Bay 415-548-6116.*** *Dancing and meditating influence massage for release of tension and energy balancing. Esalen with Trager (vibration and manipulation of joints and muscles).*

***BETH WITROGEN, 2 Coronado #38, Daly City 94015, 415-992-8731.*** *Reiki healing, energy reading and balancing, Shiatsu.*

# Bodywork

## Medical /Nutritional Counseling

See also Yellow Pages under Chiropractic, Hospitals, Physicians, Orthomolecular.

**ALAMEDA-CONTRA COSTA MEDICAL ASSOCIATION, 6230 Claremont Ave., Oakland 94618, 415-654-5383.** Gives names of certified doctors.

**CALIFORNIA PODIATRIC MEDICAL CENTER, 1700 block of Eddy St. (near Scott St.), SF, P.O. Box 7855, Rincon Annex SF 94120, 415-563-3444.** Clinic and college specializing in problems of the foot. Free monthly foot exams. Treatment of sprains, injuries, corns, callouses, bunions, toed-in feet, flat or highly arched feet, walking difficulties, etc. Clinic hours: 9 a.m. to 4:30 p.m., Mondays through Fridays; 9 a.m. to noon Saturdays.

**CENTER FOR ATTITUDINAL HEALING, 19 Main St., Tiburon 94920, 415-435-5022.** Nutrition and healing, preventive medicine.

**DEVTA BODY SHOP, Marin, 415-924-6106 or 924-0406.** Nutrition, diet, kinesiology, tai chi ch'uan. Body as a reflection of consciousness.

**THE DIET CENTER, INC., 1501 North Point, SF 94123, 415-929-8002.** Anne Lawrence. Diet for athletes, etc. Four phase program to establish and maintain good eating habits.

**INTERNATIONAL SCHOOL OF MASSAGE.** See MASSAGE.

**ORTHOMOLECULAR MEDICINE AND CLINICAL NUTRITION, 3031 Telegraph Ave., Berkeley 94705, 415-548-7384.**

**MACROBIOTICS, SAN FRANCISCO BAY AREA EAST-WEST CENTER, 1425 Broadway, Suite 22, Burlingame 94010, 415-347-5366.** Applying universal order to a change in lifestyles, including selection, preparation and manner of eating food. Classes in Bay Area include Shiatsu, Oriental medicine, cooking.

## Medical/Nutritional Counseling

***PODIATRY CLINIC, First United Methodist Church, 625 Hamilton, Palo Alto 94301, 415-323-6167.***

***RAPID GROWTH THERAPY, 316 Miller Ave., Mill Valley 94941, 415-388-7367.*** *Loyal Davis, licensed hypnotherapist and psycho-nutrionist. For those who want to change patterns of insecurity, shyness, depression, etc., quickly.*

***TOTAL HEALTH MEDICAL CENTER, Carolyn Hobbs, East Bay, 415-655-8217.*** *Lifestyle fitness counseling, nutrition, etc.*

***DANA ULLMAN, East Bay, 415-548-4788.*** *Classes in homeopathy through Fort Mason Foundation (see GROUPS). Day long and ongoing workshops. Based on the idea that if a remedy is applied that produces symptoms similar to those of a disease, the illness can be cured. Treats the person according to natural laws of healing, and one remedy for any given stage of illness.*

***WHOLISTIC HEALTH AND NUTRITION INSTITUTE, 150 Shoreline Highway, Mill Valley 94941, 415-332-2399.*** *One of the area's first sources for wholistic health. Staff of doctors, healers, devoted to health and preventive medicine.*

# Bodywork

## *Reichian/Bioenergetics*

*Reichian therapy is the father of body-oriented therapies, using several techniques to release repressed sexual/emotional tension and to restore the natural free flow of the body's energy; hence, restore health.*

**HEALING OURSELVES CENTER, 2547A Eighth St., Berkeley 94710, 415-841-6911.** *Office hours: Tuesdays through Fridays 10 a.m. to 1 p.m.; Tuesdays and Fridays, 5:30-7:30 p.m. Programs in Reichian-bioenergetic bodywork, martial arts, dance, massage. Individual body work is Reichian breath work and massage, including therapeutic stretching and manipulation, and Trager method. Essence of process is staying with the breath and body sensations.*

*Dance jam Friday nights, experienced and non-experienced dancers welcome.* *See also HALLS/Rentals.*

**INSTITUTE FOR BIOENERGETICS AND GESTALT, 1307 University Ave., Berkeley 94702, 415-841-5555.** *Michael Conant, Ph.D., director. When emotions are disturbed, tensions develop in the body. If they become chronic muscle contractions, they disturb the flow of energy. In Bioenergetics, physical and verbal therapies are integrated toward self-awareness, increased energy and self-expression. Workshops and counseling in San Francisco and Berkeley for groups and individuals.*

**INSTITUTE OF POSTURAL INTEGRATION AND REICHIAN RELEASE, 1057 Steiner St., SF 94115, 415-929-0119.** *Training in connective tissue manipulation, acupuncture and movement awareness. Program leads to certification of Reichian practitioners.*

**METAMORPHOSIS, 1710 Grant St., Berkeley 94703, 415843-4981, 841-5000.** *Dedicated to self-discovery and integration of body/-mind/spirit. Reichian therapy, Gestalt, polarity, acupressure* *massage to aid in manifesting potentialities. Monthly workshop on body therapies. Marie Jorgensen Brewer and John Taylor, associates.*

***OSHADAGEA, 1367 Church St., SF 94114, 415-285-7310.*** *Neo-Reichian techniques.*

## Rolfing

*Rolfing is a deep tissue manipulation to realign the body along its vertical axis. The rolfer works to remold the connective tissue surrounding the muscle which, through earlier trauma, holds tension, pain and disease.*

***THE ROLFING ASSOCIATES, 2859 Sacramento (near Divisadero), SF 94115, 415-922-3478.*** *Lecture/demonstration in poor posture, back, neck and other body pains, inadequate body alignment or structural body stress. Rolfing brings the body into alignment for greater balance, ease and fluidity of motion. Marc Reisman, Neal Powers, Marshall Levin, Donna LaFlamme, Penny Crow (body movement analysis).*

***ROLFING-BIOFEEDBACK CLEARING SERIES, 415-688-5330.***

## Tai Chi

*Tai chi is the dance of the martial arts. The focus is on balance, power and beauty through non-exertion, non-control. Strengthening without strain, the movements improve circulation and increase the body's energy flow. Movements are taken from nature.*

***MASTER CHOY, SF, 415-392-9159.***

***A CIRCLE FOR MEDITATIVE MOVEMENT, Box 150, 1820 Union St., SF 94123, 415-563-1383.***

**CREATIVE BODYWORK CENTER.** *See MASSAGE, above.*

***DEVTA.*** *See NUTRITION.*

***EVERYBODY'S CREATIVE ARTS CENTER.*** *See MODERN, EB.*

***INTEGRAL CHUAN INSTITUTE, 424 Vidal Dr., SF 94132, 415-334-9280.*** *Tai chi is more than a martial or health art; it is a lifestyle which promotes natural self-discipline, respect and unfoldment. Practice of the art will fill one's day with purpose and joy that come with re-integration of self with nature. Yang School of the art. Classes in San Francisco, Berkeley; free lectures and demonstrations first Tuesday of each month, 8 p.m., Fort Mason Center Bldg. 312, Laguna and Marina Boulevards.*

***CHEN HSIN SCHOOL of Internal Martial Arts, 6601 Telegraph Ave., Oakland 94609, 415-658-0802.***

***LIDA (LI LI TA) SCHOOL OF TAI JI QUAN, St. John's Center, 2727 College Ave., Berkeley 94705, 415-841-2903.*** *Mornings and evenings. Call for schedule. Learned Tai ji quan in China, Wu School; has taught in U.S. for 10 years.*

***NISSEN'S SCHOOL OF DANCE.*** *See BALLET, CCC.*

# Bodywork

## *Tai Chi*

***TAI CHI CH'UAN INNER RESEARCH INSTITUTE, 1135 Mission St., SF 94103, 415-621-2681.*** *Classes year round.*

***UNIVERSAL TAI CHI ASSOCIATION, 2901 Clement St., SF 94121, 415-221-0944.***

***UCSF.*** *See EDUCATION.*

***WHOLE LIFE CENTER, 3437 Alma St., Palo Alto 94306, 415-493-0561.***

***TAI CHI AS AN ART FORM, 2629 Woolsey St., Berkeley 94705, 415-841-2903.*** *Also: 5332 College Ave., Oakland, 415-655-8696. Beginning classes Mondays, Tuesdays and Wednesdays. Okay to watch.*

## Yoga

*Yoga postures promote fitness, flexibility and relaxation, bringing under control the senses, emotions and mind so the body becomes a pure habitation for the soul. There are many forms of yoga; the most commonly taught, whether as an adjunct to dance or not, is hatha yoga. All forms are geared to health and spiritual evolution of the being. For more listings, see Yellow Pages, Yoga Instruction.*

**ACADEMY OF DANCE ARTS.** *See BALLET, SJ.*

**BALLET THEATRE WEST.** *See BALLET, Marin.*

**MAGANA BAPTISTE.** *See BELLY, SF. Cosmic and Hindu yoga.*

**CONTRA COSTA ACADEMY OF DANCE.** *See BALLET, CCC.*

**CREATIVE BODYWORK CENTER.** *See BODYWORK, Massage.*

**DANCE SOURCE.** *See MODERN, SF.*

**DEVTA.** *See MEDICAL.*

**DIABLO VALLEY YOGA INSTITUTE, 3369 Mt. Diablo Blvd., Lafayette 94549.**

**HYDE AND GREEN STUDIO.** *See BALLET, SF.*

**INTEGRAL YOGA INSTITUTE, 70 Dolores St., SF 94110, 415-824-9600.** *Nine years offering a system of self-improvement to bring body, mind and spirit into harmony and allow the experience of inner joy. Informal sharing times with meals; guests welcome.*

**KALANJALI.** *See FOLK/Indian.*

## Yoga

***MARIN CIVIC BALLET SCHOOL.*** *See BALLET, Marin.*

***MARIN SCHOOL OF YOGA, 5627C Paradise Dr., Corte Madera 94925.***

***PURE WINE DANCE COMPANY.*** *See OTHER DANCES/Creative.*

***SAN FRANCISCO DANCE SPECTRUM.*** *See BALLET, SF.*

***SAN MATEO CITY.*** *See GROUPS/SPONSORS--City.*

***THE YOGA ROOM, 2640 College Ave. (Epic West), Berkeley 94704, 415-548-4340.*** *Iyengar method emphasizing body awareness and correct alignment in the poses. Beg. through adv., pre-natal, yoga for seniors, drop-in OK. Varied fees.*

***YOGA SOCIETY OF SAN FRANCISCO, 2872 Folsom St., SF 94110, 415-285-5537.*** *Yoga therapy for healing through movement of energy and spirit. Lectures, programs, concerts. See also INTERNATIONAL SCHOOL OF MASSAGE.*

***THE YOGA STUDIO, 6152 California St. (at 24th Ave.), SF 94121, 415-668-8800.*** *Center for the study and practice of movement and psychic sciences. Beginning modern dance and Iyengar style yoga.*

# Education

*Dance in education first appeared as a form of recreation, and was usually limited to folk dance. This pattern was strong for 50 years. The 1950's saw the growth of college performing groups, usually modern, though trained in ballet. Now dance education programs, though many are still offered under departments of physical education, are coming into their own, with classes including several levels of technique in various styles, composition, music, dance history and criticism, notation, anatomy and kinesiology, technical theater. For a complete list of dance education in the U.S., see* Dance Magazine *COLLEGE GUIDE (MAGAZINES) listing. Also check university and college music, drama, theater arts and P.E. departments for dance-related classes.*

Education

# *Education*

**CALIFORNIA INSTITUTE OF THE ARTS, School of Dance, Valencia, CA 805-255-1050.** *Focus is modern; students are trained as choreographers-performers in the belief that these disciplines are mutually dependent. Program designed to produce inventive, experimental and independently creative artists. Courses in modern, ballet, improvisation, dance design and production (lighting, costuming, stage management). Performance theaters and rehearsal studios available; sound recording and mixing studios, costume and property shops all accessible. Degrees: B.F.A. (4 years) and M.F.A. (2 years), certified and fully accredited by Western Association of Schools and Colleges, National Association of Schools of Art, National Association of Schools of Music. Student ratio is about 7:1, with about 700 students total. Scholarships, work/study, grants, loans available. Interaction among the performing arts is a founding premise of the school. Admission based on talent/audition. Director of admissions: Renee Levine.*

**AMERICAN DANCE FESTIVAL, P.O. Box 6097-K, College Station, Durham, NC 27708, 919-684-6402.** *Classes in modern; brochure available.*

**ASSOCIATION OF COLLEGE, UNIVERSITY AND COMMUNITY ARTS ADMINISTRATORS, INC. (ACUCAA), P.O. Box 2137, Madison, WI 53701, 608-262-0004.** *William Dawson, executive director. Established 1957 for those who choose professional arts events on campus.*

**BERKELEY HIGH SCHOOL, 2246 Milvia St., Berkeley 94705, 415-644-6855.** *Jane Reaves, Marcia Singman. Beg. jazz and modern (Ailey, Louis, Lewitsky styles); creative composition, improvisation and social dance from 1890's to today. Intermediate dance; adv. dance on teacher recommendation. Dance production fall semester (advanced students audition) culminating in formal concert series in January at Florence Schwimley Little Theater.*

*Profits go for scholarships, films, records, master classes, costumes. (This class has been in existence since early 1900s at BHS.)*

*Dance projects (teacher recommendation), spring semester, research on therapy, movement therapy, informal concerts, lecture/demonstrations.*

*Performing arts dept. courses in mime, Israeli folk dance (beg.-adv.) and beg. and inter. tap. African-American studies dept. (Paula Fleury), African-Haitian dance, beg.-adv. (emphasis on understanding techniques of such dance and its contributions to the world); advanced techniques from Haiti, Ghana, Congo, Nigeria, etc. Performance at various colleges and community functions available.*

*Principal's permission to adjust schedule to take outside dance possible.*

***CABRILLO COLLEGE, Aptos.*** *Classes in modern by Diana Crosby, Tandy Beal (see MODERN, SJ).*

***CALIFORNIA COLLEGE OF ARTS AND CRAFTS, Broadway at College, Oakland 94618, 415-653-8118.*** *Students may take, for credit, classes at Shawl-Anderson Modern Dance Center by signing up in the college's student records office. Fee is $10 per unit for recording fee.*

***CALIFORNIA DANCE EDUCATORS ASSOCIATION, Humboldt State University, Women's P.E. Dept., Arcata 95521, 707-826-3558.*** *Nancy Camp, membership. Non-profit, professional organization dedicated to advancement of dance as an art form at all levels of education in California. Membership open to professionals, students, writers, musicians, managers, therapists, friends. Goal is to improve communications among classrooms, administrative offices, private studios, art organizations and state legislature. Workshops, master classes, seminars, informal dinners and conferences; reduced rates for members. Christmas workshop in San Francisco; film festival, dance for children workshop, etc. Fees from $5 to $25, tax deductible.*

# *Education*

## *Education*

**CALIFORNIA STATE UNIVERSITY, FRESNO.** *B.A., M.A. dance major in P.E./Art. Ballet, modern, dance therapy. Resident performing company, the Portable Dance Troupe (see MODERN).*

**CALIFORNIA STATE UNIVERSITY, FULLERTON, 92634, 714-870-3347.** *Professional Artists in Residence, Office of Cultural Events, Wallace Farrelly, director.*

**CALIFORNIA STATE UNIVERSITY, HAYWARD, Dept. of Kinesiology and Physical Education, 25800 Hillary St., Hayward 94542, 415-881-3061.** *Cynthia Berrol, chairman. Study of scientific, cultural and artistic foundations of motion in many styles. Dance option program develops these bases, provides foundation for special interest (dance therapy, education and choreography), increases skill in variety of dance forms. Interdisciplinary special majors geared to personal interests, such as dance as a theater art or recreational dance therapy. Degrees: undergraduate B.S./major in P.E. with dance option; B.A./special major. Graduate M.S./P.E. with dance emphasis or M.S./special interdisciplinary major.*

*Faculty: Dr. Cynthia Berrol, coordinator of certification program in special P.E. and special graduate major in dance/ movement therapy; Akili Denianke, ethnic and theater dance (Harambee troupe director); Adele Wenig, coordinator CSUH dance program; Lynda Knapp (directs own modern company).*

*Courses: Afro-Haitian, folk, jazz, ballroom/disco, modern, square, tap, belly, yoga, tai chi ch'uan, aikido. Core classes: kinesiology, biomechanics, dance performance, composition and production, movement analysis and awareness, dance history, dance therapy, anthropology of dance, dance for children, dance theory.*

*The Certificate in Special P.E. trains students to develop and implement modified physical programs for primary and secondary school age pupils with functional psycho-motor disabilities. A special graduate major is also offered that joins dance/-movement therapy and counseling to accomodate those whose interests are tied to an integrated use of movement and counseling as therapy.*

# Education

## Education

***CALIFORNIA STATE UNIVERSITY, SACRAMENTO, Division of Health and Physical Education, P.E. Dept., 6000 J St., Sacramento 95819.*** *Revay Anderson, associate professor. Full dance program with extensive literary syllabus; special guest lecturers (Massine), programs, demonstrations, films, etc. Classes include ballet technique, appreciation of dance as a visual art.*

***CANADA COLLEGE, 415-364-1212.***

***CHABOT COLLEGE, 25555 Hesperian Blvd., Hayward 94545, 415-782-3000, ext. 410.*** *Santiago Garza, associate dean community services; ACUCAA.*

***COLLEGE OF ALAMEDA, 555 Atlantic Ave., Alameda 94501.*** *Yvonne Daniel, dance program. AA degree in dance. First year: introduction to dance and dance history, technique, rhythmic analysis; second year, technique, composition, performance workshops. Electives: improvisation, exposure to dance and other performing arts, jazz, ballet, modern, ethnic dance.*

***COLLEGE OF MARIN, Kentfield 94904, 415-485-9319.*** *Drama Department; classes in belly (Ilyana), others. Sydney R. Goldstein, director public events (ACUAA).*

***COLLEGE OF NOTRE DAME, 1500 Ralston Ave., Belmont 94002, 415-593-1601.***

***COLLEGE OF SAN MATEO, 1700 W. Hillsdale Blvd., San Mateo 94010, 415-574-6161.***

***COMMITTEE ON RESEARCH IN DANCE EDUCATION, 675D, Dance Department, New York University, 35 W. Fourth St., NY 10003, 212-598-3459.***

***CONTRA COSTA COLLEGE, 2600 Mission Bell Dr., San Pablo 94806, 415-235-7800.*** *Deborah Vaughan, head of Dance Department. (See also DIMENSIONS DANCE THEATER, MODERN, EB.)*

*Education*

# *Education*

***CONTRA COSTA SCHOOLS DIRECTORY, published by the Contra Costa County superintendent of schools, 75 Santa Barbara Rd., Pleasant Hill 94523.***

***DANCE EDUCATORS OF AMERICA, INC., 40 Box 470, Coldwell, NJ 07006, 201-228-5547.***

***DOMINICAN COLLEGE, 1520 Grand Ave., San Rafael 94901, 415-457-4440.*** *Movement Education Department sponsors classes in cooperation with Marin Civic Ballet School to provide a dance major with emphasis on ballet technique, with housing at the college. Fall 1979 began four year program for B.A. with major in dance. (See also BALLET, Marin.) Workshops in movement therapy and education for handicapped, seniors, etc. Classes in ballet, modern, jazz, composition, dance history, labanotation, kinesiology.*

***DONALD ERYCK, c/o Contra Costa Ballet, 2040 W. Broadway, Walnut Creek 94596, 415-935-7984.*** *Lecture/demonstrations on development of classical ballet technique.*

***FINE ARTS MUSEUMS OF SAN FRANCISCO, Golden Gate Park, SF 94118, 415-588-2887.*** *Bruce Merley, assistant curator of educational programs (ACUCAA).*

***FOOTHILL/De ANZA COMMUNITY COLLEGE, Dance Dept., 12345 El Monte Rd., Los Altos Hills 94022, 408-996-4832.*** *Dance appreciation, ballet theory and technique, modern theory and technique, pointe, tap, history and philosophy of dance, repertory company (Assortment Dance/Theatre Company), creative dramatics, dance composition. Newsletter, De Anza Dance News. A.A. degree available; W. Grant Gray, director. Special workshops, choreography and performances.*

***GOLDEN GATE UNIVERSITY, 536 Mission St., SF 94105, 415-442-7000.*** *Graduate programs in arts administration. Established 1972. Students may enroll as candidates for the M.S.*

*degree in arts administration or on a non-degree basis as candidates for the Certificate in Arts Administration. Fundraising, finance and budgeting, internships, legal aspects, marketing and public relations, human problems, computer technology. Advisory committee includes those in the local arts management profession. Jean Squair, director (ACUCAA).*

***LANEY COLLEGE, 900 Fallon St., Oakland 94607, 415-834-5740.*** *P.E. Department offers ballet, body conditioning, modern, modern-jazz, Afro-Haitian, dance production and rhythmic analysis. Laney Theater sponsors performances. Morning and evening classes. Also offered: theater arts, mime, production, stagecraft, principles and theory of acting and improvisation.*

***MERRITT COLLEGE, 12500 Campus Dr., Oakland 94619, 415-531-4911.*** *P.E. Department offers dance production workshop, int. and adv. modern, survey and history of dance, Afro-American, ballet, tap, disco, body conditioning, modern-jazz, social dance, yoga.*

***MILLS COLLEGE DANCE DEPT., Box 9942, Oakland 94613.*** *Eleanor Lauer, chairman. One of the most noted departments in the West, emphasizing the nature of dance and its relation to society. Technical and theoretical work with emphasis on communicative functions of dance. Basic preparation for dancers and dance teachers is available, with focus on modern.*

*The major requires 13 semester courses (including Labanotation, kinesiology, independent choreography). Classes include technique, theory, Afro-Haitian, ballet, improvisation, jazz, modern. Students who are not majors may enroll for credit or without credit. The masters of arts degree program allows for extensive choreography and performance, research in dance history, dance education or therapy. Completion of the eight required courses usually takes two years.*

*Graduate dance concerts are offered at the Walter A. Haas pavilion. Intensive summer program of three weeks, for students and teachers, co-sponsored by CSUH. Daily classes in technique, improvisation, effort/shape, repertory, dance/move ment for the handicapped (1979 program), special presentations on baroque dance. (See also CSUH, above.)*

**NEW COLLEGE OF CALIFORNIA, 777 Valencia, SF 94110, 415-626-1694.** *Some classes in modern, improvisation.*

**OPEN EDUCATION EXCHANGE, 6526 Telegraph Ave., Oakland 94609, 415-655-6791.** *Dance, movement, holistic health, yoga, meditation. Free publication in newsracks; teachers always needed.*

**ORPHEUS ALTERNATIVE UNIVERSITY, 1119 Geary Blvd., SF 94109, 415-474-3775.** *Classes offered in forms of dance, holistic health, meditation, yoga, etc.*

**PACIFIC SCHOOL OF RELIGION, 1798 Scenic, Berkeley 94708, 415-848-0528.** *See MISCELLANEOUS/Sacred Dance.*

**PERALTA COMMUNITY COLLEGE DISTRICT, 300 Grand Ave., Oakland 94610.** *Publishes Peralta Pathways, listing courses in all colleges under its jurisdiction, including Alameda, Laney and Merritt.*

**ST. MARY'S COLLEGE, Dept. of P.E. and Intercollegiate Athletics, Drawer RC, Moraga 94575, 415-376-4411.** *Though there is no dance department, classes are offered through the P.E. Dept. in jazz, ballet, square, social and tap. As well, the external degree program sometimes offers classes, and the special events people bring in guest companies for the public--sometimes free of charge.*

**SAN FRANCISCO CITY COLLEGE, 50 Phelan Ave., SF 94112, 415-239-3000.** *Disco, ballroom, tap classes. Irene Weed. Beg. and inter. ballet taught by Theresa Gensler.*

**SAN FRANCISCO CONSERVATORY OF BALLET AND THEATRE ARTS, Nova Academy.** *See BALLET, SF.*

# Education



***SAN FRANCISCO STATE UNIVERSITY, Dept. of P.E., 1600 Holloway Ave., SF 94132. School of Theatre Arts: 415-469-1341; Box Office, 585-7174; School of Creative Arts, 469-1471,*** *(A. James Bravar, dean). Home of Ethnic Dance Ensemble (see FOLK); classes in Kathakali Indian dance by Kunhiraman, other folk dance. Summer concert series; sponsors of Music of the Whole Earth Festival. Also sponsors summer technique workshops (e.g., Afro-Haitian-jazz); Dolores Cayou, SFSU, 415-469-2244, ext. 1559. World Arts Academy summer master classes and lecture courses in Javanese, Balinese, Indian, Japanese, jazz, Middle Eastern, African-Haitian dance, theatrical dance; 469-2467. Co-sponsored by Center for World Music.*

***SAN JOSE CITY COLLEGE, 2100 Moorpark Ave., San Jose 95128, 408-298-2181.*** *Classes in ballet by Benjamin Reyes, Santa Clara Ballet.*

***SAN JOSE COMMUNITY COLLEGE DISTRICT, 4750 San Felipe Rd., San Jose 95121, 408-274-6700.***

***SAN JOSE STATE UNIVERSITY, San Jose 95192, 408-277-2763 (School of Theater Arts).*** *Ted Gehrke, project director, ACUCAA, Room 350 Student Union, 277-3294. Performances in Studio Theatre.*

***SKYLINE COLLEGE, 3300 College Dr., San Bruno 94066, 415-355-7000.***

***SONOMA STATE COLLEGE, 1801 East Cotati Ave., Rohnert Park 94928; Divison of Humanities, Dept. of Theatre Arts, 707-664-2474.*** *Ann B. Woodhead, chairperson. B.A. in theatre arts available, emphasis in dance. Two studios; group of students and faculty tour colleges and universities. Faculty: Christopher Beck, Fred Curchack, Carla Guggenheim, Nancy Lyons, Linda Magarian, Peter Maslin, Judy Navas, Wendy Rogers, William Sherman, Ann Woodhead.*

# Education



*Study of theater arts within the liberal arts setting is approached through direct participation in making of theater events as a means of personal growth and human understanding. Productions include dance concerts; program is intended to prepare student to work in theater or for further study at graduate or professional levels. Theater arts classes introduce student to basics and techniques of drama, dance and theater production and design. Original dance and drama as well as experimental approaches are encouraged through classes such as choreography, directing and dance and drama ensemble workshops. Senior project offers independent work within framework of an ensemble theater with support of faculty. Dance emphasis major of eight required classes includes modern dance, design, performance and history of dance; eight required stage II classes, in modern, choreography, research, senior projects, etc.; and a stage II elective including kinesiology, ballet, musical theater, adv. modern, choreography and dance for children. Catalog available upon request.*

***STANFORD UNIVERSITY, P.E. Department, Stanford 94305, 415-497-4895.*** *Also: Director of Public Events, Press Courtyard, Santa Theresa St., Stanford 94305 (ACUCAA), 415-497-2551. Master classes available. Also through music department, summer workshops in Baroque music and dance, 18th century notation; John Planting, Dept. of Music, Stanford University, Stanford 94305, 415-497-3811.*

***UNIVERSITY OF CALIFORNIA, BERKELEY, Dept. of Dramatic Art, 101 Dwinelle Annex, Berkeley 94720, 415-642-1677.*** *David Wood, director. Bay Area Repertory Dance Company open to students or former students within the program. Performs works on West Coast by variety of choreographers, including Wood, Carolyn Brown, Irini Nadel, Marni Thomas, Carol Egon, Carol Murata.*

*Requirements for undergraduate major: declaration of major after 45 units in College of Letters and Science and consultation with Wood. Admission by audition in a technique class. Dance technique courses span beg., inter. and adv. modern and company class. Department of dramatic art has a graduate program, but only in exceptional cases will students interested in dance be accepted for work toward the M.A. Admission by special arrangement includes audition. Other courses: intro. to acting and dramatic literature, rhythmic analysis, survey of dramatic literature, intro. to choreography, dance analysis, adv. choreography, repertory and production.*

***UNIVERSITY OF CALIFORNIA EXTENSION, 55 Laguna St., SF 94102, 415-861-6833; 2223 Fulton St., Berkeley 94704, 415-642-4111; Santa Cruz 95064, 408-429-2971.*** *The San Francisco Ballet Free Speaker's program is available to any group of at least high school age. It consists of talks illustrated with slides, films or live demonstrations. For information call Laura Levick, community relations director, 751-2141, ext. 220, or number above. Also co-sponsor tours overseas; in 1979 it offered a tour of British ballet.*

***UNIVERSITY OF CALIFORNIA, IRVINE, Irvine 92717, 417-833-5113.*** *School of Fine Arts, Clayton Garrison, dean. Chairman of Dance Dept., Eugene Loring. Undergraduate major in dance focuses on the creative process. Requirements include extensive studio and workshop experience. Studio experiences in fundamental knowledge and technique of classical ballet and contemporary dance (modern and jazz). Program is designed for those preparing to continue as dancers, choreographers or teachers, as well as those with serious interest in theory, practice and history of dance. Master of Fine Arts also available with emphasis in choreograhy or teaching dance. Eugene Loring, professor of dance and chairman of dance; with Anthony Tudor as lecturer, among others. Catalog upon request.*

***UNIVERSITY OF CALIFORNIA, LOS ANGELES. DANCE DEPT., 213-825-3951.*** *Offers a program in Management in the Arts.*

# *Education*

# *Education*

***UNIVERSITY OF CALIFORNIA, SAN FRANCISCO, 500 Parnassus Ave., SF 94122, 415-666-1800 (Millberry Union Recreation Department, Central Desk).*** *Afro-Latin, ballet (adult and children), disco (beg. and inter.), belly (beg. and inter.), eclectic dance, exercise training, Feldenkrais, folk, jazz, relaxation, pre-natal exercise, Shiatsu massage, tai chi ch'uan, tap, women's exercise, yoga for health.*

***UNIVERSITY OF CALIFORNIA, SANTA BARBARA 93106.*** *Department of Dramatic Art; Rona Sande, coordinator. B.A. in dance.*

***UNIVERSITY OF SAN FRANCISCO, Golden Gate and Parker Avenues, SF, 415-666-6292 or 666-6507 (women's P.E.).*** *Summer dance/movement workshops for teachers with artists in residence. (See also Carol Le Blanc, 902 N. Third St., Burbank, CA 91504, 213-846-7121, ext. 105.)*

***UNIVERSITY OF SANTA CLARA, 95053.*** *Theater Arts, ballet program; Janet Shaw, adjunct lecturer, 408-984-4516, 984-4565. Recently redesigned into a four year plan. Students obtain B.A. in theater arts with dance option. Courses: basic dance I-III, a one year sequence offered two days/week ballet and two days/week modern; inter. dance I-III, second year continuance of basic; advanced modern I, II, III for those completing inter. III; choreography I-II, movement analysis, dance history, liturgical dance workshop (one quarter course), independent study, light and sound, costume design, make-up, dance therapy, theater arts.*

*Guest artist once per quarter for master class. Students give two studio concerts and one major concert a year in Mayer Theater. Department has three studios (main is 45 x 150 with skylights); others are 25 x 60 and a small working studio of 30 sq. ft. (not for rent).*

Education

# Education

**UNIVERSITY OF CALIFORNIA, SANTA CRUZ 95064.** *Aims to liberate student to freely choose unique paths after school, and to recognize other styles, schools and uses of dance outside performance. Curriculum is designed to develop strong sense of self through exposure to contemporary American dance. Core lies in foundation of physiologically correct movement mechanics, conscious use of movement for performance and choreography, and a variety of styles in performances, history and ethnology, individual advising and observation.*

*Faculty: Tandy Beal, lecturer in theater arts with specialty in dance improvisation (see MODERN, SJ); Ruth Solomon, formerly with Jean Erdman Dance Theater, founder of USCS Dance Program; Shirley Wynn, assoc. professor in Theater Arts (dance), director of the Baroque Dance Ensemble and specialist in recreation of ballroom and ballet from original dance manuals and notation scores of 18th and 19th centuries; Byron Wheeler, assistant professor of theater arts, formerly with Donald McKayle and NYU Dance Ensemble, for whom he also choreographed.*

*Summer Dance Theater Institute is an intensive six week program to allow talented and committed persons to get immersed in many aspects of dance as a creative process and a performing art; for students, performers, choreographers and teachers. Admission by audition; enrollment 75. Classes in technical theater, dance lighting and design, technique.*

**UNIVERSITY OF SAN FRANCISCO Dance Program, Dept. of P.E., SF 94117, 415-666-6507.** *Lynda Knapp and Terry Meyers, co-directors. B.A. in Liberal Arts with a major in P.E./dance, with options in teaching and credential preparation and/or performance and choreography. Linked to the former dance program at Lone Mountain College, which folded June 1978. Courses at all levels as well as intensive study for students in the major.*

## *Education*

*Ballet, jazz, modern (Hawkins, Cunningham and Limón), disco, tap, choreography, aesthetics, repertory, production, music analysis for dance, history, teaching experience, exercise physiology and kinesiology. Regularly scheduled workshops and special events with guest artists. Co-sponsor events with Bay Area Dance Coalition and California Dance Educators Association (CDEA). Program also produces dance concerts using the ballroom and main auditoriums at Lone Mountain campus. USF also hosts the dance and movement workshop for CDEA, early summer (also see GROUPS, CDEA).*

*A new dance company that grew out of an interest in continuing to work with some of the dancers at Lone Mountain has been formed, called Lynda Knapp, Terry Meyers and Dancers. Call Kathi Gallagher, dance program coordinator, Dept. P.E., 666-6614 or 666-6563, for brochure on program.*

*Knapp received B.F.A. from NYU School of the Arts, and M.A. from Ohio State. Performed with several companies and directed own for two years. Taught at several colleges and universities. Meyers holds B.A. from UC Santa Cruz and M.F.A. from NYU School of Arts. Choreographer and performer, former director of Lone Mountain dance program.*

***UNIVERSITY OF SOUTHERN CALIFORNIA, IDYLLWILD SCHOOL OF MUSIC AND THE ARTS, Idyllwild, CA 92349.*** *Summer program in modern dance, classical ballet, jazz.*

# Funding Booking

*The United States did not have a program to fund the arts directly until September, 1965 when Congress established the National Endowment for the Arts (NEA). Nevertheless, the federal government has been the largest financial supporter of the arts and humanities for a long time.*

*There are currently more than 15,000 foundations and private trusts in the country, and countless corporations. Since few dance companies survive on bookings alone, they often look to private groups for funding. More corporate funds ARE being given to the arts.*

*Most profit-making corporations can deduct up to 5 per cent of their taxable income for gifts to certain tax-exempt charities. Traditionally not much money has gone to the arts, but a new trend of greater support has benefited the growth of dance in America. The National Corporate Fund for Dance (130 W. 56th St., NYC 10019) solicits contributions from business for its members. Some smaller dance companies are tailoring creative works to fit funding source requirements. Individual choreographers have received corporate funds through umbrella organizations, but amounts smaller than $1,000 are best obtained from banks, suppliers and creditors (who may release some unpaid bills). Big oil corporations, for example, have given more than $1 million to the arts in one fiscal year.*

*Federal tax laws distinguish between gifts and charitable contributions. Most private donors (individuals), therefore, make sure their contributions are tax deductible by giving to non-profit, tax-exempt organizations. Note: people with windfalls usually need deductions before the end of the tax year. See also Yellow Pages, Foundations, Philanthropic.*

*This chapter is divided into local and national funding sources, printed funding references, local and national booking firms, and local entertainment for hire.*

# Funding Booking

## *Funding*
## *Local/State*

***BOTHIN HELPING FUND, 215 Market St., SF 94105, 415-495-0611.***

***CALIFORNIA ARTS COUNCIL, 115 I St., Sacramento 95814; local dance touring coordinator, 415-346-1062.*** *Began in 1976 to supercede the ineffectual California Arts Commission. Council's legal responsibilities include: encourage artistic awareness, participation and expression; increase accessibility and participation in arts, help independent local groups develop own arts programs; promote employment of artists; enlist aid of all state agencies to ensure fullest expression of artistic potential. The council implements California's part of the NEA Dance Touring Program, which helps sponsors book outstanding touring dance companies in all parts of the state. CAC also supports Artists in the Schools, communities and social institutions, arts in education, and innovative projects.*

*The CAC touring program aims to make the variety of California dance, from ballet, ethnic and modern to experimental groups and solo performers more available to audiences. CAC provides subsidies of up to 30% of a company's minimum fee. For information on eligibility criteria, sponsors, support amounts, application forms, etc., write CAC; or, if sponsors or companies have questions, write Dance Touring Coordinator, P.O. Box 795, SF 94101, 415-346-1062. There are various programs that a dance company can apply under, though there is no dance category as such.*

***FINE ARTS DEVELOPMENT FOUNDATION, Friends of Fine Arts, 141 Kearny St., SF 94108, 415-421-1000.*** *Sponsors events at the Opera House, Masonic Auditorium and Paramount Theater.*

***MORTIMER FLEISHHACKER FOUNDATION, 120 Montgomery, SF 94104, 415-781-5000.***

## Funding
## Local/State

***THE FOUNDATION CENTER, 312 Sutter St., SF 94108,415-975-1120.*** *Local arm of The Foundation Center, 888 Seventh Ave., NYC 10019, 212-975-1120. Only independent non-profit U.S. organization that gathers, analyzes and disseminates information on 15,000 philanthropic organizations.*

***WALLACE ALEXANDER GERBODE FOUNDATION, 149 9th St., SF 94103, 415-861-0770.***

***EVELYN AND WALTER HAAS, JR., FUND, 2666 Broadway, SF 94115, 415-921-2024.***

***WILLIAM R. HEARST FOUNDATIONS, 690 Market St., SF 94105, 415-781-8418.***

***WILLIAM AND FLORA HEWLETT FOUNDATION, 220 Bush St., SF 94104, 415-986-5179.***

***HOTEL TAX OF SAN FRANCISCO, PUBLICITY AND ADVERTISING FUND, 289 City Hall, SF 94102.*** *Chief administrative officer, 415-558-4851. Grants are made for the fiscal year beginning July 1; deadline is usually March 31. Send name, etc. of applicant; list of governing body (board, officers, staff); information on non-profit status; statement of purpose and objectives of group; proposed budget, and additional explanatory material (reviews, audience size, publicity packets, etc.). Grants have ranged from $1,000 to nearly $200,000 for large companies.*

*The Hotel Tax Fund also sponsors the Bay Area Ethnic Dance Festival, which has been held annually for two years; 415-931-0984 for information.*

***LOUIS B. LURIE FOUNDATION, 555 California St., SF 94104, 415-392-2470.***

***GARRET W. McENERNEY MUSIC, DRAMA AND ARTS FUND, 500 Sansome St., SF 94111, 415-981-0920.***

# Funding
## Local/State

***THE SAN FRANCISCO FOUNDATION, 425 California St., Suite 1602, SF 94104, 415-982-1210.*** *Accepts applications throughout the year. Last year 195 grants for more than $3.6 million were approved. Dance companies receiving support have included Footloose, Oakland Ballet, SFB and Dance Spectrum, in support of production, program planning and assistance, new ballets, scholarship funds and general support. The application procedure includes filling out a project information form, in addition to a formal proposal. The foundation has a small brochure explaining how to apply for a grant. The foundation provides financial aid to agencies and organizations for the betterment of life in the Bay Area. Preference given to activities in counties of Alameda, Contra Costa, Marin, SF and San Mateo. The foundation also funds the PAS ticket voucher program (see GROUPS). Between $500 and $80,000 can be granted.*

***THE ZELLERBACH FAMILY FUND, 260 California St., Suite 1010, SF 94111, 415-421-1247.*** *Accepts grant applications throughout the year. The current priorities include continuing support of performing arts programs and initiation of projects to improve quality of life; short term support for demonstration projects; provision of critical maintenance support to ongoing programs. Funds are directed primarily, though not exclusively, to programs and projects within the Bay Area. Programs are reviewed each year for continued support. There are six steps in applying for a grant, available from the fund, including itemized budget, half-page summary of project, evidence of non-profit status, project evaluation. Direct service projects in arts that strive to improve the quality of life for all people in the urban community receive priority.*

## *Funding*
## *National*

***JOHN SIMON GUGGENHEIM MEMORIAL FOUNDATION, 90 Park Ave., NYC 10016, 212-687-4470.*** *Available for choreographers' new works and to dance critics and historians for research projects.*

***NATIONAL ENDOWMENT FOR THE ARTS, Columbia Plaza, 2401 E St. NW, Washington, DC 20506; dance program, 202-634-6383.*** *NEA was created in 1965 to encourage and assist the nation's cultural resources. It is advised by the National Council on the Arts. Its major goals are to encourage creative depth of the nation's finest talents, make the arts more available to the public, and preserve U.S. cultural heritage.*

*The NEA Dance Program assists individuals and professional dance organizations with high artistic standards. The program funds innovative as well as traditonal, large and small companies that present the heritage of U.S. and world dance as well as new expressions of form and technique.*

*The NEA is concerned with raising artistic standards, strengthening administration and financial stability of the organizations, and disseminating dance productions of the highest quality to the widest possible audiences.*

*The Dance Program assists all forms of professional dance. Grants are awarded:*

*1) To individual choreographers (fellowships) at all stages of professional careers, generally based on past work. These do not require matching funds, but provide time and money for artistic growth. They also do not require culmination in a performance.*

*2) To individual choreographers of national stature, up to $10,000;*

*3) To individual dance companies and other organizations for dance film/video, to preserve and document major works, or experiment in extending the art of dance. Guidelines from Media Arts Program of NEA, above address, 202-634-6300;*

*4) To individuals and organizations who provide services to dance companies, dancers and choreographers, with national or regional impact. "General Services to the Field" category.*

# Funding National

*5) To dance companies for choreography, professional companies in residence, rehearsal support, production, artistic personnel, management and administration;*

*6) To support long-term dance engagements, sponsor local companies.*

*Brochures are available listing deadlines, eligibility and legal requirements, with application forms for all above categories. Call 202-634-6383, or write address above.*

*The NEA also has sponsored for almost 13 years a Dance Touring Program in cooperation with state art councils and community groups (see California Arts Council, above). The purpose is to make available the best of professional dance to the largest audience possible, by stimulating local dance company residencies; may include performances, master classes, lecture/demonstrations, seminars, children's programs and open rehearsals.*

*Professional companies must meet certain quantitative (not qualitative) criteria for the touring program. For brochure write Dance Touring Program Coordinator, CAC, above. Sponsors may write state arts agencies for copies of the DTP guidelines and the Directory of Dance Companies (California Arts Council, Clark Mitze, executive director, 115 I St., Sacramento 95814, 916-445-1530).*

*The Dance Touring Program currently has 109 companies under its auspices. It makes available to sponsors up to 30 per cent of a company's minimum fee. It is the intent of the program to make possible touring engagements that otherwise would be out of financial reach. (This is not the only kind of touring available, however.) Local sponsors are listed under GROUPS/SPONSORS.*

*NEA also publishes statistics on dance audience growth, dancers wages, allocations, touring, number of sponsors, etc.*

*Notes: NEA fiscal year is Oct. 1 to Sept. 30. For a booklet entitled Guide to Programs, send $1.30 to Superintendent of Documents, U.S. Government Printing Office, Washington, DC 20402, stock #036-000-00033-3. It takes six to nine weeks for grant approval by advisory panels and chairmen.*

## *Funding National*

***NATIONAL ENDOWMENT FOR THE HUMANITIES, 806 15th St. NW, Washington, DC 20506, 202-382-7465.*** *Sister of NEA. Created by Congress in 1965 to support projects of research, education and public acitivity in the humanities, including history and criticism of the arts. NEH encourages the understanding of ideas, values and experiences that have been and will be formative in our culture, and to relate the study of the humanities to national concerns. It does not offer support for creative works in the arts or for performances or training. Historical, theatrical and critical studies in the arts are eligible for NEH support.*

*Categories: research grants, fellowships, education programs, public programs, state programs, special programs, challenge grants to stimulate fund-raising.*

*The NEH has funded some projects with performance components, annotation of dance films, etc. It provides limited fellowships to creative and performing artists of exceptional talent.*

*The brochure lists who is eligible, how to apply, how grants are awarded, requirements of each division, Office of Special Projects, Office of Youth Programs, and the challenge grant program, as well as deadlines, etc.*

*Write NEH at the above address. For more information locally write or call the California Council on the Humanities in Public Policy, 312 Sutter St., Suite 601, SF 94105, 415-543-3865.*

# Funding/Booking

## References

***(DUN AND BRADSTREET'S) REFERENCE BOOK OF CORPORATE MANAGMENT, Dun and Bradstreet, Marketing Services Division, 99 Church St., NYC 10007, $95;*** *available at libraries. List of 2,400 top corps. Also publishes Million Dollar Directory of 45,000 large corporations and a "middle market" directory of 30,000 smaller companies.*

***FINANCIAL MANAGEMENT FOR THE ARTS: A Guidebook for Arts Organizations, ACA Publications, 1564 Broadway, NYC 10036,*** *Charles A. Nelson, Frederick J. Turk, authors. $4.50 including postage.*

***THE FOUNDATION CENTER, 888 7th Ave., NYC 10019, 212-489-8610.*** *Provides information on philanthropic corporations and extensive library service. Unique repository on fundraising. Publishes Foundation News with extensive current grant announcements.*

***THE FOUNDATION DIRECTORY, Columbia University Press, 136 S. Broadway, Irvington, NY 10533. $30.*** *Extensive listing, by Foundation Center, of 2,500 foundations having assets over $1 million. Arranged by state and gives information on purpose, areas of funding interest.*

***THE GRANTMANSHIP CENTER NEWS, The Grantmanship Center, 1015 West Olympic Blvd., LA 90015.*** *$15/yr. (8 issues). Useful periodical covering a single area of funding. Back issues available. The center sponsors a five day intensive introduction to fundraising throughout the country.*

***POOR'S REGISTER OF CORPORATIONS AND DIRECTORS, Standard and Poor's Corp., 345 Hudson St., NYC 10014.*** *$150/yr. or available at library. Lists 37,000 corporations, biog. of 70,000 corp. officers.*

## References

***THE SOCIAL REGISTER, Social Register Assn., 381 Park Ave. South, NYC 10016,*** *$28.50, available at libraries.*

***TAFT INFORMATION SYSTEM, Taft Products, Inc., 1000 Vermont Ave. NW, Washington DC 20005, 202-347-0788.*** *A directory of foundations in U.S. giving at least $100,000 a year in grants. From the Foundation Reporter, new every six months listing contact people at each foundation, application procedures, examples of projects funded, etc. Monthly monitors, bulletins periodically.*

## *Booking*

*Many companies do in-house bookings. Some buy the time of an outsider to sell them, on a retainer basis or contingent fee. Other companies have arrangements with not-for-profit management organizations that offer booking services on similar fee bases. Bookings may also be made by a commercial management business, which usually charge substantial fees and provide a big sell. They often get bookings and help with travel and publicity, but rarely help with internal management or touring details. See also Yellow Pages, Entertainment Bureaus, Professional Talent Management and Theatrical Agencies.*

# *Funding/Booking*

## *Booking*
### *Local*

*AIMEE ENTERTAINMENT ASSN., Suite 104, 14241 Ventura Blvd., Sherman Oaks 91423, 213-872-0374.*

*ARTS UNLIMITED, 515 John Muir Dr., SF 94132, 415-584-6333.* Ruth McCreery, director.

*BREBNER AGENCIES, INC., 161 Berry St., SF 94107, 415-495-6700.*

*CALIFORNIA DANCE MANAGEMENT, c/o Reuben Mack Associates, Suite 300, 5820 Wilshire Blvd., Los Angeles 90036, 213-936-5123.*

*COLUMBIA ARTISTS MANAGEMENT, INC., 7060 Hollywood Blvd., Los Angeles 90028, 213-461-3401.*

*DANCERS A LA CARTE, 100 N. Winchester Blvd., Santa Clara 408-984-6606.*

*BERNARD DOVE PRODUCTIONS, SF, 415-775-7136 or 981-1260.*

*GREAT PERFORMANCES, INC. One Jackson Place, 710 Sansome St., SF 94111.*

*INTERNATIONAL SOCIETY OF PERFORMING ARTS ADMINISTRATORS. Samira Baroody, 1310 Jones St., #1001, SF 94109, 415-928-8139.* Arts promotion and counseling.

*HAYMOND BOOKING AGENCY, 26 O'Farrell St., SF 94108.* Artists Department: *415-391-7216.*

*HOSPITAL AUDIENCES, INC., Bldg. 312, Fort Mason, Laguna and Marina Boulevards, SF 94123, 415-776-9171.* Brings dance and arts events to patients, or vice versa.

*INTERNATIONAL CONCERTS EXCHANGE, 9015 Wilshire Blvd., Beverly Hills 90211, 213-272-5539.* Irwin Parnes, director.

## *Booking*
## *Local*

***OBERLIN DANCE COLLECTIVE.*** *See MODERN, SF.*

***P.R.O.J.E.C.T. E.D.E.N. PRODUCTIONS, Marin, 415-332-9100.***

***S.F. BAY AREA PROFESSIONAL TALENT AGENCY, 511 Cortland Ave., SF 94110, 415-641-1618.***

***THAYER ADVERTISING, 499 Hamilton Ave., Palo Alto, 415-328-0975 or 591-3871. Mail Address: P.O. Box 581, Belmont.*** *Professional talent directory; photo catalog of talent distributed to advertising agencies, TV studios, film producers, shopping centers, etc.*

***THEATRE COMMUNICATIONS CENTER OF THE BAY AREA, 1182 Market St., SF 94103, 415-431-2448.***

***WINDFALL ARTISTS MANAGEMENT, INC., 335 Beach Rd., Burlingame 94010, 415-342-9264.***

***YOUNG AUDIENCES OF THE BAY AREA, 55 New Montgomery St., Suite 606, SF 94105, 415-495-8380.*** *Mrs. Robert Sutton, chairman. (Also Young Audiences of San Jose, 123 S. Third St., San Jose 95113, 408-292-8301, Arline Cox, president; Young Audiences of Napa Valley, P.O. Box 2440, Yountville 94599, Robert Zaro, chairman; 115 E. 92nd St., NYC 10028, 212-831-8110, Warren Yost, executive director.)*

*Since 1949, Young Audiences has brought live professional music to schools. This nationwide organization aims to connect the arts and education of children. It has introduced more than a million school children to a live performing arts experience. Programs now include dance, music and theater.*

## Booking
### Local

**AYRES ENTERTAINMENT COORDINATORS, P.O. Box 23555, San Jose 95123.** *Beverlee Ayres, 408-255-1663. Includes Tahitian and belly dancing.*

**BELLY DANCERS BOUTIQUE, 1235 Boulevard Way, Walnut Creek 94595, 415-937-7852.**

**ENTERTAINMENT WORLD, 2536 Coconut Dr., San Jose 95122, 408-274-1024.**

**FOLKLORICO MEXICANO el GALLO, P.O. Box 207, Selma (San Jose area), 209-896-4298.** *Professional mariachis dancers and singers.*

**JITTERBUG KING AND QUEEN OF SAN FRANCISCO, 415-552-4990.**

**MILLENIUM ENTERTAINMENT, 415-938-4444 (Walnut Creek).**

**MYRIAD TALENT PRODUCTIONS, 3004 16th Ave., SF 94116, 415-863-1429.**

**NICKELODEON, 3001 S. Winchester Blvd., Campbell, 408-866-1404.**

**MARY ANN'S DANCE CENTER, 1487 Franklin, Santa Clara 95050, 408-247-5550.**

**SANTA CLARA DANCE STUDIO, Mele Alohi Dancers, 408-262-8840.**

**MARGO TEMBEY DANCERS, 2022 Lewelling Blvd., San Leandro 94579, 415-351-8116.**

**IRENE WEED.** *See TAP, SF.*

# Funding/Booking

## *Booking National*

***AMERICAN ASSN. OF MUSEUMS, 2233 Wisconsin Ave. NW, Washington DC, 10007.*** *Growing source of bookings; sponsors conferences and monthly bulletin of museum activities, and bi-monthly "Museum News." The Official Museum Directory is published biennially ($35); lists members. Program includes dance. Some bookings qualify for NEA support under DTP.*

***AMERICAN SYMPHONY ORCHESTRA LEAGUE, Symphony Hill, P.O. Box 66, Vienna, VT, 22180, 702-938-2822.*** *National organization of symphony orchestras. Members are beginning to include dance on subscription programs. Write for membership list and information about conferences at which members can be contacted for potential bookings. Some qualify for NEA support under DTP. Local groups included.*

***ARTISTS-IN-SCHOOLS, Charles Reinhart Mgmt., Inc., 1860 Broadway, NYC 10023, 212-586-1925.*** *Project administered by Education Program of NEA. Companies and individual teachers (as movement specialists) are sent into district schools for two week teaching residencies. Companies and specialists chosen by state art councils and local sponsors from list approved by an NEA panel.*

***ASSOCIATION OF COLLEGE, UNIVERSITY AND COMMUNITY ARTS ADMINISTRATORS, P.O. Box 2137, Madison, WI 53701, 608-262-0004.*** *Organization of sponsors; runs biggest and most important booking meetings for dance. Regular membership includes most college and university concert series people. Affiliate membership ($150) gives right to rent table to display and distribute publicity material during national conferences.*

***HOSPITAL AUDIENCES.*** *(See GROUPS.) Sponsors variety of performances and workshops in prisons, nursing homes, hospitals. Provides program advice, referrals and a little money. Main office: 1540 Broadway, NYC 10036, 212-575-7679.*

## *Booking*
## *National*

***INTERNATIONAL SOCIETY OF PERFORMING ARTS ADMINISTRATORS, Mershon Auditorium, 30 W. 15th Ave., Columbus, Ohio 43210, 614-422-5785.*** *Association of buyers and sellers of large cultural attractions.*

***NATIONAL ENTERTAINMENT CONFERENCE, P.O. Box 11489, Capital Station, Columbia, SC 92911, 803-253-4365 or 5751.*** *Assn. of sponsors that holds national and regional conventions of people hiring entertainment for college campuses. Assoc. memberships ($100) enable one to rent exhibit space at national and regional conventions. Growing source of dance bookings. Possible for member companies to do 20 minute performance as part of variety show at conventions. Immense budget. Publishes Student Activities Programming magazine for members, and sends out regularly updated directories of contact people at 1,000 member schools during the year.*

***S.F. BAY AREA DANCE COALITION.*** *See GROUPS. Guidelines available.*

***WESTERN ALLIANCE OF ARTS ADMINISTRATORS, c/o Jay Doty, Garrison Theatre, Claremont Colleges, Claremont, CA 91711, 714-626-8511.*** *Fall booking meeting of ACUCAA-type sponsors from western states.*

***YOUNG AUDIENCES, National Coordinating and Administration Office, 115 E. 92nd St., NYC, 10028, 212-831-8110.*** *Sends dancers and musicians into schools. Open to approaches from dance companies, especially small ones. Bookings only in company's area of residence.*

# groups Sponsors

*The following chapter lists alphabetically groups associated with all aspects of dance, nationwide and local. If there isn't a local branch, check the New York office for Bay Area information. Also check local Chambers of Commerce.*

# groups sponsors

## Groups

**AMERICAN COUNCIL FOR THE ARTS, 1570 Seventh Ave., NYC 10018, 212-354-6655.** *Links all state and local art councils in U.S. Many publications.*

**AMERICAN COLLEGE DANCE FESTIVAL ASSOCIATION.** *See MODERN, California State University, Fresno.*

**AMERICAN DANCE GUILD, Suite 828, 152 West 42nd St., NYC 10036, 212-977-0183.** *Promotes dance with forums for professional excellence, studies, communication. Monthly newsletter; semi-annual Dance Scope, with reviews, personal interviews.*

**AMERICAN GUILD OF MUSICAL ARTISTS, 100 Bush St., SF 94104, 415-986-4060.** *Dancers' union. AGMA hotline (433-6266) announces by recorded messages current auditions, etc.*

**AMERICAN GUILD OF VARIETY ARTISTS, 6430 West Sunset Blvd., LA 90028, 213-464-8281.** *The union of such artists in films.*

**ARTISTS-IN-SCHOOLS DANCE COMPONENT, Charles Reinhart, national coordinator. Charles Reinhart Management, Inc., 1860 Broadway, NYC 10023, 212-586-1925.** *See also FUNDING/-BOOKING.*

**ART RISE, San Bruno.** *See MODERN, Therklesen, Peninsula.*

**ASIAN ARTS ACADEMY:** *Summer concerts at San Francisco State University (Javanese, Japanese, Indonesian, South Indian dance and music). See EDUCATION.*

# groups Sponsors

## Groups

***ASSOCIATED COUNCILS OF THE ARTS, 1564 Broadway, NYC 10036, 212-586-3731.*** *Michael Newton, president. National membership organization representing state, regional and community arts councils and commissions. Administers NEA's technical assistance program for state and community arts agencies. It includes the Advocates for the Arts, a citizens' action project with national membership, focusing on arts-related legal issues. ACA publishes bi-monthly ACA Reports ($30/yr.). Word from Washington covers federal funding for the arts, legislation, etc. Arts Advocate, monthly, carries legislative and legal news.*

***ASSOCIATION OF AMERICAN DANCE COMPANIES, 162 West 56th St., NYC 10019, 800-223-6753.*** *John Gingrich, president. National organization for dance companies. Aids organizational and administrative development. Available to non-members as a resource for job referrals, counseling and placement. Offers inexpensive booking representation for members, produces a variety of dance publications and organizes national and regional conferences.* ***CALIFORNIA ASSOCIATION OF DANCE COMPANIES*** *is local regional division:* ***910 Second St., Sacramento 95814, 916-444-9579.*** *Ann Doyle, director. Communication, research and referral for state's dance community. Newsletter and California Dance Directory. Annual conferences.*

***BAY AREA ARTS SERVICES (BAAS), 415-626-5553.*** *Coalition of nine Bay Area arts and service organizations; provides free or low cost technical aid to artists and art groups in SF, Alameda, Contra Costa, San Mateo, Santa Clara counties. Conferences, clinics and individual consultations on bookkeeping, PR, booking, touring, etc. Applications processed weekly; simple procedure.*

***BAY AREA CONTACT NETWORK (BACN), 1033 Cole St., SF 94117.*** *Group of contact improvisation teachers and performers that coordinates and promotes contact locally. Monthly newsletter with information on classes, jams, workshops, performances.*

# groups sponsors

## Groups

***BUSINESS COMMITTEE FOR THE ARTS (BCA), 1700 Broadway, NYC 10019, 212-765-5980.*** *Gideon Chagy, vice pres. Supports more giving to the arts by business. Monthly and quarterly newsletters for arts and business organizations. Publishes 126 Ways to Support the Arts.*

***CALIFORNIA ARTS COUNCIL.*** *See FUNDING.*

***CALIFORNIA ASSOCIATION OF DANCE COMPANIES, 1412 Van Ness Ave., SF 94109.*** *See AADC, above.*

***COMMITTEE ON RESEARCH IN DANCE, c/o Dr. Patricia A. Rowe, School of Education, New York University, 35 W. Fourth St., NYC 10003.*** *Membership organization that encourages research in all areas of dance. Information center, newsletter.*

***COUNCIL FOR THE ARTS, PALO ALTO (CAPA) and mid-Peninsula area, CAPA/Community Box Office, 1305 Middlefield Rd., Box 11564, Palo Alto 94306, 415-329-2623.*** *Cultural events calendar covering three months, listing dance, film, arts events. CAPA calendar editor, 1313 Newell Road, Palo Alto 94303, 415-329-2605.*

***COUNTRY DANCE AND SONG SOCIETY OF AMERICA, 55 Christopher St., NYC 10014, 212-255-8895.*** *Traditonal folk dance and music promotions; 50 regional centers.*

***DANCE CRITICS ASSOCIATION, 789 West End Ave., NYC 10025.*** *Kitty Cunningham, director.*

***DANCE DEVELOPMENT CENTER FOR THE MID-PENINSULA, Twin Pines Cultural Center, 1219 Ralston Ave., Belmont 94002, 415-595-2888.***

## Groups

***DANCE THEATER WORKSHOP, c/o ATL, 219 W. 19th St., NYC 10011, 212-691-6500.*** *David White, executive director. Membership service group whose benefits include job placement, rental rates, mailing service, discount advertising and telephone service, national dance sponsor list, dance video access.*

***THE DANCE WORKS, INC., 2212 Parker St., Berkeley 94704, 415-548-5962.*** *(See JAZZ, EB). Justin Asher Zitler, director. Sponsors intensive performance/choreography workshops with guest artists, the Berkeley Dance Company, more.*

***DANCEWAYS, 393 West End Ave., 14-F, NYC 10024, 212-799-2860.*** *Non-profit organization established with help of Volunteer Lawyers for the Arts to educate dance consumers and promote the growth of dance. Researching and compiling Guide to Dance in New York.*

***FORT MASON CENTER FOR THE ARTS, HUMANITIES, RECREATION, EDUCATION, AND ECOLOGY, Laguna and Marina Blvds., SF 94123, 415-441-5705.*** *Classes and workshops include international folk dance, 1950's jitterbug, tap, disco-jazz, improv. theater, body fitness, health, acumassage therapy, diet, Feldenkrais awareness through movement, yoga, tai chi ch'uan, theater and music.*

*Fort Mason Foundation office (Bldg. 308) also sponsors dance events, bringing in groups, local and other, to perform or give lecture/demonstrations, etc. Monthly calendar. Memberships are tax deductible and help pay operating expenses, publicity, etc.*

***Groups Located in Fort Mason Include:***
***Building 310:***

*Bay Area Lawyers for the Arts, 775-7200.*
*Marina Theatre, 441-5705.*

# groups Sponsors

## Groups

***Building 312:***
*Center for World Music, 838-8989.*
*Hospital Audiences, Inc., 776-9171.*
*S.F. Bay Area Dance Coalition, 673-8172.*
*S.F. Central YMCA, 885-0460.*
*S.F. Folk Music Center, 441-8910.*
***Building 314:***
*Marina Music Hall, 441-5705.*
*Media Alliance, 441-2557.*

***INTERNATIONAL SOCIETY OF THE PERFORMING ARTS ADMINISTRATORS, INC., E.J. Thomas Hall, University of Akron, OH 44325.***

***INSTITUTE OF MOVEMENT STUDIES, Julia Morgan Center for the Arts (formerly Epic West), 2640 College Ave., Berkeley 94704.*** *See RESOURCES, Notation.*

***INSTITUTE FOR SOCIAL DANCE STUDIES, Suite 609, 24 W. 57th St., NYC 10019, 212-757-6661.*** *Grants scholarships for teacher training, facilities and staff. Reference library, audio-visual, historicals, for loan to education agencies; teaching materials.*

***INTERNATIONAL ALLIANCE OF THEATER STAGE EMPLOYEES (IATSE), 1270 Avenue of the Americas, NYC 10021, 212-245-4369.*** *Union of theater stage employees (stage hands, wardrobe, make-up artists). IATSE Local No. 16, 230 Jones St., SF 94102, 415-441-4601 or 474-6881 (special department).*

***INTERNATIONAL ASSOCIATION OF BLACK AND AFRICAN CHOREOGRAPHERS, P.O. Box 49199, Chicago, IL 60649.*** *Goals: educational journal, information center, encyclopedia on Black and African dance.*

*groups sponsors*

# *Groups*

***INTERNATIONAL SOCIETY OF PERFORMING ARTS ADMINISTRATORS, 1310 Jones St., #1001, SF 94109, 415-928-8139.*** *Arts promotion and counseling.*

***NATIONAL ASSOCIATION OF DANCE AND AFFILIATED ARTISTS, INC.: National Headquarters, 50 Victoria Ave., Millbrae, 415-692-2951. SF area chapter 7, 1948 Camden Ave., San Jose 95124;*** *sponsors master classes, youth programs.*

***THE NATIONAL COUNCIL OF DANCE TEACHER ORGANIZATIONS, INC., c/o Eleanor Rubino, 77 White St., East Boston, MA 92128, 617-569-0459.*** *Examine and grade tests by Board of Directors of Performing Arts Dept. of NCDTO.*

***NATIONAL DANCE ASSOCIATION (AMERICAN ALLIANCE FOR HEALTH, P.E. AND RECREATION), 1201 16th St. NW, Washington DC. 20036, 202-833-5557.*** *Dr. Margie Hanson, executive secretary. Dance in education; Focus on Dance, bi-annual publication; newsletter, Dance Dynamics, twice yearly.*

***NATIONAL ENTERTAINMENT AND CAMPUS ACTIVITIES ASSN., c/o membership secretary, P.O. Box 11489, Columbia, SC 29211, 803-799-0768.***

***NATIONAL RESEARCH CENTER OF THE ARTS, 1270 Avenue of the Americas, NYC, 10020.*** *Louis Harris, chairman. Research services for the arts. Write for list of available studies.*

***PERFORMER REFERRAL SERVICE, ONSTAGE-BACKSTAGE, San Rafael, 415-459-2555.***

***PERFORMING ARTS SERVICES, 1182 Market St., SF 94102, 415-552-3505.*** *A tax-exempt organization serving the non-profit theater, dance and music communities in SF, Alameda and Contra Costa counties. The PAS voucher program was designed to increase attendance at performances by offering subsidized admissions. Those eligible include senior citizens, physically* *disabled persons, high school students, union members, clerical workers, artists and members of community-based service organizations. Calendar of events and lists of groups accepting vouchers; events guide gives information on voucher policies for each event.*

**PUBLISHING CENTER FOR CULTURAL RESOURCES, 27 West 53rd St., NYC 10019, 212-489-9595.** *Assists non-profit groups in any aspect of publishing process. Supports publication of some books and pamphlets by providing loans against future sales, or by acting as a distributor.*

**ST. FRANCIS HEIGHTS DANCE AND MUSIC GUILD, 405 Lakeshore Dr., Daly City, 415-992-1934.**

**SAN FRANCISCO/AFFILIATE ARTISTS OPERA PROGRAM, Affiliate Artists, Inc., 155 W. 68th St., NY 10023, 212-580-2000.** *First U.S. program for the professional advancement of young opera singers and related artists.*

**SAN FRANCISCO BAY AREA DANCE COALITION, Building 312, Fort Mason, Laguna at Marina, SF 94123, 415-673-8172.** *Sukey Lilienthal, executive director. Non-profit membership/-service organization whose purpose is to promote, assist and represent the dance community of the Bay Area. Founded in April, 1973, by a group of dancers and dance managers, the coalition has pledged to draw together the scattered interests of the dance community. Currently at least 80 companies and 500 individual memberships. The coalition publishes an invaluable monthly dance calendar listing events, notes, classifieds, etc. The dance information center assembles and distributes information. Members receive the calendar monthly with 20% discount on advertising rates, discounts on fees for workshops and performances, access to low cost sound and lighting equipment, services of a graphic designer at low cost, and more.*

*The coalition is also a resource center for dance related information, such as a list of Bay Area technical resources, media lists, job referral, performance schedule clearing house, lighting equipment, consulting, resource library, dance resource files. Cost to join ranges from $6 (dancer) to $1,000 (sponsor's council). The agency is supported in part by the SF Hotel Tax Fund.*

**SAN FRANCISCO COUNCIL OF FOLK DANCE GROUPS.** *See ASHKENAZ, FOLK, International or KIRSCHNER, FOLK, Israeli.*

**SAN FRANCISCO DANCERS "ACTION" FORUM, P.O. Box 11748, SF 94101.** *Tance Johnson, director, 415-397-3764, 968-5959. Founded in 1968 to give SF audiences more opportunities to see quality entertainment through performances, youth events, and dance activities incorporating related arts, as well as to build more outlets for skilled professionals. Includes music training, guest artist series, guest artists in schools, master classes, dance samplers, ethnic dance. Annual festival of dance highlights.*

*This non-profit sponsoring/producing organization has paid teachers, scholarship students, dancers to appear as guest artists, musicians, costumers, dance technicians; has produced more than 225 performances. Available on request: arts awareness program (booking, choreography) costuming and mask-making, layout, management; videotapes of SF Dancers Forum performances; a personalized community information service reaching 25 states.*

*More than 3,000 young people were included in dance and art events last season; 500 limited income and minority high school students received extensive free dance training; 40 field trips were sponsored to major dance and art events; 15-30 performances in schools and communities, free; 20 Dancers Forum students now with major companies. Workshop performing outlets throughout the year and professioal paid concerts spring, summer and fall events.*

# Groups Sponsors

## Groups

***SCREEN ACTORS GUILD, 100 Bush St., SF 94104, 415-391-7510.*** *Also Screen Extras Guild. All performances, including dancers in films.*

***TAMALPAIS DANCE GUILD, 10 Olive St., Mill Valley 94941, 415-388-5146.***

***THEATRE DEVELOPMENT FUND, 1501 Broadway, NYC 10036, 212-221-0013.*** *Dance vouchers in NYC; 48,000 costumes in collection rented for nominal fee. Work study in costume design.*

***VOLUNTEER LAWYERS FOR THE ARTS/Bay Area Lawyers for the Arts, Fort Mason Center, Bldg. 310, SF 94123, 415-775-7200.*** *Can help with many legal matters, including formation of general or specific contracts for bookings, etc. NYC office at 36 W. 44th St., NYC 10036, 212-575-1150. Local newsletter The Working Arts, published bi-monthly.*

***WESTERN ASSOCIATES OF PERFORMING ARTS MANAGERS, 3221 22nd St., SF 94110, 415-824-5044.*** *Anne Smith.*

# Groups Sponsors

## *Educational*

***FOOTHILL-De ANZA COMMUNITY COLLEGE DISTRICT, 12345 El Monte Rd., Los Altos Hills 94022,*** *Rowland K. Chase, director of community services.*

***MENDOCINO COLLEGE, Box 3000, Ukiah 95482.*** *Robert Alto.*

***SAN JOSE STATE UNIVERSITY, San Jose 95192,*** *Janet Van Swoll.*

***STANFORD UNIVERSITY, Office of Public Events, Stanford 94305.*** *Vicky Holt, director.*

***COMMITTEE FOR ARTS AND LECTURES (CAL), 101 Zellerbach Hall, University of California, Berkeley 94720.*** *Betty Connors, manager.*

***CAL, University of California, Davis, 150 Memorial Union, Davis 95616.*** *Alison Cramer, manager.*

***UNIVERSITY OF CALIFORNIA, LOS ANGELES, Fine Arts Production, B324 Murphy Hall, UCLA 90024.*** *Edmond G. Harris, director.*

***UNIVERSITY OF CALIFORNIA, SANTA CRUZ, Committee for Arts and Lectures, Santa Cruz 95064.*** *Narrye Caldwell.*

***UNIVERSITY OF SOUTHERN CALIFORNIA—IDYLLWILD, School of Music and the Arts, P.O. Box 38, Idyllwild 92349.*** *Allen Koenig, manager.*

# groups Sponsors

## City

*Most cities have budgets for departments of parks and recreation; many such departments sponsor dance or exercise classes. Those known to offer classes are listed below. Otherwise, look in the White Pages under the name of the city, then Department of Parks and Recreation (or Recreation and Parks). Usually these classes are offered at low rates, and are geared to people seeking exercise rather than dance careers. City parks are often sites of free dance performances.*

*Additional information is available from Chambers of Commerce.*

***ALAMEDA COUNTY ART COMMISSION, 1730 Franklin, Oakland 94612, 415-874-5937 (administration office).***

***TOWN OF ATHERTON, REDWOOD CITY PARKS AND RECREATION DEPT., Holbrook Palmer Park, 94025, 415-324-4521.*** *See also SUGANO-JONSSON, BALLET, Peninsula.*

***BERKELEY RECREATION AND PARKS AND COMMUNITY SERVICES DEPT., 2180 Milvia St., Berkeley 94704, 415-644-6530.***

***CONCORD LEISURE SERVICES, 2974 Salvio, Concord 94519, 415-671-3270.***

***EL CERRITO COMMUNITY CENTER, El Cerrito Parks and Recreation Dept., 7007 Moeser Lane, El Cerrito 94530, 415-525-6747.***

***MARIN COUNTY PARKS AND RECREATION, Civic Center, San Rafael, 415-479-1100.***

***MOUNTAIN VIEW PARKS AND RECREATION OFFICE, 201 S. Rengstorff Ave., Mountain View 94040, 415-969-3890.***

***OAKLAND PARKS AND RECREATION DEPT., 1520 Lakeside Dr., Oakland 94612, 415-273-3091.*** *See also DANCE ARTS of OAKLAND, FOLK.*

# Groups Sponsors

## City

PALO ALTO PARKS AND PLAYGROUNDS program information, 415-329-2585; Dance and Music program, 329-2527; Recreation Dept., 1305 Middlefield Rd., 415-329-2661.

RICHMOND DEPARTMENT OF RECREATION AND PARKS, Civic Center and Barrett Avenue, 415-232-1212.

SAN FRANCISCO CITY AND COUNTY, Art Commission, 165 Grove St., SF 94102, 415-558-3464 (ask for dance activities); Neighborhood Arts Program, 431-8650; Community cultural facilities, see HALLS/RENTALS.

SAN FRANCISCO RECREATION AND PARKS DEPT., Drama and Dance Advisory Committee, Dance Center, 50 Scott St., SF 94117, 415-558-3601.

SAN JOSE PARKS AND RECREATION DEPT., 151 W. Mission St., SJ 95110, 408-277-4661. Fine Arts Commission, 408-277-5144. Center for Performing Arts, 255 Almaden Blvd., 408-277-5277.

CITY OF SAN MATEO DANCE DEPT., Central Recreation Center, 50 East Fifth Ave., San Mateo 94401, division of Parks and Recreation, 364-5600. Cultural arts division of the parks department offers an extensive program in dance for children and adults under Mary Joyce, director, and Jill Daly, assistant director. Progressive program for children (grades 1-8) includes Dance I-V, workshop and Young Performers. Technique is based on fundamentals common to both ballet and modern. Young Performers (9-13) are available during May for performances. Additional children's classes include kinderdance, ballet, tap, jazz and disco. A summer dance at La Honda for girls 10-16 is co-sponsored by the San Mateo Dance Association.

For adults: aerobic, ballet, belly, dancersize, disco, folk, hula, jazz, social, square, tap and yoga. A performing group, Interchange, is available for performance year-round.

# groups Sponsors

## City

*The city department has five studios which it shares when available. "Our purpose is to free the dance within the child. Our method is to teach from the inside out-- from feeling and muscular states—so that the child not only builds skill, but dances with the total environment of mind, body and spirit."*

***SANTA CLARA PARKS AND RECREATION, 298 Garden Hill Dr., Los Gatos 95030, 408-356-7151 (administration).***

***SUNNYVALE PERFORMING ARTS PROGRAMS (Parks and Recreation), 408-738-5521.***

***WALNUT CREEK CIVIC ARTS, 1445 Civic Dr., WC 94596, 415-935-3300.*** *Leisure services; very active in dance. Publishes newsletter, seasonal catalog of events and calendar.*

# groups Sponsors

## *Community*

*YMCAs and YWCAs are good local sources of beginning and intermediate dance and body fitness classes at low cost. Following is a partial list. For more information look in the Yellow Pages under Playgrounds and Parks, Recreation Centers, Religious Organizations, Youth Organizations and Centers.*

***ALAMEDA COUNTY:***

***YMCA Berkeley, 2001 Allston Way, Berkeley 94704, 415-848-6800.*** *Feldenkrais, massage, etc.*

***YMCA, 2101 Telegraph Ave., Oakland 94612.*** *See MODERN, EB.*

***YWCA Oakland, 1515 Webster St., Oakland 94612, 415-451-7900.*** *Disco classes by Crispin Pierce; drop in basis.*

***CONTRA COSTA COUNTY:***

***YMCA Mt. Diablo, 350 Civic Center Dr., Pleasant Hill 94523, 415-687-8900.***

***YWCA of Contra Costa, 1543 Sunnyvale Ave., Walnut Creek 94596, 415-939-9167; 3230 MacDonald Ave., Richmond, 415-234-1270.***

***MARIN COUNTY:***

***YMCA, 241 N. San Pedro Rd., San Rafael 94903, 415-472-1301.***

***YWCA, 1618 Mission Ave., San Rafael 94901, 415-456-0782.***

# *Groups Sponsors*

## *Community*

*SAN FRANCISCO COUNTY:*

***YWCA, 620 Sutter St., 415-775-6500, 94102.*** *Ballroom for seniors.*

***YMCA, 166 The Embarcadero, SF 94111, 415-392-2191.*** *Dancercise I and II.*

***YMCA, 220 Golden Gate Ave., 94102, 415-885-0460.***

***YMCA, FORT MASON CENTER, Marina at Laguna, SF 94123, 415-885-0460.***

***MISSION YMCA, 400 Mission, 94105, 415-586-6900.*** *Jazz and disco.*

***RICHMOND YMCA, 1834 Clement St., 94121, 415-668-2060.***

*SAN MATEO COUNTY (Peninsula):*

***YMCA OF PALO ALTO, Los Altos, Mt. View, Stanford, 3412 Ross Rd., Palo Alto 94303, 415-494-1883.***

***YWCA THE MID-PENINSULA, 4161 Alma St., Palo Alto 94306, 415-494-0972.***

***YWCA SAN BRUNO, 560 El Camino Real, San Bruno 94066, 415-952-8500.***

***YWCA PENINSULA, 240 N. El Camino Real, San Mateo 94402, 415-342-5228.***

# groups Sponsors

## Community

*SAN JOSE:*

***YMCA OF SANTA CLARA VALLEY**, 1190 Emory St., SJ 95126, 408-298-3888.*

***YWCA SAN JOSE**, 375 Third, 408-295-4011.*

# Space

*These listings include sites of dance performances by Bay Area and visiting companies, as well as studios that rent space. More space can be located by looking in the phone book under City/Community Centers, White Pages; or in the Yellow Pages, under Churches, Clubs, Halls and Auditoriums, Playgrounds and Parks, Recreation Centers, Religious Organizations, Theaters and Youth Recreation Centers. See also newspaper classified under Performing Arts and Rentals, and Classified Flea Market under Rentals (see MAGAZINES).*

# *Contra Costa County*

***CONCORD PAVILION, 2000 Kirker Pass Rd., Concord 94501, 415-671-3282; 798-3316.*** *8,000 seats; wheelchair access. Rental $1,500 and up.*

***DIABLO VALLEY COLLEGE AUDITORIUM, 321 Golf Club Rd., Pleasant Hill, 94523, 415-685-1230.***

***EAST BAY MUSIC CENTER, 2369 Barrett Ave., Richmond 94804, 415-234-5624.***

***PINOLE VALLEY HIGH SCHOOL THEATRE ARTS DEPT., 2900 Pinole Valley Rd., Pinole 94564, 415-758-8281.***

***RICHMOND ART CENTER, 25th and Barrett Ave., Richmond 94804, 415-234-2396.***

***ST. MARY'S COLLEGE AUDITORIUM, Moraga 94556, 415-376-4411.***

***WALNUT CREEK CIVIC ART GALLERY/CENTER THEATER, 1641 Locust St., Walnut Creek 94597, 415-935-6000 ext. 256, or 939-0355.*** *450 seats; wheelchair access. Michael Raines, community arts supervisor.*

***WILLOWS THEATRE, 1975 Diamond Blvd. at Willow Pass Rd., Concord 94520, 415-798-6525.*** *198 seats; wheelchair access.*

***ASHKENAZ FOLK DANCE COOPERATIVE.*** *See FOLK/INTERNATIONAL.*

***BELLY DANCE ARTS STUDIO.*** *See BELLY, EB.*

***THE BERKELEY ART CENTER, 1275 Walnut Ave., Berkeley 94709.*** *Carl Worth, director; Richard Sargent, curator.*

***BERKELEY COMMUNITY THEATER, Allston Way at Grove, Berkeley, 415-845-2308.***

***BERKELEY MOVING ARTS, 2200 Parker St., Berkeley 94704, 415-848-4878.*** *85 seats; no wheelchair access.*

***BLAKE STREET THEATER, 2019 Blake St., Berkeley 94704.***

***JANE BROWN FOUNDATION FOR THE DANCE.*** *See OTHER DANCE, Creative.*

***CALIFORNIA STATE UNIVERSITY, HAYWARD, P.E. Bldg., Carlos Bee Boulevard, Hayward 94542, 415-881-3061.***

***CHABOT COLLEGE AUDITORIUM, 15555 Hesperian Blvd., Hayward 94545, 415-786-6800.*** *Little theatre proscenium, 220 seats; auditorium, 1,500 seats. Dr. Santiago Garza, assoc. dean of community services.*

***CLASSICAL BALLET CENTER.*** *See BALLET, EB.*

***CREATIVE DANCE THEATER, 659 Arlington, Berkeley 94707, 415-526-9783.***

***EAST BAY BALLET THEATRE.*** *See BALLET, EB.*

***EAST BAY CENTER FOR THE PERFORMING ARTS, Berkeley Center, 1819 Tenth St., Berkeley 94710.***

***EVERYBODY'S CREATIVE ART CENTER, 354 21st St., Oakland 94612, 415-863-1830 or 826-6355.*** *New, large studio.*

***FINNISH BROTHERHOOD HALL, 1970 Chestnut St., Berkeley 94705, 415-845-5352.***

***FIRST UNITED METHODIST CHURCH, 2352 Broadway, third floor, Oakland 94612, 415-444-8171.***

***FULL SPECTRUM STUDIO.*** *See BALLET, EB. $2.50/hr. days; barres, mirrors, stereo.*

***WALTER HAAS PAVILION, Mills College, Oakland 94613, 415-632-2700.***

***HEALING OURSELVES CENTER, 2547A 8th St., Berkeley (at Dwight Way), 94710, 415-841-6911.*** *Office hours: Tues.-Fri. 10-1, Tues. (&) Fri. 5:30-7:30 p.m. Dance studio for rent, suitable for dance, bodywork, etc. 1,600 sq. ft. maple floor (40 x 40), off floor carpeted area (8 x 40), massage tables, hanging trapezes, foam mats and pillows, plenty of natural light, quadraphonic sound system, electrical circuits for theater lights, adequate parking. Rates: weekend nights, Sat. & Sun. only, $50/evening. Weekend days: $40, or $24 for half day. Weekdays: $5/hr. Entire weekend, $150 (first and last weekends only). Stereo fee, $5; available to see during office hours, and Fridays 8:30 to 10:30 p.m. at dance jam.*

***HEARST GYMNASIUM, University of California, Berkeley 94720, 415-642-6000.***

***LANEY COLLEGE THEATRE, 900 Fallon St., Oakland 94607, 415-444-4695.***

# Spaces

## East Bay

***LIVE OAK THEATRE, 1301 Shattuck Ave., Berkeley 94709, 415-841-5580.*** *150 seats; no charge for performance in theater. Wheelchair access.*

***METROPOLITAN THEATRE, 1426 Alice (off 14th St.), Oakland 94612, 415-523-9333.***

***JULIA MORGAN CENTER FOR THE ARTS, 2640 College Ave., Berkeley 94704, 415-548-2687.*** *Classroom, rehearsal, performance space available. Three studios, from 720 to 2,400 sq. ft. Hourly rates. Two performance spaces, raised stage on open floor.*

***MOVING PARTS, 2212 Parker at Fulton, Berkeley 94704.***

***OAKLAND AUDITORIUM, 10 Tenth St., Oakland 94607.*** *Proscenium, 2,000 seats; arena, 6,000. Norvel "Bud" Alexander, auditorium supervisor.*

***OAKLAND MUSEUM, 1000 Oak St., Oakland 94607.***

***PARAMOUNT THEATER, 2025 Broadway, Oakland 94612, 415-465-6400.*** *3,000 seats; wheelchair access.*

***RALPH'S STUDIO, 2547 Eighth at Dwight Way, Berkeley 94710, 415-653-2088.***

***ST. ALBAN'S CHURCH, 1501 Washington Ave. at Curtis, Albany 94707, 415-525-1716.***

***ST. CLEMENT'S CHURCH, 2837 Claremont Ave., Berkeley 94705, 415-843-2678.***

***ST. JOHN'S PRESBYTERIAN CHURCH, 2727 College Ave., Berkeley 94705, 415-845-6830.*** *350 seats; wheelchair access.*

# Spaces

## East Bay

***ST. MARK'S EPISCOPAL CHURCH, 2300 Bancroft Way, Berkeley 94704, 415-841-6500.*** *400 seats; no wheelchair access.*

***SANDS, 1933 Broadway, Oakland 94612, 415-451-8892.***

***FLORENCE SCHWIMLEY THEATRE, Allston Way and Grove St., Berkeley.***

***RALPH'S STUDIO, 2547 Eighth St., Berkeley 94710, 415-653-2088.***

***SKYLIGHT STUIDO, 2547 Eighth St., Berkeley 94710.***

***SPACE I, 2547 Eighth St., Berkeley 94710, 415-841-9576.***

***THEATER METAMORPHOSE, 2525 Eighth St. at Dwight Way, Berkeley 94710, 415-548-7677.*** *99 seats; wheelchair access.*

***UNITARIAN FELLOWSHIP, 1924 Cedar, Berkeley 94709, 415-841-4824.***

***UNIVERSITY ART MUSEUM, 2626 Bancroft Way, Berkeley 94720, 415-642-5317 or 642-1207.*** *300 seats; more than 50 per cent dance. No rentals.*

***YOSHI'S JAPANESE RESTAURANT, 6030 Claremont Ave., Oakland 94618, 415-652-9200.*** *Talent auditioned for paid performances in connection with restaurant, in newly designed upstairs space.*

***ZELLERBACH AUDITORIUM, University of California, Berkeley 94720, 415-642-5550.*** *Russell McGrath, manager. Proscenium, 2,100 seats; multi-form, 500-700 seats.*

***RENTABLES:***

***415-548-7677,*** *fully equipped 99 seat theater, rates negotiable.*

***415-845-9250, 534-3630 (a.m.), 1800 Dwight Way, Berkeley;*** *music, art and dance center.*

***415-843-3973.*** *16 x 36 floor, mirrors, barres, stereo, tape, piano. $4/hr.*

***415-536-9783.*** *40 x 60; $6/hr. mornings, evenings, weekends. View, dressing room. North Berkeley Hills.*

***415-841-6911.*** *40 x 40, piano, quadraphonic sound system, skylights, good parking. Day $5/hr. Weekend rates, $50. West Berkeley.*

***415-547-9939 or 653-1513.*** *60 x 75, showers, wood floor. Telegraph Avenue at 51st, Oakland.*

# Space

## *Marin/Sonoma*

*ALMONTE HALL, 104 Almonte Blvd., Mill Valley 94941.*

*ANGELICO THEATER, DOMINICAN COLLEGE. See EDUCATION.*

*BALLET THEATRE WEST. See BALLET, Marin.*

*BAY TERRACE THEATRE/MIRA THEATRE GUILD, 51 Daniels Ave., Benicia 94510, 415-644-3262.*

*BELROSE STUDIO THEATER, 1415 Fifth Ave., San Rafael 94901.*

*BENICIA OLD TOWN GROUP THEATER, 140 West J St., Benicia 94510, 415-745-9957.*

*CINNABAR THEATER, 3333 Petaluma Blvd., Petaluma 94952, 707-763-8920.*

*COLLEGE OF MARIN Fine Arts Theater, Kentfield 94904, 415-485-9560. Rental through drama dept.; 604 seats.*

*THE DANCE PALACE, Main Street, Pt. Reyes Station 94956, 415-663-1075.*

*THE FAIRFAX PAVILION, 142 Bolinas Rd., Fairfax, 415-454-9689.*

*SONOMA STATE UNIVERSITY, Warren Auditorium (Ives 101), 1801 East Cotati Ave., Rohnert Park 94928, 707-664-2353.*

*TAMALPAIS DANCE CENTER. See BALLET, Marin.*

# Spaces

## Peninsula

**ACADEMY OF DANCE ARTS.** *See BALLET, Peninsula.*

**THE BALLET SCHOOL.** *See BALLET, Peninsula.*

**CANADA COLLEGE, 4200 Farm Hill Blvd., Redwood City 94061, 415-364-1212.**

**THE CIRCLE STAR THEATRE, 1717 Industrial Rd., San Carlos 94070, 415-364-2550.**

**COLLEGE OF SAN MATEO THEATER, 1700 W. Hillsdale Blvd., San Mateo 94402, 415-697-9422,** *for information.*

**COMMUNITY THEATER, 1305 Middlefield Rd., Palo Alto 94301, 415-320-2526.**

**FINE ARTS THEATRE, 429 California Ave., Palo Alto 94306, 415-327-6655.**

**MITCHELL PARK COMMUNITY CENTER, 3800 Middlefield Rd., Palo Alto 94303, 415-329-2487.**

**SAN MATEO PERFORMING ARTS CENTER, 650 N. Delaware, San Mateo 94401, 415-343-8485.**

**SKYLINE COLLEGE, 3300 College Dr., San Bruno 94066.**

**SPANGENBERG THEATER, 780 Arastradero Rd., Palo Alto 94306, 415-855-8242.**

**STANFORD MEMORIAL AUDITORIUM, Office of Public Events, Stanford 94305, 415-497-2551.** *Rental by arrangement; 1,332 seats.*

**MARLENE THERKELSEN DANCE STUDIO.** *See MODERN, Peninsula.*

**ZOHAR SCHOOL OF DANCE.** *See BALLET, Peninsula.*

# Spaces

## *San Francisco*

***ARABESQUE CONCERT DANCE, 456 Post St., SF 94102, 415-397-3764.*** *300 seats; wheelchair access.*

***ASIAN ART MUSEUM, Golden Gate Park, SF 94118, 415-558-2993.***

***BAYVIEW OPERA HOUSE, 4705 Third St., SF 94124.***

***BETHANY UNITED METHODIST CHURCH, 1268 Sanchez St., SF 94114, 415-647-8393.***

***MIRIAM BORNE'S DANCE AND YOGA STUDIO.*** *70 seats. See OTHER DANCES/Creative.*

***BRAND X STUDIO, 855 Folsom St., SF 94107, 415-757-1633.*** *60 x 23 space; seats 70. Rents for $5/hr; $100/weekend. Barbara Roesch.*

***CABRILLO MUSIC CENTER, 442 Shotwell St., SF 94110, 415-482-1419.***

***CALIFORNIA PALACE OF THE LEGION OF HONOR, 34th Ave. and Clement, Lincoln Park, SF 94121, 415-558-2881.*** *340 seats; wheelchair access.*

***CENTER FOR WORLD MUSIC, Fort Mason Bldg. 312, SF 94123.*** *See SPONSORS.*

***CENTERSPACE, 2840 Mariposa, SF 94110, 415-839-3267.*** *No rentals; 55-80 seats. No wheelchair access.*

***CHINA BASIN DANCE THEATRE.*** *See OTHER DANCES/Creative. Rental $5/hr.*

***CHINESE CULTURAL CENTER, 750 Kearny St., SF 94108.***

***CROATIAN-AMERICAN HOME ASSOCIATION, INC., 3416 19th, SF, 415-431-7729.***

***80 Langston Street, SF, 415-626-5416.*** *Pays honoraria to dancers, etc., presenting works.*

***EUREKA VALLEY RECREATION CENTER, Collingwood and 18th Streets, SF 94114.***

***THE EXPLORATORIUM, 3601 Lyon St., SF 94123, 415-563-7337.***

***THE FARM, 1499 Potrero, SF 94110.***

***FIRST UNITARIAN CHURCH, 1187 Franklin St., SF 94109, 415-776-4580.***

***FOOTLOOSE.*** *Rental. See MODERN, SF.*

***FORT MASON CENTER.*** *See GROUPS/SPONSORS.*

***GUMPTION, 1563 Page St., SF 94117.*** *100 seats, no rentals.*

***HELLMAN HALL, San Francisco Conservatory of Music, 1201 Ortega St., SF 94122.***

***INTERSECTION THEATRE, 756 Union St., SF 94133, 415-397-6061.***

***JAPAN CENTER THEATRE, 1881 Post St., SF 94115, 415-567-4820.***

***MARGARET JENKINS.*** *See MODERN, SF. Rental contracts available based on number of days needed, etc. Extensive details available regarding newly expanded space, 415-863-7580.*

## San Francisco

**THE LOFT, 132 Bush St., SF 94104, 415-392-9300.**

**LONE MOUNTAIN COLLEGE, 2800 Turk Blvd., SF 94118, 415-752-7000, ext. 272.** *Main Theater, 532 seats; WABE Theater, 120 seats.*

**MANDALA DANCE CENTER.** *See FOLK/INTERNATIONAL. Daytime rental, $5/hr., 415-552-4990.*

**MARINES MEMORIAL THEATER, 609 Sutter at Mason, SF 94102, 415-771-4917.** *640 seats; wheelchair access.*

**MASONIC AUDITORIUM, 1111 California St., SF 94108, 415-776-4917.** *3,165 seats; wheelchair access.*

**MERCURY ATHLETIC CLUB, 404 Clement St., SF 94118, 415-387-3574.**

**MODERN JAZZ WORKS.** *See JAZZ, SF.*

**NEIGHBORHOOD ARTS THEATER, 220 Buchanan St., SF 94102, 415-431-8650.** *Ethnic and experimental. 200-500 seats; wheelchair access.*

**NEW COLLEGE OF CALIFORNIA Stage, 777 Valencia, SF 94110, 415-626-1694.** *150 seats; no wheelchair access, no rentals.*

**NOE VALLEY PRESBYTERIAN CHURCH, 1021 Sanchez St., SF 94114, 415-282-2317.**

**OLD FIRST CENTER FOR THE ARTS, (Old First Presbyterian Church), 1751 Sacramento St., SF 94109, 415-776-5552.** *550 seats; no wheelchair access.*

**PALACE OF FINE ARTS, 3301 Lyon St., SF 94132, 415-563-6504.** *Laurie Zien, administrator. 1,003 seats; wheelchair access. $225 for an eight hour performing day.*

***PANGAEA CENTER FOR THE ARTS, 517 Cortland Ave., SF 94110, 415-285-3331.*** *90 seats; wheelchair access.*

***PEOPLE'S CULTURAL CENTER, 721 Valencia St., SF 94110, 415-431-9329.***

***PERFORMING ARTS WORKSHOP/ARTISTS INTERCHANGE, 340 Presidio, SF 94115, 415-931-9228.*** *100 seats; wheelchair access.*

***AMY POWELL STUDIO.*** *See DISCO. Low rates.*

***RECONSTELLATION, 253 or 255 Leavenworth, SF 94102.*** *See BALLET, SF.*

***RED SHIELD YOUTH CENTER, 95 McCoppin, SF, 94103, 415-431-4341.***

***PROJECT ARTAUD, 499 Alabama St., SF 94110, 415-552-4014 or 552-4190.*** *Home of Mangrove.*

***SAN FRANCISCO ART COMMISSION neighborhood center: South of Market Cultural Center, 552-2131; Chinese Cultural Center 957-1146; Bayview Opera House, 824-1283; Mission Cultural Center, 821-1155; Western Addition Cultural Center, 921-7976. (All area code 415.)***

***SAN FRANCISCO DANCE ARCHIVES, 3150 Sacramento St., SF 94115.*** *See REFERENCE.*

***SAN FRANCISCO DANCE SPECTRUM.*** *See BALLET, SF. 80 seats; rental $25 bare space, more for lights and sound.*

***SAN FRANCISCO DANCE THEATRE, Community Theatre Space, 1412 Van Ness Ave., SF 94109, 415-673-8101.*** *Alan Shratter. Rents for $65/performance with $50 refundable deposit. Tech or rehearsal time, $45/day. 30 x 35 stage, 12 foot ceilings; seats 125-200. Sound, lights.*

***SAN FRANCISCO JEWISH COMMUNITY CENTER, 3220 California St., SF 94118, 415-346-6040.***

***SAN FRANCISCO MUSEUM OF MODERN ART, Van Ness Ave. at McAllister, 415-863-8800 or 431-1210.*** *500 seats; 35 per cent dance events. No rental.*

***SAN FRANCISCO PERFORMANCE GALLERY, 3153 17th St., SF 94110, 415-863-6606.*** *See also Oberlin Dance Collective, MODERN, SF.*

***SAN FRANCISCO PUBLIC LIBRARY, Civic Center, 415-558-3191.*** *Hosts free dance concerts.*

***SAN FRANCISCO WAR MEMORIAL OPERA HOUSE, Van Ness at Grove St., SF 94102, 415-661-6600.*** *Donald Michalske, managing director. Proscenium, 3,252 seats. Rental rates differ depending on weekend or weekday use, ranging from $450-$700.*

***SHOWCASE THEATER, 430 Mason St., SF 94102, 415-998-3167.***

***SOUTH SAN FRANCISCO OPERA HOUSE, 4705 Third St., SF 94124, 415-824-1283.***

***STUDIO EREMOS WORKSHOP, 499 Alabama St., SF 94110, 415-552-3451.*** *50-60 seats; wheelchair access.*

***SUN DANCE STUDIO, 301 Eighth St., SF 94103.***

***SYNERGIC THEATER, 545 Haight St., SF 94117, 415-431-1171, 552-2742.*** *$3-4/hr. rental rates.*

***TEMPLE UNITED METHODIST CHURCH, 19th Avenue at Junipero Serra Blvd., 415-586-1444.***

***THEATRE OF MAN, 1350 Waller St., SF 94117, 415-285-3719.*** *99 seats; no wheelchair access. Dance and experimental theater companies. Suspended wood floor, heat, piano; for performance or rehearsal.*

***THEATRE FLAMENCO DANCE CENTER, 465 S. Van Ness Ave., 415-431-6521.*** *$2.50 to $5/hr. Sunny.*

***THE STUDIO.*** *See MODERN, SF.*

***VETERAN'S AUDITORIUM, 465 So. Van Ness Ave., SF 94103, 415-431-6521.*** *700 seats; wheelchair access.*

***VICTORIA THEATRE, 2961 16th St., SF 94103.*** *See also FOLK/Spanish, Theatre Flamenco.*

***VORPAL GALLERY, 393 Grove St., SF 94102, 415-397-9200.***

***WALKABOUT STUDIO, 1360 Howard St., SF 94103.***

***WOMEN'S BUILDING OF THE BAY AREA, 3543 18th St., Ibsen Hall, SF 94110, 415-863-5225 or 346-2384.***

*RENTABLES:*

***415-281-1178.*** *SF dance studio.*

***415-863-8598.*** *SF dance/theater space for classes, rehearsals, auditions, low rates.*

***415-626-3131.*** *Igbal Lewis, prime SF location.*

# Spaces

## *San Jose*

*THE DANCE CLUB*, ***San Jose.*** *See BALLROOM, SJ.*

***FLINT CENTER, De Anza College, Cupertino 95014, 408-996-4817 or 996-4832.*** *2,600 seats; rental by arrangement.*

***LOUIS B. MAYER THEATRE, University of Santa Clara, 408-984-4242.***

***SAN JOSE CENTER FOR THE PERFORMING ARTS, 255 Almaden Blvd., San Jose 95113, 408-277-5277; after 5 p.m. and weekends, 408-288-7469.***

***SUNNYVALE PERFORMING ARTS CENTER, Sunnyvale Community Center, 500 E. Remington Ave., P.O. Box 607, Sunnyvale 94088, 408-739-0531, 735-8340.*** *Proscenium, 3,200 seats. Pat Plant, performing arts coordinator.*

***UNIVERSITY OF CALIFORNIA, SANTA CRUZ, new Performing Arts Complex. See EDUCATION.***

# Resources

*The growing abundance of resources available in the dance field can overwhelm anyone looking for help. Since it is impossible to list every person or group, view this chapter as an introduction to a variety of dance resources. It includes events, dance therapy, music and theater, notation, dance archives, technical resources, film and video, media and supplies.*

# *Events*

***AMERICAN COLLEGE DANCE FESTIVAL ASSN., Dance Program, Swarthmore College, Swarthmore, PA 19081.***

***AMERICAN DANCE FESTIVAL, Southern California Visitors Council, 705 West Seventh St., LA 90017.*** *Annual, late May; features Bay Area groups including Balasarawati (see FOLK/Indian).*

***AMERICAN DANCE FESTIVAL, P.O. Box 6097P, College Station, Durham, NC 27708.*** *Courses in nearly 20 subjects, including technique, kinesiology, music for dance, injury problems, stagecraft, therapeutic massage. Workshops in dance therapy, critics conference, dance on television. Performances by a dozen companies, including modern, ethnic; for brochure write above address.*

***ARTHUR MURRAY WEST COAST DANCE OLYMPICS.*** *See BALLROOM, SF.*

***CALIFORNIA ARTS SPRING FAIR, California Institute of the Arts, Valencia 91355.*** *Annual, May.*

***CARMEL FESTIVAL OF DANCE, Sunset Community and Cultural Center, P.O. Box 5066, Carmel 93921, 408-624-3996.*** *Richard Tyler, director.*

***CITY OF SAN JOSE, Spring Arts in Education Week.*** *Summer Talent in Tapestry festivals feature local dance companies.*

***FAIRE EXTRAORDINAIRE, Oakland;*** *annnual summer event on College Avenue, featuring modern, jazz, ballet and much dance-related material. Danceworks Production; see JAZZ, EB.*

***FESTIVAL OF THE ARTS, c/o Bea Everson, 340 San Gorgonio, San Diego 92106.*** *Annual since 1974, Aug.-Sept.*

# Resources

## *Events*

***SPRING DANCE CONCERT FESTIVAL, Allen Hancock College, 800 South College, Santa Maria 93454, 805-922-6966, ext. 232.*** *Annual since 1969; April.*

***STANFORD SUMMER FESTIVAL OF THE ARTS, P.O. Box 3006, Stanford 94305.*** *Annual since 1964; mid-June to mid-July.*

***STERN GROVE FESTIVAL, P.O. Box 3250, SF 94111, 415-398-6551.*** *James Friedman, executive secretary. Annual, June-August.*

***SUMMER DANCE, produced by Events in cooperation with Intersection, 756 Union St., SF 94133, 415-221-3333 ext. 456.*** *Yearly in August at Palace of Fine Arts Theater.*

Resources

# *Dance Therapy*

*Dance therapy, as defined by the American Dance Therapy Association, is "the psycho-therapeutic use of movement to further the emotional and physical integration of an individual." It has developed from early ritual healing ceremonies to serve day care centers, correctional facilities, geriatric centers, etc.*

**ACADEMY OF DANCE ARTS, 988 W. El Camino Real, Sunnyvale 94087, 312-739-7182; 312-733-4234.** *Terri L. Owens, teacher of meditation, self-awareness, massage. Terri is a minister who counsels and does therapy with invalids, etc. The school offers a program for body therapy to correct physical defects.*

**ADVENTURES IN MOVEMENT FOR THE HANDICAPPED, 945 Danbury Rd., Dayton, Ohio 45420.** *National, non-profit organization to help blind, deaf, retired people. Registered by ADTA (see below). Physiotherapy, licensed massage, kinesiotherapy, chiropractics, osteopathy, orthopedics for emotionally and physically handicapped.*

**AMERICAN DANCE GUILD, 1133 Broadway #1427, NYC 10010, 212-691-7773.** *Careers information sheet with several sources.*

**AMERICAN DANCE THERAPY ASSOCIATES, Suite 230, 2000 Century Plaza, Columbia, MD 21044, 301-977-4040.** *Founded 1966. Promotes research, education, annual conferences, workshops, newsletter published six times a year. Also publishes the American Journal of Dance Therapy, semi-annually. Joanna Harris, editor. Registry of professional standards; more than 1,000 members in 12 countries.*

**CALIFORNIA STATE UNIVERSITY, FRESNO.** *See EDUCATION.*

# Resources

## *Dance Therapy*

***CALIFORNIA STATE UNIVERSITY, HAYWARD.*** *See EDUCATION.*

***CENTER FOR ENERGETIC STUDIES, 2045 Francisco St., Berkeley 94709, 415-526-8373.*** *Michael Conant, director. Workshops, seminars and private sessions on the body process as basis for individuals to form themselves and their worlds. Basic biological training and re-education. Staff includes Tamara Greenberg, registered dance therapist, who uses dance/movement to further emotional and physical integration.*

***CONSTANCE COOK, DTR, 2107 Pierce St., SF 94115, 415-346-2911.*** *ADTA registered.*

***TAMARA GREENBERG, DTR, 2045 Francisco St., Berkeley 94709, 415-841-1611.***

***JOANNA HARRIS, 2714 Woolsey St., Berkeley 94705, 415-653-8111.***

***HEALING OURSELVES CENTER, 2547A Eighth St., Berkeley 94710, 415-841-6911.***

***HEALTH EDUCATION SEMINARS, P.O. Box 14472, SF 94114, 415-626-2044.*** *Dance therapy, polarity, psychokinesis, private consultations.*

***JANLYN DANCE COMPANY.*** *See MODERN, Santa Clara.*

***ANNE KRANTZ, 9448 Graton Rd., Sebastopol 95472, 707-823-0377.***

# Resources

## Dance Therapy

**NITZE BRODIE-MILLER, 2 Frederick Court, Menlo Park 94025, 408-328-7191.** Registered movement psychotherapist. Individual and groups, weekend workshops, training and counseling.

**URSULA MILLETT.** See BALLET, SJ. Therapy referrals.

**NEW SCHOOL OF MASSAGE.** See BODY WORK, Massage.

**OPEN SPACE STUDIO, 2118 Vine St., Berkeley 94709, 415-848-8403 or 848-4947.** Lorie Kranzler-Kennedy, movement specialist. Movement therapy for individuals, families and groups; consultation, creative dance. Nine-week courses limited to six people, by interview only.

**PACIFIC SCHOOL OF RELIGION.** See EDUCATION.

**PRATT INSTITUTE, Dance Therapy Department, East Building, Brooklyn, NY 11205.** Masters degree program.

**PURE WINE DANCE COMPANY, 3316 24th St., SF 94110, 415-282-4020 (at Samuel Lewis Studios.)** Chinese therapeutic movement, Eastern dance, whirling dance, fundamentals of dance.

**SAN FRANCISCO DANCER'S WORKSHOP.** Feldenkrais. See OTHER DANCES/Creative.

**KATHLYN STENTZ, 541 Cowper St., Palo Alto 94301, 415-321-3126.** DTR, ADTA.

**THE STILL POINT, 514 High St., Palo Alto 94301, 415-321-3126.** Kathlyn Stentz, Patricia Burbank. Creative dance and dance therapy.

## *Dance Therapy*

### *References*

***SUSAN WALLOCK, 77 Murray Ave., Larkspur 94939.*** *DTR, ADTA, Ph.D.*

***NANCY ROBERTSON ZENOFF, 3 Calladi Way, Atherton 94025, 408-854-1981.***

***UNIVERSITY OF SANTA CLARA.*** *See EDUCATION.*

### *References*

***AMERICAN JOURNAL OF DANCE THERAPY (ADTA), Suite 230, 2000 Century Plaza, Columbia, MD 21044.*** *Semi-annual; $11-$15/yr. Joanna Harris, editor. Newsletter six times a year.*

# Resources

## *Media*
## *Print/Local*

*This list covers magazines and newspapers, radio and television stations that offer interviews, criticisms, discussions about local dance companies, choreographers, etc. Also: call the Dance Coalition and ask for their Bay Area press list (673-8172) and check the Yellow Pages.*

***ARTS AND LEISURE PUBLICATIONS, division of the Hagen Group, 950 Battery St., SF 94111, 415-956-6262.*** *Publishes dance programs.*

***BAY GUARDIAN DAY AND NIGHT, Guardian Building, 2700 19th St., SF 94110.*** *Free weekly tabloid with full Bay Area arts listing.*

***THE BERKELEY MONTHLY, 2275 Shattuck Ave., Berkeley 94704.*** *Calendar listings, occasional articles and reviews on local dance and theater arts.*

***CITY ARTS MONTHLY, City Celebration, Inc. 640 Natoma St., SF 94103, 415-552-4387.*** *Elliot Katz, editor. Non-profit corporation producing free and low cost music, theater and dance events. Newspaper is free, monthly and offers a calendar, interviews, a forum for artists, photography, etc. A $10 year contribution buys membership and subscription. Distributed free at local clubs, BASS outlets and City Celebration functions.*

***CLASSIFIED FLEA MARKET, PO Box 2078, Oakland 94604, 415-530-3870.*** *Classified and display ads for performances, rentals, body work, etc.*

***COMMON GROUND, 1300 Sanchez St., SF 94131,*** *$1 to be on mailing list. New Age groups listed, as well as individuals offering alternative healing methods, creative dance, nutrition, yoga etc. Published quarterly; available free at many health food stores, metaphysical shops and the like.*

Resources

# *Media*
# *Print/Local*

***DIRECTORY OF PHONE NUMBERS FOR PRESS, RADIO, TV. Pacific Telephone News Bureau, Room 712B, 370 Third St., SF, 94107.*** *Yearly pamphlet.*

***DAILY CALIFORNIAN, 2490 Channing Way, Suite 300, Berkeley 94704.*** *Calendar items must be submitted by Wednesday noon for Fridays' entertainment list.*

***DANCE MAGAZINE, Carol Egan, 1601 Milvia St., Berkeley 94704.***

***DANCE NEWS, 1120 Broderick St., SF 94115.*** *Renee Renouf.*

***EXPRESS, PO Box 32 3198, Berkeley 94703, 415-653-7332.*** *John Raeside, editor. Weekly, free.*

***GROUNDSWELL NEWS, PO Box 916, San Jose 95113.*** *Lists local disco spots, alternative health information. Monthly.*

***KICKS, Dance around the Bay, 610A Cole St., SF 94117, 415-661-KICK.*** *Monthly, free.*

***MARIN SCOPE, Harbor Dr., Sausalito 94965, 415-332-3778.*** *Robert Stephens, dance critic/writer. In depth interviews and opinions on local and guest artists, companies.*

***MEDIA ALLIANCE, Bldg. 314, Fort Mason, Laguna and Marina, SF 94123, 415-441-2557.***

***NETWORKS Newsletter, Bay Area Video Collection, 2940 16th St., Room 200, SF 94103, 415-861-3283.***

***PACIFIC SUN, 21 Corte Madera, Mill Valley 94941, 415-383-4500.*** *Stephanie von Buchau, dance critic.*

Resources

## Media
## Print/Local

***PENINSULA MAGAZINE, 260 Sheridan Ave., Suite B1, Palo Alto 94306, 415-327-6666.***

***PERFORMING ARTS MAGAZINE, 651 Brannan St., SF 94107, 415-781-8931.*** *J. Friedman.*

***PERFORMING ARTS FORUM, Suite 605, 515 John Muir Dr., SF 94132, 415-584-6333.***

***SAN FRANCISCO BAY GUARDIAN, 2700 19th St., SF 94110, 415-824-7660.*** *Calendar lists, dance highlights, compilations, etc. Janice Ross, dance critic.*

***SAN FRANCISCO CHRONICLE, 925 Mission St., SF 94103, 415-777-1111.*** *People, entertainment sections. Interviews, press releases. Sunday pink section listings, reviews.*

***SAN FRANCISCO EXAMINER, 110 Fifth St., SF 94103, 415-777-2424.*** *Daily and Sunday Scene sections (interviews, press releases); Calendar of events sections; arts department (reviews, press releases), under Scene Section; California Living Sunday Magazine (articles, interviews.)*

***SAN FRANCISCO MAGAZINE, 631 Howard St., SF 94105.*** *Stephanie von Buchau, dance critic.*

***THE SENTINEL, 522 Hayes St., SF 94102, 415-864-2178.*** *Steve Steinberg, dance writer/critic. In dept reviews of local and guest dance artists and companies.*

***UNIVERSITY OF CALIFORNIA, BERKELEY, Calendar, Office of Public Information, 101 Sproul Hall, Berkeley 94720, 415-642-3734.*** *Reports activities open to campus and public. Must be received before noon Friday for publication following Friday.*

# Resources

## Media
## Print/National

***THE WORKING ARTS, Bay Area Lawyers for the Arts, Fort Mason Center, Bldg. 312, SF 94132, 415-775-7200.*** *Bi-monthly: articles on use of contracts, etc.*

***ACUCAA (ASSOCIATON OF COLLEGE, UNIVERSITY AND COMMUNITY ARTS ADMINISTRATORS) Newsletter, P.O. Box 2137, Madison, WI 53701.***

***AMERICAN DANCE GUILD BOOK CLUB, P.O. Box 109, Princeton, NJ 08540.*** *Free brochures.*

***ARTS MANAGEMENT, 408 West 57th St., NYC 10019.*** *Alvin Reiss, editor. Financial, management, case studies, reviews, recent publications in the field. $10/yr. for five issues.*

***THE ARTS REPORTING SERVICE, 9214 Three Oaks Dr., Silver Spring, MD 20901.*** *Charles C. Mark, publisher. Hotline for funding for the arts, labor relations, publicity, legislation, conferences, arts education, and much more. $30/yr. for 24 issues.*

***BALLET NEWS, The Metropolitan Opera Guild, Inc., 1865 Broadway, NY 10023, 212-582-7500.*** *$18/yr. subscription.*

***BUSINESS COMMITTEE FOR THE ARTS (BCA) Newsletter.*** *See GROUPS/SPONSORS.*

***CALIFORNIA DANCE DIRECTORY, California Association of Dance Companies, 910 Second St., Sacramento 95814, 916-444-9579.***

***COMMITTEE ON RESEARCH IN DANCE (CORD) newsletter.*** *See GROUPS/SPONSORS.*

***COMMUNITY ARTS AGENCIES HANDBOOK AND GUIDE, American Council for the Arts, 570 Seventh Ave., NYC 10018.*** *$12.*

# Resources

## *Media*
## *Print/National*

***COMPOSERS AND CHOREOGRAPHERS THEATER REVIEW, 25 West 19th ST., NYC 10011.*** *Quarterly; annual, $10.*

***DANCE AND DANCERS, Hanson Books, Ltd., Artillery Mansions, 75 Victoria Station, London SW1, England.*** *Monthly; $14.60/yr. Editor, Peter Williams.*

***DANCE CHRONICLE, Marcel Dekker, Inc., NYC 10016.*** *Semi-annual; $7.50 annual rate.*

***DANCE DIMENSIONS, Wisconsin Dance Council, Marquette University, Dept. of Philosophy, 134 Coughln Hall, Milwaukee, WI 53233.*** *Quarterly; annual, $5.*

***DANCE HERALD, P.O. Box 686, Ansonia Station, NYC 10023.*** *$3/yr.*

***DANCE LIFE, Box 1236 Stuyvesant Station, NYC 10009.*** *David Lindner, publisher and editor. Published three times a year/$5.*

***DANCE MAGAZINE, 10 Columbus Circle, NYC 10019.*** *Danad Publishing Co., Inc., William Como, editor. Reviews, calendars, notes, classified ads, articles on dance injuries, diets, anatomy, etc. Monthly; $15/yr.*

***DANCE MAGAZINE COLLEGE GUIDE; address above.*** *Degree programs, summer programs, performance opportunities, etc.*

***DANCE MOTION PRESS, 22 W. 77th St., NYC 10024.***

***DANCE NEWS, 119 W. 57th St., NYC 10019.*** *Helen Atlas, editor. Monthly except July and August; $7/yr.*

Resources

## *Media Print/National*

***DANCE PERSPECTIVES, 270 Madison Ave., NYC 10016.*** *Marcel Dekker, Inc., publishers. Selma Jeanne Cohen, editor. $12.50/yr., student and professional rate.*

***DANCE SCOPE, American Dance Guild, publishers, Suite 828, 152 West 42nd St., NYC 10036.***

***DANCE THEATER WORKSHOP (DTW) newsletter.*** *See GROUPS/SPONSORS.*

***DECADE, 11 Beacon St., Boston, MA 02108.*** *New national arts magazine dedicated to thought-provoking articles about the fine and performing arts. About 10 articles per issue, illustrated with photographs and art reproductions. Steven G. Barkus, editor and founder.*

***FOOTNOTES, F. Randolph Associates, Inc., 1300 Arch St., Philadelphia, PA 19107, 800-621-8318.*** *Catalog of ballet and theater trips, supplies, educational opportunities, etc.*

***NEW PERFORMANCE, Oberlin Dance Collective quarterly.*** *See MODERN, SF.*

***THE OFFICIAL MUSEUM DIRECTORY, American Association of Museums, 2233 Wisconsin Ave. NW, Washington DC 20007.*** *Biennial publication; $35. For bookings.*

***PERFORMING ARTS JOURNAL, P.O. Box 858, Peter Stuyvesant Station, NYC 10019.*** *Published three times a year; $8.*

***PERFORMING ARTS REVIEW, LAW-ARTS Publishers, Inc., 453 Greenwich St., NYC 10013, 212-925-4978.***

# Resources

## *Media*
## *Print/National*

***PRESERVING THE MOVING IMAGE, Corporation for Public Broadcasting, 888 16th St. NW, Washington DC 20006.*** *Ralph N. Sargent. $3.95.*

***STUDENT ACTIVITIES PROGRAMMING, National Entertainment Conference, P.O. Box 11489, Capitol Station, Columbia, SC 92911.*** *Booking information.*

***VARIETY, 1654 W. 46th St., NYC 10036.*** *Weekly; $35/yr.*

***VILITIS, P.O. Box 1226, Denver, CO.*** *Folk dance. Bi-monthly; $7/yr.*

***THE WASHINGTON INTERNATIONAL ARTS LETTER, P.O. Box 9005, Washington, DC 20003, 1321 Fourth St. SW, Washington, DC 20024.*** *Covers funding sources, developments in the arts, recent publications, etc. $32/yr.*

Resources

# Media Radio/TV

***KALW-FM (91.7), 2905 21st, SF, 415-648-1177.*** *"Meet the San Francisco Ballet," a program of interviews with company members. Host, Alan Farley; Fridays 10 p.m. and Sundays 4 p.m.*

***KCBS (740 AM), 1 Embarcadero Center, SF, 415-982-7000.*** *Throughout the season, members of SFB and artists associated with the ballet are featured on the station's "On Stage" program. Host, Steve Baffrey.*

***KKHI AM (1500), Hotel St. Francis, SF, 415-986-2151.*** *Interviews.*

***KPFA-FM (94.1), 2207 Shattuck Ave., Berkeley, 415-846-6767.*** *Interviews, etc. Commentator on the arts, Irene Oppenheim.*

***KQED-FM (88.5), 500 Eighth St., SF 415-864-2051.*** *News and interviews pertaining to SFB can be heard on "Matters Musical," Tuesdays and Fridays at 8:45 a.m. and 12:15 p.m. Host, Alan Ulrich.*

***KUSF-FM (90.3), 2130 Fulton St., SF 94117, 415-666-6206.*** *USF radio station. Weekly calendar of events, dance community interviews.*

***CABLE TV, Viacom, Channel 8, 1171 Potrero, SF.*** *$3/hr to show video on TV. 415-285-0776.*

***KGO-TV, 277 Golden Gate Ave., SF, 415-863-0077.*** *"Perspectives."*

***KPIX-TV, The Evening Show and Community Billboard, 2655 Van Ness Ave., SF, 415-776-5100.***

***KQED-TV Open Studio, 1011 Bryant St., SF, 415-864-2000.***

# Music Classes

*Music theory, musical comedy, music theater: music in general is the essence of much of the feeling dancers and dance lovers have for the art. Studios which are offering music-related studies to round out the expression of self, are slowly increasing in numbers. This section is divided into three parts: classes; reference sources; and music groups that have dance.*

***CONTRA COSTA COUNTY:***

**CONTRA COSTA ACADEMY.** *See BALLET, CCC. Musical comedy.*

**DANSE BOUTIQUE.** *See BALLET, CCC. Music education.*

***EAST BAY:***

***JANE BROWN FOUNDATION FOR THE DANCE AND RELATED ARTS.*** *See OTHER DANCES/Creative. Music theory.*

***EAST BAY CENTER FOR THE PERFORMING ARTS.*** *See BALLET, EB. Music education.*

***MARIN:***

***BALLET THEATRE WEST.*** *See BALLET, Marin. Music theater.*

**CONSERVATORY OF BALLET.** *See BALLET, Marin. Musical comedy.*

***DANCE ARTS OF MARIN.*** *See BALLET, Marin. Music theater.*

**BELROSE ACADEMY.** *See BALLET, Marin. Musical comedy.*

*PENINSULA:*

***DANCE ARTS CENTER AT MARLIN COVE.*** *See BALLET, Peninsula. Voice.*

*SAN FRANCISCO:*

***OBERLIN DANCE COLLECTIVE.*** *See MODERN, SF.*

***PURE WINE DANCE COMPANY.*** *See OTHER DANCES/Creative.*

***UNIVERSITY OF SAN FRANCISCO.*** *See EDUCATION.*

*SAN JOSE:*

***MARIE STINNETT.*** *See JAZZ, SJ. Musical comedy.*

# Resources

## *Music References*

***ALGORITHM STUDIO, SF, 415-658-5021.*** *Compose music for and/or with dancers.*

***AMERICAN MUSIC CENTER, 250 W. 57th St., NYC 10019, 212-247-3121.*** *Tony Greenberg, executive director. Official U.S. center for music. Membership allows use of information files, library of sources by U.S. composers, bi-monthly newsletter. Group publishes the Contemporary Music Performance Directory, which lists spaces and sponsoring organizations for music performance around the country.*

***AMERICAN SOCIETY OF COMPOSERS, AUTHORS AND PUBLISHERS, One Lincoln Plaza, NYC 10023, 212-595-3050.*** *Information on royalties; index department.*

***BERKELEY SCOTTISH PLAYERS, 2312 Parker St., Berkeley 94704.*** *Six to nine members play for dance events; two albums on the market. Barbara Bowsma and Robert McOwen.* *See also ROYAL SCOTTISH COUNTRY DANCE SOCIETY, FOLK/-NORTHERN EUROPE.*

***BROADCAST MUSICIANS, INC., 40 West 57th St., NYC 10019, 212-586-2000.*** *Concert music administration; royalties information.*

***CENTER FOR WORLD MUSIC, Bldg. 312, Fort Mason, Laguna and Marina, SF 94123, 415-848-8989.*** *Special events include Indonesian, Flamenco dance and music. Also at Fort Mason is the SF Folk Music Center and Marina Music Hall. Co-sponsors summer workshops at SFSU.*

# Resources

## *Music References*

***COMPOSERS AND CHOREOGRAPHERS THEATRE, 25 West 19th St., NYC 10011.*** *Laura Foreman, director. Membership service organization for dance and music. Advice and training in promotion, publicity, internal management, fund raising, production, etc. Tape library of contemporary music, job listings, video equipment, mailing lists and reservation service available to members.*

***MUSIC JOURNAL ARTISTS DIRECTORY, 370 Lexington Ave., NYC 10017, 212-889-9350.*** *Lee Clark Newmeier, editor.*

***MUSICAL AMERICA: International Directory of the Performing Arts. ABC Leisure Magazine, publishers, 130 E. 59th St., NYC 10022, 212-587-7777.*** *George Dickey, rates and information.*

***TERPISCHORE RECORDS, P.O. Box 9025, Berkeley 94709.*** *Records for ballet study. Massine: Movements and Variations; Richard Gibson; Leon Danielian.*

***LARK IN THE MORNING, 5080 Little Lake St., Mendocino 95460, 707-937-5824.*** *Folk instruments—medieval, French, Celtic, Balkan, African, Russian. Catalog $2.*

***THE NEW YORK PUBLIC LIBRARY AT LINCOLN CENTER, 111 Amsterdam Ave., NYC 10023, 212-799-2200.*** *General Library of the Performing Arts, music section, has an extensive record collection that can be checked out. The Music Collection of the Research Library of the Performing Arts (same building) has records, tapes and scores that can be studied.*

***PACIFIC DANCE THEATRE LIBRARY, 1929 Irving St., SF 94112, 415-731-4454.*** *Ballet orchestrations for sale or rent.*

*As well, most major universities in the Bay Area have extensive sheet music and record collections available for study. The music library at UC Berkeley is one.*

# Music Groups

*Orchestras are beginning to feel more comfortable including dance soloists, pas de deux, etc. in a concert. Some sponsor one company per season on the subscription lists, or commission a dance company to create works premiered under their auspices.*

***DIABLO SYMPHONY ORCHESTRA.*** *See CONTRA COSTA BALLET CENTER, BALLET, CCC.*

***MARIN SYMPHONY, P.O. Box 127, San Rafael 94902, 415-456-0880.***

***OAKLAND SYMPHONY ORCHESTRA, Paramount Theater of the Arts, 2025 Broadway, Oakland 94612, 415-444-3531.***

***MUSIC THEATER.*** *See FORT MASON, GROUPS. Music Theater Association, c/o Robert Hall, 5 Westland Rd., Hamden, CT 06517.*

***SAN FRANCISCO CHILDREN'S OPERA ASSOCIATION.*** *P.O. Box 18143, SF 94118; studio at 245 10th Ave., SF, 415-386-9622.*

***SAN FRANCISCO OPERA ASSOCIATION, War Memorial Opera House, SF 94102, 415-861-4008.*** *Spring and fall opera season auditions. Number of operas with dancers varies, as does number of dancers used in each opera. All must be AGMA members, though not in order to audition. Auditions are announced through the press, AGMA hotline (433-6266), dance studios, etc. Dancers paid union scale, in spring they are paid hourly for rehearsal time and per performance; in fall, a core is retained and paid a weekly salary. Shoes are provided in the fall.*

***SAN JOSE SYMPHONY, 170 Park Center Plaza, SJ 95113, 408-287-7383.***

***SPRING OPERA THEATER. Lenore Naxon, coordinator; Opera House, 415-431-1463.***

## *Music Groups*

***SAN FRANCISCO SYMPHONY, Room 107, War Memorial Veterans Building, SF 94102, 415-861-6240.***

***WESTERN OPERA THEATER, Opera House, 415-861-4074.***

## *Notation*

*Some think the origin of movement notation was Egyptian hieroglyphics. Whatever the truth, the goal of modern notation has been a kind of shorthand adaptable to all forms of dance. Notation is also a valuable aid in seeing a clearer perspective of space, movement and the physiological source of movements.*

*Labanotation, or kinetographie, is not shorthand but pictures of the body and its positions in space. With this script any ballet can be analyzed and reconstructed, step by step.*

*Margaret Mom's system is written with abstract symbols based on movement around an imaginary axis (<u>1928 Notation of Movement</u>).*

*The Benesh dance notation system was copyrighted in 1955, and since 1956 has been included in London's Royal Academy of Dancing teacher's training course. It is also called choreology and is a system of shorthand. (<u>An Introduction to Benesh Dance Notation System</u>, A & C Black, Publishers, London, 1956.)*

*Two other systems are effort/shape, and Sutton Movement Shorthand.*

***BENESH INSTITUTE OF CHOREOLOGY, LTD., 4 Margravine Gardens, Barons Court, London W6 8PH, England 01-741-0511.***

***DANCE NOTATION BUREAU, 19 Union Square West, NYC 10003, 212-989-5535.*** *Herbert Kummell, executive director. Total training in Labanotation, Benesh.*

# Resources

## *Notation*
## *Reference/Libraries*

***DOMINICAN COLLEGE.*** *See EDUCATION.*

***DOROTHY GROVER, 17 Ascot Court, Oakland 94611.*** *Certified Labanotation teacher.*

***INSTITUTE OF MOVEMENT STUDIES, Julia Morgan Center for the Arts (formerly Epic West), 2640 College Ave., Berkeley 94704, 415-524-7798 or 707-763-4537.*** *Intensive Effort-Shape/Space Harmony workshops based on principles of human movement developed by Rudolf Laban. Instructors: Ellen Cohen, Carla Guggenheim, Betsy Kagan, Suzanne Manning.*

***BETSY KAGAN.*** *See MODERN, EB. Certified reconstructor and teacher of Labanotation.*

***KAHNOTATION.*** *See MASON/KAHN STUDIOS, TAP, SF.*

***LABANOTATION INSTITUTE OF MOVEMENT STUDIES, 151 W. 19th St., NYC 10011.*** *Irmgard Bartenieff, founder.*

***MILLS COLLEGE, Dept. of Dance, Oakland 94613.*** *(See EDUCATION.) Mary Ann Kinkead, certified Labanotation teacher, reconstructor, kinetographer and teacher of kinetography. President, International Council of Kinetography and Labanotation.*

***THE MOVEMENT SHORTHAND SOCIETY (Sutton Movement Shorthand), P.O. Box 4949, Irvine 92716, 714-644-8342.***

## *Reference/Libraries*

*For more listings see Yellow Pages under Libraries; White Pages under county or city offices, Libraries, Public. Local libraries often lend or rent dance films for a small fee. Many universities have active film rental services.*

# Resources

## *Reference / Libraries*

***ARCHIVES FOR THE PERFORMING ARTS, 3150 Sacramento St., SF 94115, 415-922-6750.*** *Russell Hartley, director. A public resource of inestimable value, the Archives is an exhibition museum of dance and other memorabilia in photographs, documents, costumes, books, paintings, clippings. The emphasis is on a century of local theatrical history. Hartley himself began the study of ballet at age 17, and spent four years with SFB in the 1940's. He has a career as set and costume designer for more than 30 ballets with SFB and NYCB. The paintings he did "in the wings" during those years are part of the Archives' collection.*

***AUDIOVISUAL ARCHIVES, Div. of the National Archives and Records Service, Washington DC 20408, 202-655-4000.***

***DANCE ARCHIVES, Harvard College Theater Collection, Houghton Library, Cambridge, MA 02138, 617-495-2445.*** *Dance with 18th and 19th century specialization.*

***LESLIE GETZ, 239 El Camino Real, Menlo Park 94025.*** *Private library (appointment only) of 1,100 books, 2,500 periodicals, 250 programs in several languages; 20th century and earlier.*

***LAWTON HARN'S MEMORIAL LIBRARY OF FOLK DANCE MATERIALS, University of the Pacific, Stockton 95211.*** *8,000 folk dance records; extensive cross reference card file.*

***THE LIBRARY OF THE PERFORMING ARTS, Dance Collection, Lincoln Center, 111 Amsterdam Ave., NYC 10023, 212-799-2200.*** *Records, tapes, scores, etc. to study. Appointments only. Special collections include Denishawn, Nijinsky, Duncan.*

***L.A. PUBLIC LIBRARY, 630 West 15th St., LA 90015, 213-626-7461.***

***PACIFIC DANCE THEATER LIBRARY, 1929 Irving St., SF 94122.*** *Orchestrations of ballet classics and original music; purchase or rental.*

# Resources

## Technical

For more information, call the S.F. Bay Area Dance Coalition for their Technical Resources list (673-8172). Check the Yellow Pages under Sound System and Equipment Renting, Lighting Systems and Equipment, Theater Supplies, Dance Supplies, Costume Designers. See also DANCE MAGAZINE's annual for listings and ads (MEDIA, NATIONAL).

**LEONARD S. AUERBACH & ASSOCIATES, 1005 Sansome St., SF 94111, 415-392-7528.** Theater planning and systems lighting design.

**BELROSE THEATRICAL HOUSE.** See SUPPLIES, Marin. Technical referrals.

**DONALD CATE, 734 Arkansas St., SF 94107, 415-826-2998.** United Scenic Artists member; costumes, lighting, scenic.

**COLLEGE OF ALAMEDA, Fashion Arts Department.** See EDUCATION.

**EVERYBODY'S.** Classes in lighting design by Bob Merrill. See MODERN, EB.

**RON HODGE, 543 Belvedere, SF 94117.** Costumes.

**KELVIN QUALITY SOUND, 415-948-2519.** Technician and audio equipment available anywhere in Bay Area.

**STUART KOPPLE, P.O. Box 99618, SF 94109, 415-355-7322.** Technical services; lighting design, sound engineering, technical direction, consultation.

**NORVID JENKINS ROSS, UC Santa Cruz Theatre Arts Dept., Santa Cruz 95064, 408-429-2974.** United Scenic Artists member; costumes, lighting, design.

# Resources

## *Technical*

***SIMON'S DIRECTORY OF THEATRICAL MATERIALS, SERVICES AND INFORMATION, Package Publicity Services, Inc., 1564 Broadway, NYC 10036.*** *Bernard Simon, editor. $8.95. Extensive commercial directory telling where to buy or rent an array of production and promotion services and equipment.*

***DEBORA STOLL, 415-641-8988.*** *Consultant in production, design, lighting, equipment.*

***JOHN SULLIVAN, 415-863-7580 (Margaret Jenkins Studio, SF).*** *Lighting instructor.*

***TECHNICAL ASSISTANCE GROUP, 463 West Street, NYC, 10014, 212-691-3500.*** *Range of technical and management help to dance companies and producing groups nationwide.*

***U.S. INSTITUTE FOR THEATRE TECHNOLOGY, 1501 Broadway, Room 1408, NYC 10036, 212-354-5360.***

***VAARKAART, design and production services, SF, 415-552-3555.***

## Theater

***ACADEMY OF DANCE ARTS.*** *See BALLET, SJ. Production classes.*

***ACADEMY OF SPEECH AND DANCE.*** *See BALLET, SJ. Drama class.*

***ALMADEN SCHOOL.*** *See BALLET, SJ. Theater arts classes.*

***ANABEL'S.*** *See BALLET, SJ. Theater arts classes.*

***BALLET THEATRE WEST.*** *See BALLET, Marin. Drama classes.*

***BELROSE STUDIO.*** *See BALLET, Marin. Theater arts classes.*

***BEA BLUM'S.*** *See TAP, Marin.*

***CIRCUS A LA MODE, 2547 Eighth St., Berkeley 94710.*** *Teaching, performing circus acts.*

***CONSERVATORY OF BALLET.*** *See BALLET, Marin. Creative arts.*

***JOYA CORY.*** *See OTHER DANCES/Creative. Physical theater.*

***DANCE ARTS OF MARIN.*** *See BALLET, Marin. Theatrical dance.*

***DANCE ARTS/MARLIN COVE.*** *See BALLET, Peninsula. Drama classes.*

***EVERYBODY'S.*** *See MODERN, EB.*

***FOOTLOOSE.*** *See MODERN, SF.*

***LANEY COLLEGE.*** *See EDUCATION.*

## *Theater*

***MENLO PARK ACADEMY.*** *See BALLET, Peninsula. Stage dancing.*

***OAKLAND VOLUNTEER BUREAU FOR ARTISTS, 415-273-3831.*** *Dancers, stage hands, etc. for productions. No experience needed. No pay.*

***PERFORMING ARTS WORKSHOP.*** *See MODERN, SF.*

***PICKLE FAMILY CIRCUS Workshop, 400 Missouri, SF 94107, 415-826-0747.*** *Circus-related acrobatics, gymnastics and tumbling for dancers. $6/class; $52/10 classes.*

***PURE WINE DANCE COMPANY.*** *See OTHER DANCES/Creative.*

***BARI ROLFE, 434 66th St., Oakland 94609, 415-658-2482.*** *Teaching Lecoq-based techniques in mime, mask, movement for actors and dancers. Available for workshops with dance companies in comedia, clown, body language, pantomime blanche.*

***SAN FRANCISCO CHILDREN'S OPERA, P.O. Box 18143, SF 94118; studio at 245 10th Ave., SF, 94118, 415-386-9622.***

***SHAWL-ANDERSON.*** *See BALLET, EB. Mime classes with Richard Frey.*

***SONOMA STATE COLLEGE.*** *See EDUCATION.*

***JAN TANGEN, 415-457-9591.*** *The art of performance; to give performers a chance to dissolve the barriers to self-expression.*

***THE DANCE CLUB.*** *See BALLROOM, SJ. Theater arts classes.*

## Ticket Offices

***ACT Box Office, 450 Geary Blvd., SF 94102, 415-673-6440.***

***BASS, 415-835-4342; San Jose area, 408-297-7552.*** *Credit card charges by telephone OK.*

***BASS TICKET SERVICE, T-E-L-E-T-I-X, 360 22nd, Oakland, 415-835-3849.***

***BASS, 912 Town and Country Village, San Jose, 408-246-1160.***

***BERKELEY COMMUNITY THEATER Box Office, Grove at Allston Way, 415-845-2308.*** *Has featured Alonso's National Ballet of Cuba, London Royal Ballet, among others.*

***BULLOCKS-BASS TICKETS, 285 Winston Dr., SF 94132, 415-665-2441.***

***CAPWELL'S.***

***CHABOT COLLEGE AUDITORIUM, 1555 Hesperian Blvd., Hayward, 94541, 415-786-6800.***

***CIVIC ARTS THEATRE TICKET OFFICE, 1641 Locust, Walnut Creek 94956, 415-939-0355.***

***COLLEGE OF MARIN FINE ARTS THEATER BOX OFFICE, Kentfield, 418-485-9385.***

***COMMITTEE FOR ARTS AND LECTURES (CAL) BOX OFFICES: UC Berkeley, 101 Zellerbach Hall, 415-642-9988; UC Davis; UC San Francisco (Millberry Union Central Desk Box Office); UC Santa Cruz; The Book Mark, Fremont; The Music Tree, Gilroy, The Music Tree, Morgan Hill.***

*CAL box offices are open for ticket sales one hour before scheduled performing times. Unpaid reservations held three* *working days or until 5:30 p.m. of working day before performance. Special student rates for most events; UC student rush tickets ($2) available just before curtain time if not sold out. Parking information available.*

***COMMUNITY BOX OFFICE, 1305 Middlefield Rd., Palo Alto 94301, 415-329-2623.***

***DOWNTOWN CENTER BOX OFFICE, 325 Mason St., SF 94102, 415-775-2021.***

***EEYORE BOOKS, Cotati, 707-795-8301.***

***EMPORIUM/CAPWELL'S.***

***FINE ARTS BOX OFFICE, 141 Kearny, SF 94108, 415-421-1000.*** *Tickets for all major dance events; visiting companies.*

***FLINT CENTER BOX OFFICE, Cupertino 95014,408-257-9555.***

***HINK'S OF BERKELEY, Shattuck and Kittredge, Berkeley, 415-845-1100.***

***HOTEL ST. FRANCIS THEATRE TICKET AGENCY, Powell at Geary, SF, 415-362-2324, 397-7000.***

***MacARTHUR-BROADWAY BOX OFFICE, Oakland 94163, 415-654-8255.***

***MACY'S.***

***MARIN CENTER BOX OFFICE, Civic Center Dr., San Rafael, 415-472-3500.***

***MENDOCINO COLLEGE, Box 3000, Ukiah 94582.***

## *Ticket Offices*

*MILLS COLLEGE BOX OFFICE, Seminary at MacArthur Blvd., Oakland, 415-654-4222.*

*MUNTER MUSIC CO., 501 Georgia, Vallejo, 415-643-5427.*

*MUSIC COOP, Petaluma, 707-823-7664.*

*PENINSULA BOX OFFICE, Village Corner Shopping Center, Los Altos, 415-941-3100.*

*PEOPLE'S MUSIC, Sebastopol, 707-823-7664.*

*SAN FRANCISCO STATE UNIVERSITY BOX OFFICE, 415-585-7174.*

*SAN FRANCISCO SYMPHONY ASSN. BOX OFFICE, War Memorial Opera House, SF 94102; special events, 415-431-5400 (Joffrey, etc.).*

*SAN FRANCISCO TICKET CENTER, 724 Pine St., SF 94108, 415-397-1612.*

*SAN JOSE BOX OFFICE, 912 Town and Country Village, San Jose 95128, 408-246-1160.*

*SANTA CRUZ BOX OFFICE, 408-427-1984.*

*STANROY'S MUSIC, Santa Rosa, 707-545-4827.*

*NELL THRAMS TICKET AGENCY, 2131 Broadway, Oakland 94512, 415-444-8575.* Opera, symphony, theater, Circle Star Theater.

*TICKETRON, Inc., 427 Merchant St., SF 94111, 415-788-2828.*

*TRESIDDER BOX OFFICE, Stanford University, Stanford 94305, 415-497-4317.*

# *Resources*

## *Ticket Offices Video/Film*

***UNION STREET BOX OFFICE, 1793 Union St., SF 94123, 415-474-6660.***

***UC SANTA CLARA, Mayer Theatre Box Office, 95064, 408-429-2826.***

***WILLOWS THEATER, Concord, 415-798-6525.***

## *Video/Film*

***AMERICAN DANCE VIDEO, 1330 Campus Dr., Berkeley 94708, 415-841-1548.*** *Dance filmmakers.*

***AMERICAN FILM INSTITUTE, JFK Center for the Performing Arts, Washington DC 20566.*** *"Access," sources of equipment to film or tape your own dance.*

***AUDIO-VISUAL SOURCE DIRECTORY, Motion Picture Enterprises, Tarrytown, NJ.***

***BALLET RESEARCH ASSOCIATION, 145 Upper St., London N1 1QY, England.*** *Leningrad-Kirov training film.*

***BAY AREA VIDEO COALITION, 2940 16th St., Room 200, SF 94103, 415-861-3282.***

***CANYON CINEMA COOP, Suite 338, 2325 Third St., SF 94107, 415-626-2255.*** *For sale or rental.*

***CORPORATION FOR PUBLIC BROADCASTING, 1111 16th St. NW, Washington DC 20036, 202-293-6160.***

***DANCE FILM ARCHIVE, University of Rochester, Rochester, NY 14627.*** *John Mueller.*

# Resources

## *Video/Film*

***DANCE FILM DIRECTORY (ballet and modern), Princeton Book Co., 1978.***

***DANCE FILMS ASSOCIATION, Inc., Room 2201, 250 W. 57th St., NYC 10019, 212-586-2142.*** *Non-profit, tax-exempt educational organization promoting the use of audio-visual material. Services available in the U.S.; records of dance for teaching aids and dance appreciation. 16mm and video of dancers, choreographers, technique, therapy; catalogue of films; newsletter.*

***DANCE VIDEO WORKSHOPS, Skip Sweeney, 415-648-9094.***

***DEMystivision, 79 Langton St., SF 94103, 415-391-6967.***

***EXTENSION MEDIA CENTER, UC Berkeley, CA 94720, 415-642-4111.***

***FILM WRIGHT, Diamond Heights, Box 31441, SF 94131.*** *Sale or rental. Films include Anna Halprin, Merce Cunningham.*

***FILMMAKERS LIBRARY, 290 West End Ave., NYC 10023, 212-877-4486.***

***FRANCISCAN FILMS, Box 6116, SF 94101, 415-388-9372.***

***MATIJA GUBEC.*** *See FOLK/RUSSIAN. Color, one hour video cassette of group in live performance; for promotion, education.*

***HISTORICAL FILMS, Box 46505, Hollywood 90046, 213-463-7111.*** *Dance films dating from 1894.*

***IVY FILM, 165 West 46th St., NYC 10036, 212-765-3940.*** *Includes Violette Verdy's "Ballerina," Nureyev and Fonteyn pas de deux.*

***RUTH C. LERT, 1 San Antonio Place, SF 94133, 415-397-6480.*** *Modern dance, Bauhaus films. Lecture/demonstrations.*

***GWEN LEWIS.*** *See FOLK/AFRO. Videotapes available.*

***DEBORAH MANGUM, 1349 47th Ave., SF 94122, 415-661-0256.*** *Video dance consultant; independent director, documentarian.*

***NIELS MELO, Telepros, P.O. Box 1116, Belmont 94002, 415-595-1169.*** *Film and video.*

***NATIONAL ASSOCIATION OF EDUCATIONAL BROADCASTERS, 1346 Connecticut Ave. NW, Washington DC 20036, 202-785-1100.***

***NATIONAL AUDIO-VISUAL CENTER, U.S.I.A. Films, National Archives and Records Service, Washington DC 20409.*** *Collection of more than 8,000 films that can be rented or bought. Referrals to other agencies that loan films.*

***ORIGINAL FACE VIDEO, 3580 21st St., SF 94114, 415-824-2254.*** *Joanna Luther and Joseph Tieger. Video for documentation and self-expression. Full color video production, editing and complete post production services by arrangement. For classes, rehearsals, performances, documentation, self-teaching. Gift certificates available.*

***SAN FRANCISCO DANCERS ACTION FORUM.*** *See GROUPS/-SPONSORS.*

***TEMPO FILMS, #2 Ninth Ave., San Mateo 94401, 415-348-8114.*** *Japanese coal mining dance, Japanese folk dance.*

***TRICONTINENTAL FILM CENTER, P.O. Box 443, Berkeley 94704.*** *Alicia Alonso on film.*

***UC EXTENSION MEDIA CENTER, Berkeley 94720, 415-642-0460.*** *Extensive dance film collection.*

# Resources

## *Video/Film*

***VIDEO FREE AMERICA, 442 Shotwell St., SF 94110, 415-648-0077.***

***#10 Olive St., Mill Valley, 415-388-5146.*** *Dance Film Festival headquarters.*

***UC THEATRE, 2036 University Ave., at Shattuck, Berkeley 94704, 415-843-6267.*** *Continuing films on Baryshnikov, Kirov, Fonteyn and Nureyev.*

# Supplies

*This chapter is divided into two sections: nationwide name distributors with local outlets carrying dance supplies, and smaller stores that primarily sell dancewear, music, books, etc.*

# Supplies

## National

**ALBERT'S HOSIERY AND DANCE WEAR (Danskin, Selva pointe shoes; discounts for teachers and dance students):** *530 Southland Mall, Hayward, 415-735-8166; 867 Market St., SF, 415-421-2135; 377 Sun Valley Mall, Concord, 415-825-1322; 110 Serramonte Center, Daly City, 415-994-0110; 110 Tanforan Shopping Center, Daly City/Colma, 415-873-6688; 7 Stockton, SF, 415-362-7788; 307 Eastridge Center, San Jose, 408-274-2228.*

**CAPEZIO DISTRIBUTORS (leotards, tights, shoes, etc.):** *Capezio Dance Theatre Shop, 5914 College Ave., Oakland 94618, 415-658-8198; Capezio of SF, 126 Post St., 415-421-5657; Encore Theatrical Supply Co., 20662 Redwood Rd., Castro Valley, 415-537-5647; Martin Dance Supply Co., 7395 Village Parkway, Dublin, 415-828-8037; Martin Theatrical Supply, 1370 Locust, Walnut Creek, 415-934-8037; Vallco Fashion Park, Cupertino, 408-996-9283; 467 Saratoga Ave., San Jose, 408-296-3424 (24 hour mail orders); 309 South B, San Mateo, 415-344-9283 (mail order).*

**DANSKIN:** *141 Sutter St., San Francisco, 415-986-6912; 362 Kearny, SF, 415-397-9120; 71 Stonestown Mall, 415-681-3295; also Encore, Castro Valley; Martin, Dublin and Walnut Creek.*

**PARKLANE HOISERY STORES (Danskin leotards, tights, etc.):** *151 Eastmont Mall, Oakland, 415-569-4382; 58 Hillsdale Mall, San Mateo, 415-574-1471; 7120 Northgate Mall, San Rafael, 415-479-3699; Mayfield Ave., Mountain View, 415-968-8779; 29 Almaden Fashion Plaza, San Jose, 408-264-9411; 2 Westgate Shopping Center, San Jose, 408-378-1913; 436 N. Santa Cruz Ave., Los Gatos, 408-354-8848.*

# Supplies

## Contra Costa County

***CHILDREN'S SHOE BOAT, 323 Sun Valley Mall, Concord, 415-687-9910.*** *Capezio.*

***HALLOWELLS SHOE CORRAL, Ygnacio Valley Rd. at Oak Grove Rd., Walnut Creek 94598, 415-939-7664.*** *Capezio.*

***MARTIN DANCE SUPPLY, 7395 Village Parkway, Dublin 94566, 415-828-8037.*** *Danskin and Capezio.*

***MARTIN THEATRICAL SUPPLY, 1370 Locust St., Walnut Creek 94958, 415-934-8037.*** *Lycra, Capezio, Danskin, Bonny Doone.*

***SAN RAMON VALLEY DANCE ACADEMY. 415-837-4656.*** *See BALLET, CCC.*

***SULA'S BELLY DANCE WORLD.*** *See BELLY, CCC.*

***THE DANCE SHOPPE, 101 Ryan Ind. Court, San Ramon 94583, 415-837-4656.***

# Supplies

## *East Bay*

***ACT ONE COSTUMES, 1530 MacArthur Blvd., Oakland 94602, 415-530-4141.***

***BENTLEY'S OF BERKELEY, INC., 2122 Shattuck Ave., Berkeley 94704, 415-843-7595.*** *Danskin, Capezio, etc. Specials for teachers and students.*

***DANCE ETC., 5897 College Ave., Oakland 94618, 415-658-8198.*** *Catalog of books (ballet, country dance, dance therapy, ethnic, historical, mime, modern, religious, used and out of print), periodicals, posters, percussion instruments, T-shirts, souvenir programs, records and tapes.*

***DANCE REPERTORY THEATRE.*** *See BALLET, EB.*

***J & J'S COSTUME OUTLET SHOP, 4176 Thornton Ave., Fremont 94536, 415-793-0698.*** *Sales and rentals.*

***THE MUSICAL OFFERING, 2431 Durant, Berkeley 94704, 415-849-0211.***

***BONNIE WALKER OPANCI, 869 Contra Costa, Berkeley 94707, 415-526-1330.*** *Custom, Macedonian, Turkish, Romanian boots; group discounts. Send for catalog.*

***SAND DOLLAR, 1222 Solano Ave., Albany 94706, 415-527-1931.*** *Huge stock of books and programs, mostly out-of-print and a few new dance books. Hours: 10-5, Tues. through Sat. Also specialize in modern poetry, new/used and out-of-print. Over 1,000 titles in ballet available; catalog available on request. Want-lists and additions to mailing list invited. Authors include Gordon Anthony, Arnold Haskell, Serge Lifar, many more on biographies, design, history, etc.*

# Suppliers

## Marin

*BELROSE ONSTAGE-BACKSTAGE THEATRICAL HOUSE, 1629 Fifth Ave., San Rafael 94901, 415-459-2555.* Stage lights and equipment sales and rental, performer and technician referral, books, magazines, sheet music, records, makeup.

*CHILDREN'S BOOTERY McKENZIE'S, 1000 Fifth Ave., San Rafael 94901, 415-454-3850.*

*DANCEWEAR OF MARIN, 1130 Idylberry Rd., San Rafael 94903, 415-472-2980.*

*D'LYNNES CAPEZIO DANCE WEAR, 1435 Fourth St., San Rafael 94901, 415-456-4747.* Makeup; supplies for modern, folk, ballet, jazz and tap.

*MERV'S BOOTERY, 898 Sir Francis Drake Blvd., San Anselmo 94960, 415-456-2334.*

*MOSHER SHOES, 96 Throckmorton Ave., Mill Valley 94941, 415-388-0432.*

*POLLIWOG SHOP, 1004 Magnolia Ave., Larkspur 94939, 415-461-1839.* Special orders.

# Suppliers

## *Peninsula*

*BALLET ARTS CENTER.* See BALLET, Peninsula.

*CHILDREN'S BOOTERY, 149 Main, Los Altos 94022, 415-948-6283; 225 Mayfield Ave., Mountain View, 415-968-0779; 2635 Middlefield Rd., Palo Alto 94306, 415-326-1221.*

*THE DANCE FACTORY, 1660 Broadway, Redwood City 94063, 415-368-4084.*

*DANCER'S LOFT, 1163 El Camino Real, Menlo Park, 415-323-5292.*

*MENLO PARK ACADEMY.* See BALLET, Peninsula.

*MOON GODDESS IMPORTS, P.O. Box 1597, Palo Alto 94302, 415-494-6083.* Books, mail orders, publishers.

*SPORTS GALLERY, Old Mill Specialty Center, Mountain View, 415-941-5308.*

*TIGHTS PLUS, 102 University Ave. and Alma, Palo Alto 94301, 415-323-8226.*

# Suppliers

## San Francisco

***ABOUT MUSIC, 357 Grove St., SF 94102, 415-621-1634.*** *Books and music.*

***BALLET BOUTIQUE OF THE SFB; SF Ballet Association Auxiliary, P.O. Box 15415, SF 94115.*** *SFB T-shirts, calendars, memorabilia (toe shoes), etc. by mail, or during intermissions at performance.*

***BALLET INTERNATIONAL, 3051 19th Ave., SF 94132, 415-731-6440.*** *Howard Buhl. Specializing in pointe shoes (Schachtner, Zubiller-Woessner, Gamba); soft toe slipper in Polish, Gamba, Balletique. Ribbons, knit pads, Dance Magazine, Dance News, Gelabert, "Anatomy and Ballet" (Sparger). Delivery by UPS-air, where possible; surface UPS or parcel post otherwise. Price list available. Individual service.*

***MAGANA (BAPTISTE) BAZAAR BOUTIQUE, 9 Clement St., SF 94118, 415-668-6636.*** *Belly.*

***DANCE ART CO., 222 Powell St., SF 94102, 415-392-4912.*** *Leotards by Tunics of England; Danskin leotards and tights, much more.*

***DRAMA BOOKS, 511 Geary at Taylor, SF 94102, 415-441-5343.*** *Film, dance books, programs, posters, designs. Mail order; retail stores.*

***NU-BARRES, 2325 Third St., SF 94107, 415-552-1689.*** *Portables.*

***PACIFIC DANCE SUPPLIES, 1630 Taraval, SF 94116, 415-661-1100.*** *Records and apparel, ballet and tap. Danskin.*

***PACIFIC DANCE THEATRE LIBRARY, 1929 Irving St., SF 94122, 415-731-4454.*** *Ballet orchestrations for sale or rental.*

***UNIVERSAL DANCE SUPPLY CO., 185 Fifth Ave., SF 94118, 415-387-8444.*** *Freed, Gamba, Danskin. Ballet and tap.*

# Supplies

## San Jose

DEAN NENA. *See TAP, SJ.*

GENE AND MARY LOU'S DANCE SUPPLIES, 1367 East Taylor, SJ 95133, 408-292-6455. *Records, clothing, books, accessories.*

LARRY'S COSTUMES AND NOVELTY CO., 1645 W. San Carlos, SJ 95128, 408-293-6036.

MARGARET'S ARABIAN COSTUMERY, 891 Wainwright Dr., SJ 95128, 408-293-7047.

NEWMAN'S DANCE AND COSTUME SHOPPE, 10487 S. De Anza, Cupertino 95014, 408-253-2623.

THE 1887 SHOP, 109 Town and Country Village, SJ, 408-246-1887.

VICTORIA'S THEATRICAL SUPPLY, 851 W. San Carlos, SJ 95126, 408-295-9316.

# Suppliers

## *Beyond the Bay*

***KORALION PRESS, 330 N. Fairfax Ave., Los Angeles 90036.*** *Ballet posters.*

***THE DANCE MART, Box 48, Homecrest Station, Brooklyn, NY 11229.*** *Catalog available on dance studies and techniques; ballet, mime, character dance, modern, jazz, kinesiology, body conditioning, dance therapy, anatomy, religious dance, ballroom, dance for children, general works, etc.*

***ISRAELI FOLK DANCE INSTITUTE, 515 Park Ave., NYC 10022.*** *Records and publications.*

***"FOOTNOTES", F. RANDOLPH ASSOCIATES, 1300 Arch St., Philadelphia, PA 19107.*** *A mail-order catalogue for books, records, posters, T-shirts, barres, etc.*

# Appendices

## Ballet

| | |
|---|---|
| **ABT** | *American Ballet Theatre Co.* |
| **CCA** | *Cecchetti Council of America (see Groups)* |
| **CCC** | *Contra Costa County* |
| **DMofA** | *Dance Masters of America* |
| **DMofC** | *Dance Masters of California* |
| **EB** | *East Bay* |
| **LRB** | *London Royal Ballet* |
| **NYCB** | *New York City Ballet* |
| **RAD** | *Royal Academy of Dancing, London (see GROUPS)* |
| **SF** | *San Francisco* |
| **SFB** | *San Francisco Ballet* |
| **SJ** | *San Jose* |

# Appendices

## Ballet

### CONTRA COSTA COUNTY

*Contra Costa Ballet Company. See CC Ballet Center.*

*Orinda Ballet Company. See Orinda Ballet School.*

### EAST BAY

*Alameda Civic Ballet Co. See Dance Repertory Theatre.*

*Ballet D'Enfants. See Vala Bovie School.*

*Berkeley Ballet Theatre. See Classical Ballet Center.*

*Dancer's Repertory Theatre. See Dancer's Theatre Studio.*

*East Bay Ballet Theatre.*

*Metropolitian Ballet Company of Oakland. See Academy of Dance.*

*The Oakland Ballet Company, and Youth Company.*

*The Oakland Civic Ballet. See Ballet Arts Center.*

### MARIN AND SONOMA

*Ballet Theatre West Company.*

*Marin Civic Ballet Company.*

*Petaluma City Ballet.*

*Santa Rosa Ballet Company.*

*Tamalpais Dance Theatre.*

# Appendices

## Ballet

**PENINSULA**

*Palo Alto Dance Theater. See Pacific Dance Center.*

*Peninsula Ballet Theatre.*

**SAN FRANCISCO**

*Arabesque Concert Dance.*

*Ballet Celeste. See S.F. Conservatory of Ballet.*

*Janina Cywinska's Ballet Company.*

*Children's Ballet Theatre.*

*Chrysalis. See S.F. Dance Theatre.*

*Reconstellation.*

*San Francisco Ballet.*

*San Francisco Dance Spectrum.*

*San Francisco Dance Theatre.*

*Theatre Ballet of San Francisco. See S.F. Conservatory of Ballet.*

*Marc Wilde Ballet.*

**SAN JOSE**

*Eufrazia Ballet Ensemble.*

*San Jose Ballet Company.*

*Santa Clara Ballet Company.*

# Appendices

## Ethnic/Folk

**ISRAELI**

*Ami Folk Troupe.*

*Nirkoda of San Francisco.*

*Rikudom Israeli Folk Dance Group.*

**LATIN**

*Cabadbaran Cultural Dance Troupe.*

*El Cuadro Flamenco.*

*Grupo Utrera.*

*Maria Haydee.*

*Los Flamencos de la Bodega.*

*Los Lupenos de San Jose.*

*Mis Criolla.*

*Rosa Montoya Bailes Flamencos.*

*Theatre Flamenco of San Francisco.*

*Trujillo Dance Company.*

*Eloisa Vasquez.*

### PHILIPPINES

*Bagong Diwa Dance Company.*

*The Filipina Dancers of San Francisco.*

*Sons of Samoa.*

*Taire's Otea.*

### SLAVIC

*Lowiczanie Polish Dance Ensemble.*

*Matija Gubec Croatian Folklore Ensemble.*

*Russian Folk Dance Ensemble.*

*Troik Balalaikas.*

### UNCLASSIFIED FOLK

*Baroque Dance Ensemble (UC Santa Cruz).*

*Capp Street Center Dance Company.*

*Chican India Dance Group.*

*San Jose Mele Alohi Dancers.*

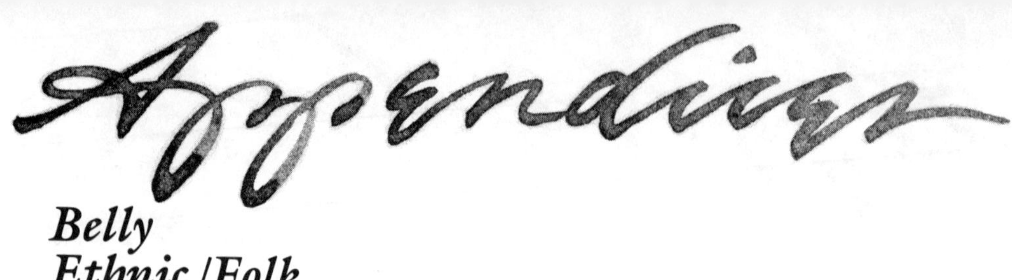

# *Belly Ethnic/Folk*

*Ar'rusala. See Molly Rodriquez, FOLK/ARABIC.*

*The Aswan Dancers. See Amina, SF.*

*Baptiste Royal Belly Dancing and East Indian Troupe. See Magaña Baptiste.*

*Farida Karoon Belly Dance Troupe.*

*Sciroccos Dance Theatre. See Ilyana.*

# *Ethnic/Folk*

## AFRO

*Aquarius Rising Dance Theatre.*

*Harambee Dance Ensemble.*

*Gwen Lewis Dance Experience.*

*Lotus African Ensemble Dance Company.*

*Wajumbe Cultural Ensemble.*

## ARABIC

*Children of Isis.*

*Zah-rah.*

# Appendices

## Ethnic/Folk

**ASIAN**

*Asian American Dance Collective.*

*Chinese Folk Dance Association.*

*Chung Ngai Dance Troupe.*

**GREEK**

*Aitos Greek Dancers.*

*Alkmini Greek Dance Ensemble.*

**INDIAN**

*Balasarawati.*

*Kalanjali.*

**INTERNATIONAL**

*Almonte Folk Dancers.*

*Khadra.*

*Kopachka Dancers.*

*SFSU Ethnic Dance Ensemble.*

*Stanford International Folk Dancers.*

*Terpsichorean International Dance Troupe.*

*Westwind International Folk Ensemble.*

# Appendices

## Jazz

*Aquarius Dance Theater/New Theater Company of Marin. See JAZZ, MARIN.*

*Berkeley Dance Company. See JAZZ, EB.*

*Company in Flight. See JAZZ, EB.*

*Dancer's Synectics Group. See JAZZ, SF.*

*Hot Energy Dance Troupe. See JAZZ, SF.*

*The Jazz Set. See Dance Center at Marlin Cove, JAZZ, Peninsula.*

*Modern Jazz Works. See JAZZ, SF (Cecelia Bowman's).*

*Rec Russell Jazz Dance Company. See JAZZ, MARIN.*

*The Collectibles. See San Carlos Dance Collective, Ballet, Peninsula.*

*West Coast Dancers/Junior Dancers. See West Coast Dance Theatre, JAZZ, EB.*

*West Coast Dance Works. See Ed Mock, JAZZ.*

# Appendices

## Modern

**EAST BAY**

*Aquarius Rising Dance Theatre.*

*Bay Area Repertory Dance Theatre.*

*Blake Street Hawkeyes.*

*Body and Soul.*

*Consort Dance Theatre.*

*Dimensions Dance Theatre.*

*East Bay Dance Perspectives.*

*Jeannde Herst Dance Company (Dancer's Theatre Studio).*

*Moving Parts.*

*Moving Space/Marcia Sakamoto.*

*Nuba Dance Theatre.*

*Right Angle Left Dance Ensemble.*

*Temple of the Wings.*

*Wendy Rodgers Dance Company.*

**MARIN AND SONOMA**

*Mercury Moving Company.*

**PENINSULA**

*Marlene Therkelsen Dance Company.*

# Appendices

## Modern

### SAN FRANCISCO

*Dance Source.*

*Dansfrancisco.*

*Earthly Co.*

*Epicenter Dance Works.*

*Footloose.*

*Margaret Jenkins Dance Company.*

*Lynda Knapp, Terry Meyers and Dancers (USF).*

*Mobius.*

*Performing Arts Workshop.*

*Ruth St. Denis/Denishawn Dance.*

*Paul Scardina Dance Company.*

*San Francisco Moving Company.*

*Sundance Company.*

*Synergic Theater.*

*Tumbleweed.*

*Shela Xoregos.*

# Appendices

## *Modern*

**SAN JOSE AND BEYOND**

*The Assortment Dance Theatre (Foothill-De Anza College)*

*Tandy Beal and Company.*

*Janlyn Dance Company.*

*Portable Dance Troupe (CSU Fresno).*

# Appendices

## Children

*Vala Bovie, Ballets D'Enfants. See BALLET, EB.*

*Children's Creative Dance Theatre.*

*Danse Boutique. See BALLET, CCC.*

*East Bay Center for the Performing Arts. See BALLET, EB.*

*Margaret Jenkins. See MODERN, EB.*

*Lee Lane. See BALLET, Peninsula.*

*Mason-Kahn, Youth on Stage. See TAP, SF.*

*Brynar Mehl.*

*Oakland Ballet Company; Youth Company. See BALLET, EB.*

*Orinda Ballet School. See BALLET, CCC.*

*Performing Arts Workshop. See MODERN, SF.*

*Planet of Dance. See MODERN, EB.*

*St. George Home, Inc., 1515 Arch St, Berkeley 94708, 415-848-2393. Dances with the Dragon seminars, workshops and adventures for those who work with children. Include body movement and guided fantasy, dance, sound in working with profoundly disturbed youngsters (schizophrenic and autistic).*

*San Francisco Children's Ballet Theatre School. See Evelyn Wenger, BALLET, SF.*

*San Francisco Conservatory of Ballet; Ballet Celeste. See BALLET, SF.*

*San Francisco Dance Spectrum. See BALLET, SF.*

# Appendices

## Children

*San Francisco Dance Theatre, junior division; Chrysalis. See BALLET, SF.*

*Santa Clara Ballet School. See BALLET, San Jose.*

*Shawl-Anderson Modern Dance Center. See BALLET, EB.*

*Star Dance Studio. See BALLET, SF.*

*Tamalpais Dance Center. See BALLET, Marin.*

*Young Performers. See San Mateo City, GROUPS/SPONSORS.*

*A woman of great and varied talents with an extraordinary commitment to this art form, Beth Witrogen is a journalist, dance photographer, and dancer. As a freelancer she's worked with The Christian Science Monitor, Washington Post, and Philadelphia Enquirer. For the past several years she's been an editor for The San Francisco Examiner.*

*Ms. Witrogen has studied ballet for many years, and has been researching and exploring the bay area dance scene ever since her arrival here in 1970. Her credentials include a Masters of Journalism from University of California, Berkeley.*

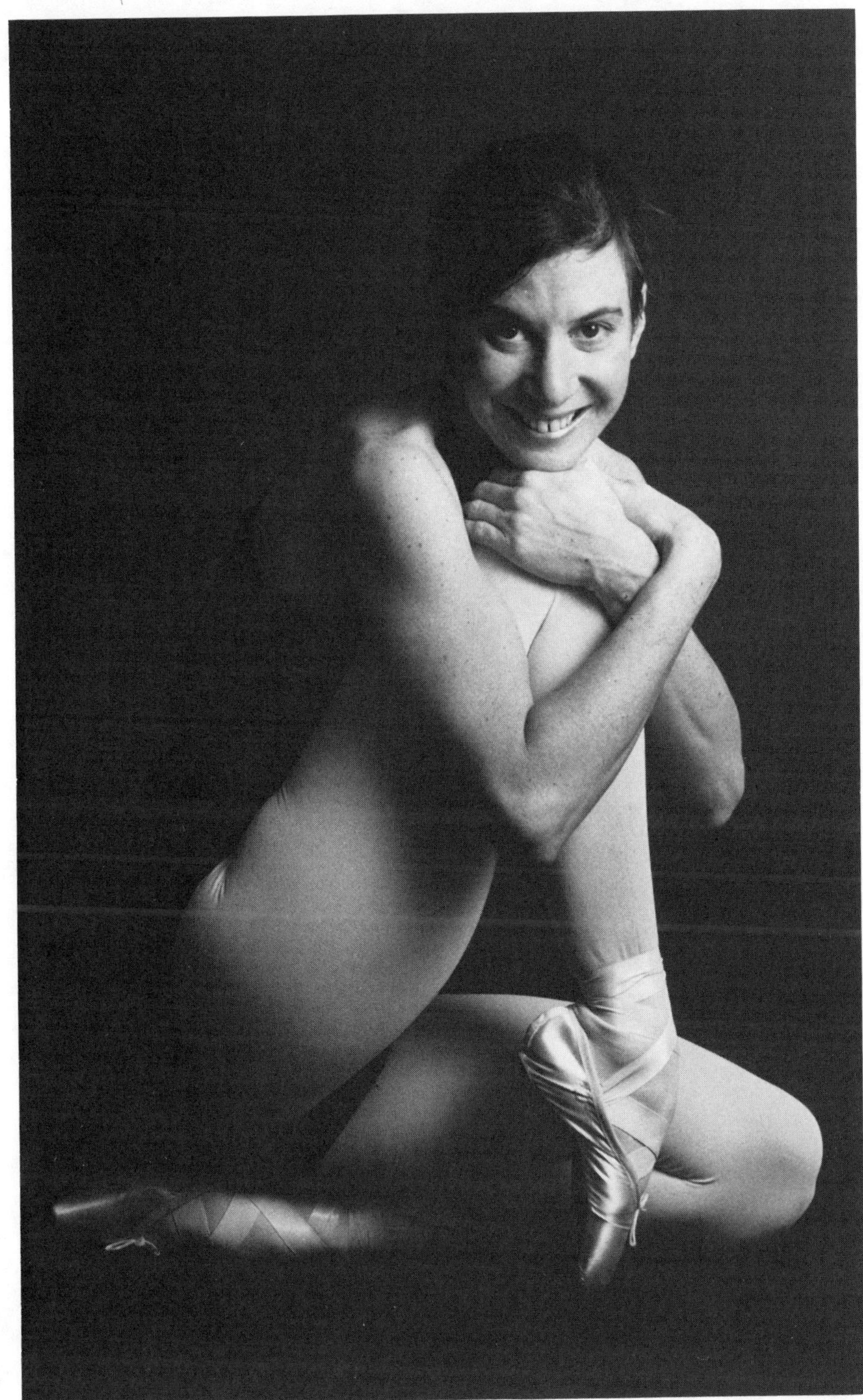

Bob McLeod